Study Guide

Automotive Encyclopedia

Fundamental Principles, Operation, Construction, Service, and Repair

Nancy Henke-Konopasek
Senior Editor

Publisher
The Goodheart-Willcox Company, Inc.
Tinley Park, Illinois
www.g-w.com

2005 Edition

Manufactured in the United States of America

International Standard Book Number 1-59070-423-1

1 2 3 4 5 6 7 8 9—05—10 09 08 07 06 05

The Goodheart-Willcox Company, Inc. Safety Notice: The reader is expressly advised to carefully read, understand, and apply all safety precautions and warnings described in this book or that might also be indicated in undertaking the activities and exercises described herein to minimize risk of personal injury or injury to others. Common sense and good judgment should also be exercised and applied to help avoid all potential hazards. The reader should always refer to the appropriate manufacturer's technical information, directions, and recommendations; then proceed with care to follow specific equipment operating instructions. The reader should understand these notices and cautions are not exhaustive.

Contents

Introduction

This Study Guide is designed for use with the *Automotive Encyclopedia* text. As you complete the questions and problems in this Study Guide, you can review the concepts and techniques presented in the text. The contents of this Study Guide are divided into chapters that correspond to the chapters in the text. After reading your assignment in the text, do your best to complete these questions and problems carefully and accurately. Each chapter in the Study Guide includes several types of questions and problems.

Automotive Encyclopedia covers vehicle construction, principles of operation, and basic service procedures. It also explores the many sciences involved in vehicle operation: the fundamentals of electricity, electronics, computers, hydraulics, pneumatics, internal combustion, power transmission, and steering and suspension geometry. Basic information on safety, hand tools, fasteners, measuring instruments, meters, analyzers, and service equipment is also included.

In-depth coverage is devoted to engine fundamentals and service, emission controls, transmissions and transaxles, front-wheel drive, four-wheel drive, and anti-lock braking. Special emphasis is given to operation and diagnosis of computer-controlled systems.

The automotive service field offers many career opportunities for anyone who is mechanically and technically inclined and has the educational background. Several career-related activities are included in this Study Guide.

This Study Guide helps provide the foundation on which a sound, thorough understanding of automotive technology is based. Once these fundamentals are learned, hands-on experience will enable you to diagnose trouble and perform needed repairs.

Nancy Henke-Konopasek

Instructions for Answering Questions

Each chapter in this Study Guide correlates directly to the same chapter in the textbook. Before answering the questions in the Study Guide, study the assigned chapter of the text and answer the end-of-chapter review questions while referring to your text. Then review the objectives at the beginning of each Study Guide chapter. This will help you review the important concepts from the textbook chapter. Try to complete as many of the Study Guide questions as possible without referring to the textbook. Then use the text to complete the remaining questions.

A variety of questions are used in the Study Guide, including Multiple Choice, Identification, Completion, Short Answer, and Matching. The sequence of the questions for each question type starts toward the beginning of each chapter and progresses through the chapter. The Study Guide questions should be answered in the following manner.

Multiple Choice

Select the best answer and write the corresponding letter in the space at the right.

1. Which of the following is used for measuring resistance? 1. C
   (A) Ammeter.
   (B) Voltmeter.
   (C) Ohmmeter.
   (D) None of the above.

2. Lubricating oil in an automobile engine _____. 2. D
   (A) lubricates the moving parts
   (B) seals between the piston rings and cylinder wall
   (C) carries heat away from engine parts
   (D) All of the above.

Identification

Specific instructions are included with each set of Identification questions. In general, you are required to identify components indicated on the illustration or photograph accompanying the questions.

Identify the items indicated on the diagram below.

3. Push rods. 3. C
4. Lifters. 4. D
5. Cylinder head. 5. B
6. Rocker arms. 6. A

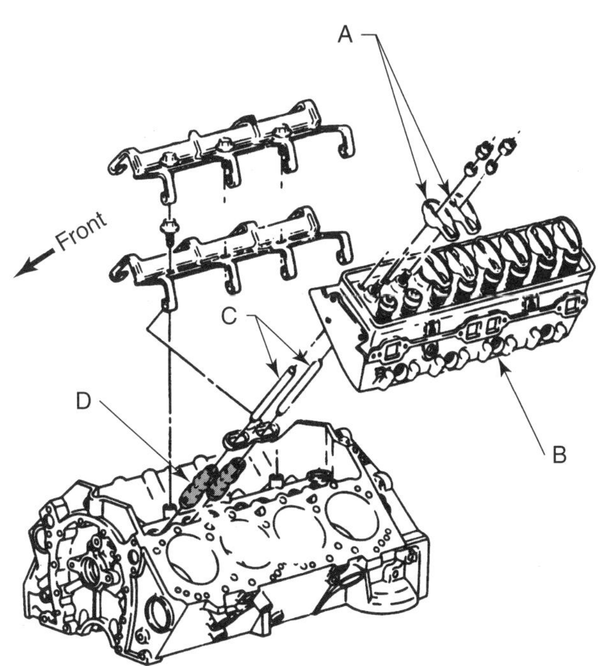

Completion

Read the following statements. Write the word or words that best complete the statement in the blank at the right.

7. The _____ _____ link the pistons to the crankshaft. 7. connecting rods
8. The _____ opens the valves at the appropriate times in the combustion cycle. 8. camshaft
9. The _____ _____ is the space within the cylinder above the piston where the burning of the air/fuel mixture occurs. 9. combustion chamber

Short Answer

Provide complete responses to the following statements.

10. List the three types of fuel injection systems.

    Single-point injection system

    Multi-point injection system

    Direct injection system

11. Explain why you should never remove a radiator cap when the coolant is hot.

    Pressurized coolant may shoot from the radiator, causing severe burns.

Matching

Match the term in the right column with its description in the left column. Place the corresponding letter in the blank.

(A) Toe-in.
(B) Caster.
(C) Camber.
(D) Steering axis inclination.

12. The angle measured between a true vertical line through the center of the wheel and the centerline through the upper and lower ball joints. 12. B
13. The angle formed by the true vertical centerline and the vertical centerline of the tire. 13. C
14. The amount in fractions of an inch or degree that the front (or rear) wheels are closer together in the front than in the rear. 14. A
15. The angle formed by the true vertical centerline and the centerline of the upper and lower ball joints. 15. D

Chapter 1

Automotive Safety

Name ____________________

Date ____________ Instructor ____________

Score ______ Textbook pages 13–20

After studying the chapter in the text and completing this section of the workbook, you will be able to:

- ❑ Describe what a clean shop should look like and why.
- ❑ State what type of eye protection should be worn for a specific job.
- ❑ Cite fire preventive measures that should be followed when working in an automotive shop.
- ❑ List the precautions that should be followed when raising a vehicle off the floor.
- ❑ List the safety measures that should be followed when using welding equipment.
- ❑ Demonstrate how to dress safely when in the shop.

Multiple Choice

1. Which of the following points is set forth in the OSHA Act?
   (A) Floors must be clean and free of grease, oil, and dirt.
   (B) Washrooms must be kept clean and sanitary.
   (C) Personal protective equipment for eyes, face, head, and extremities, as well as protective respiratory devices, shields, and barriers must be provided.
   (D) All of the above.

1. A

2. Which of the following is not combustible?
   (A) Gasoline.
   (B) Water.
   (C) Lacquer thinner.
   (D) Certain cleaning fluids.

2. B

3. No smoking signs should be _____.
   (A) prominently displayed and followed
   (B) ignored
   (C) displayed, but not followed
   (D) None of the above.

3. A

Name ______________________

4. Brake and clutch linings may contain asbestos. The dust from these items is a carcinogen. This is why you should _____.
   (A) not work on them
   (B) always wear a respirator when working on them
   (C) not wear a respirator and breathe deeply when working on them
   (D) use a fire extinguisher on them

4. B

5. Under the _____, an employer is responsible for providing employees with training and information about the characteristics of hazardous materials in the workplace as well as labeling these materials.
   (A) OSHA laws
   (B) Right-to-Know laws
   (C) EPA laws
   (D) Resource Conservation and Recovery Act

5. B

6. Files should _____.
   (A) be used without a handle
   (B) be used as pry bars
   (C) never be hammered
   (D) All of the above.

6. C

7. Which of the following should not be worn when working around machines, engines, or motors?
   (A) Long sleeves buttoned at the cuffs or rolled up past the elbows.
   (B) Sturdy shoes or boots, preferably with steel toes.
   (C) Jewelry, such as chains or rings.
   (D) Caps without brims.

7. C

8. When igniting a welding torch, use a _____.
   (A) match
   (B) cigarette lighter
   (C) friction-type lighter
   (D) All of the above.

8. C

Identification

Identify common hazards involved in automotive service and repair as indicated in the illustration on the top of the next page.

9. Hot exhaust system components. 9. E

10. High ignition system voltage. 10. C

11. Hot coolant. 11. G

12. Noxious exhaust. 12. D

13. Rotating belts and pulleys. 13. A

14. Spinning fan. 14. F

15. Hot engine components. 15. B

Name ______________________________

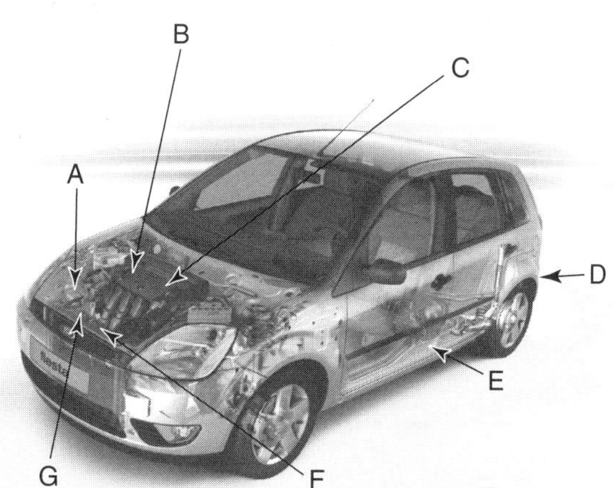

Identify the typical personal protective equipment shown below.

16. Respirator. 16. C

17. Safety glasses. 17. A

18. Safety goggles. 18. B

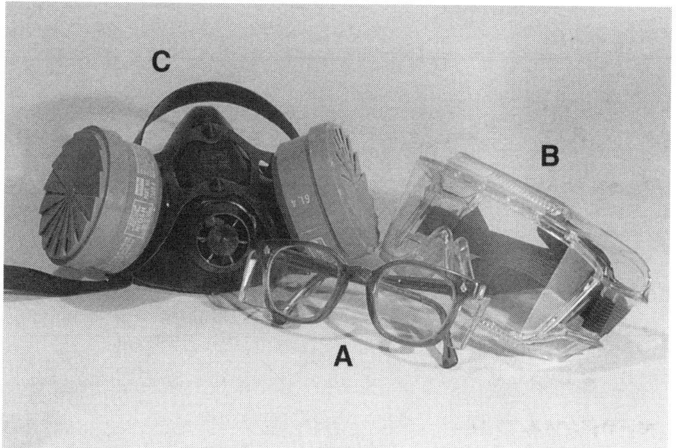

Completion

19. The Occupational Safety and Health Administration (OSHA) is a branch of the Department of Labor formed to establish and enforce ______ for all types of businesses to ensure that they are operated under conditions of maximum safety and health. 19. GUIDELINES

20. According to OSHA, electrical connections must be properly ______. 20. GROUNDED

21. Class ______ fire extinguishers are for electrical fires. 21. C

22. Class ______ fire extinguishers are for chemical fires. 22. B

23. Class ______ fire extinguishers are for ordinary combustible materials. 23. A

24. As protection against fire, always place oil and paint rags in a(n) ______ (sealed, open) container. 24. WASTE CONTAINER SEALED

Name ______________________

25. When it is necessary to observe the electrolyte level in a battery, a _____ (flashlight, flame) should be used.

25. FLASHLIGHT

26. Proper _____ is necessary in an auto shop because engine exhaust fumes contain carbon monoxide, which is a deadly poison.

26. VENTILATION SYSTEM

27. If lifts are not available and it is necessary to keep a vehicle raised, the vehicle should be placed on jack _____.

27. JACK STAND

28. When the head of a chisel becomes mushroomed, the chisel should be discarded or the head should be _____ to remove the mushroomed edges.

28. GRINDED OR FILED

29. When lifting heavy objects, keep your back straight and lift with your _____.

29. LEGS

30. When performing a grinding operation, always wear _____ to protect the eyes from flying objects.

30. SAFETY GLASSES

Short Answer

31. List the nine sections that must appear on a material safety data sheet.

PRODUCT INFORMATION
INGREDIENTS
PHYSICAL/CHEMICAL CHARACTERISTICS
FIRE AND EXPLOSION HAZARD DATA
REACTIVITY DATA
SPILL OR LEAK PROCEDURES
HEALTH HAZARD DATA
FIRST AID PROCEDURES
PROTECTION INFORMATION

32. List six hazardous wastes generated from automotive service and repair.

USED MOTOR OIL AND OTHER DISCARDED LUBRICANTS
USED OIL FILTERS
CLEANING SOLVENTS
BATTERIES
ANTIFREEZE
REFRIGERANT

Name ______________________

33. List ten safety rules that are to be followed in the automotive shop.

GET PERMISHON FIRST
USE TOOLS SAFTY
SPILLS MUST BE CLEAN
STAFFY GLASES MUST BE WORN AT ALL TIMES
TOOLS MUST BE CLEAN
GET PERMISHON TO USE SHOP LIFT
PUT RAGS IN A OILY WAST CONTAINER
NO SMOKING IN THE SHOP
USE A EXHAUST HOSE SO NO CARBONMONIXID
USE YOUR LEGS WHEN LIFTING

Chapter 2

Owner's Manuals, Service Manuals, and Repair Manuals

Name ______________________

Date ____________ Instructor ____________

Score ______ Textbook pages 21–28

After studying the chapter in the text and completing this section of the workbook, you will be able to:

- ❑ List the types of information that can be found in the owner's manual.
- ❑ Explain what type of information can be found in service manuals and repair manuals.
- ❑ Determine the difference between a service manual and a repair manual.
- ❑ Demonstrate how to use a flat rate manual.

Multiple Choice

1. The owner's manual should normally be kept in _____.
   (A) your house
   (B) the glove box of the vehicle
   (C) a safe deposit box
   (D) the garage

   1. B

2. Which of the following are covered in an owner's manual?
   (A) Specifications on the maximum weight limit that a specific vehicle can tow behind it.
   (B) How to start the engine under different conditions.
   (C) An explanation of components, gauges, and accessories.
   (D) All of the above.

   2. D

3. The VIN has 17 digits and is generally located _____.
   (A) under the hood
   (B) at the upper-left corner of the dash
   (C) in the glove box
   (D) in the trunk

   3. B

Name ______________________

4. Technical service bulletins _____.
   (A) cover only new car models
   (B) are available only to dealer service departments
   (C) help technicians diagnose certain problems
   (D) Both A and C.

4. C

Completion

5. The owner's manual contains _____ (technical, nontechnical) information for the proper operation of a car.

5. TECHNICAL

6. The owner's manual gives _____ on the types and levels of various fluids used in a vehicle.

6. SPECIFICATION

7. Service manuals and repair manuals contain very specific _____ (technical, nontechnical) information needed by a technician to make proper repairs.

7. TECHNICAL

8. A(n) _____ manual is published by the vehicle manufacturer for every different model every year.

8. SERVICE

9. A(n) _____ manual is published by a company other than that of the vehicle manufacturer.

9. REPAIR

10. To make sure you have the correct service manual for the vehicle you are working on, check the _____.

10. VIN NUMBER

11. A(n) _____ _____ manual is used to determine how much to charge a customer for needed repairs.

11. FLAT RATE

12. A flat rate manual may list that a tune-up will take 1.8 hours on a 1999 Ford V-6 engine. If the hourly rate charged by the shop is $40.00/hr., the labor for the tune-up would cost _____.

12. 72.00$

Short Answer

13. List three items of information that you should have when calling a zone office.

YEAR
MAKE
MODLE

14. Explain why you should keep a copy of all warranty repair orders after work has been done on a vehicle.

IF IT BREAKS AGEAN THE WARRANTY WILL MAKE IT GET WORKED ON AGEAN

15. Why should intermittent problems be documented?

SO ~~YOU~~ THE TEC. WILL KNOW ITS BEEN A PROBLEM BEFOR

Name ______________________

16. Why do independent shops use repair manuals?

BECUSE THE REPAIR THE CARS

17. What is the VIN and why is it important?

VEHICLE IDENTIFICATION NUMBER, IT IS IMPORTANT BECUSE IT IS USED FOR THE LICENCE AND ~~[illegible]~~ INSURANCE

18. How does using computerized information compare to using a service manual?

COMPUTERIZED IS FASTER

19. What types of information can technicians access using the Internet?

IT MIGHT HAVE MORE INFO. ON THE CAR THEN THE OWNERS MANUAL

Chapter 3

Automotive Tools

Name ______________________________

Date ______________ Instructor ______________

Score ______ Textbook pages 29–46

After studying the chapter in the text and completing this section of the workbook, you will be able to:

- ❑ Identify the various tools used to service automobiles.
- ❑ Describe the purpose of each tool used in the shop.
- ❑ Use tools safely.
- ❑ Select the right tool for the job.

Multiple Choice

1. The beginning automotive technician must learn the correct methods of using tools to _____.
   (A) perform the work as quickly as possible
   (B) complete the job with maximum safety
   (C) complete the job with maximum accuracy
   (D) All of the above.

   1. D

2. Apprentice technicians learn that time will be saved if they take good care of their hand tools by _____.
   (A) cleaning them after use
   (B) returning them to their proper storage place
   (C) leaving them where they think they will use them next
   (D) Both A and B.

   2. D

3. _____ wrenches are general-purpose wrenches and are preferred by many technicians.
   (A) Combination
   (B) Open-ended
   (C) Box
   (D) Tubing

   3. B

Name ______________________

4. The _____ screwdriver provides the tightest, most positive fit.
   (A) blade-type
   (B) Phillips
   (C) Pozidriv
   (D) Torx

4. B

5. Which type of metal shears are most frequently used?
   (A) Straight blade shears.
   (B) Curved blade shears.
   (C) Scroll pivoted snips.
   (D) None of the above.

5. A

6. When not in use, files should be _____.
   (A) placed in a drawer with other tools
   (B) hung on a rack
   (C) placed where they will be used next
   (D) left flat on a workbench

6. D

7. When using a hacksaw, the most effective cutting speed is about _____ per second.
   (A) one stroke
   (B) two strokes
   (C) three strokes
   (D) four strokes

7. A

8. For cutting angle iron, heavy pipe, brass, or copper, use a hacksaw blade with _____ teeth per inch.
   (A) 14
   (B) 18
   (C) 24
   (D) 32

8. A

Identification

Identify the various accessory handles shown below.

9. Flexible extension. — 9. F
10. Sliding T-handle. — 10. B
11. Short extension. — 11. D
12. Socket drivers. — 12. G
13. Flex handle. — 13. A
14. Long extension. — 14. E
15. Speed wrench. — 15. C

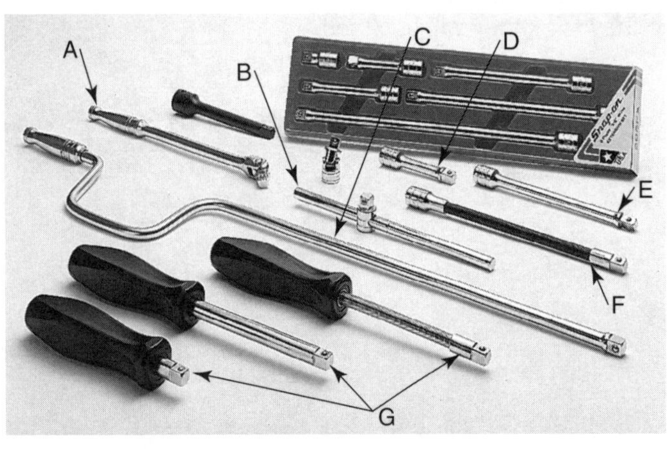

Name ______________________________

Identify the type of screwdriver that should be used with the screw heads shown below.

16. Clutch.	16.	D
17. Phillips.	17.	B
18. Blade-type.	18.	A
19. Torx.	19.	E
20. Pozidriv.	20.	C

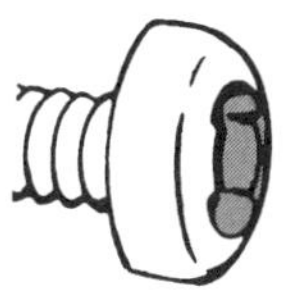
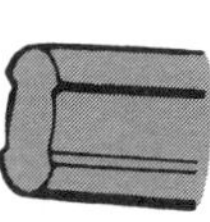

Identify the various types of chisels shown below.

21. Half round chisel.	21.	C
22. Round nose chisel.	22.	E
23. Cape chisel	23.	B
24. Cold chisel.	24.	A
25. Diamond chisel.	25.	D

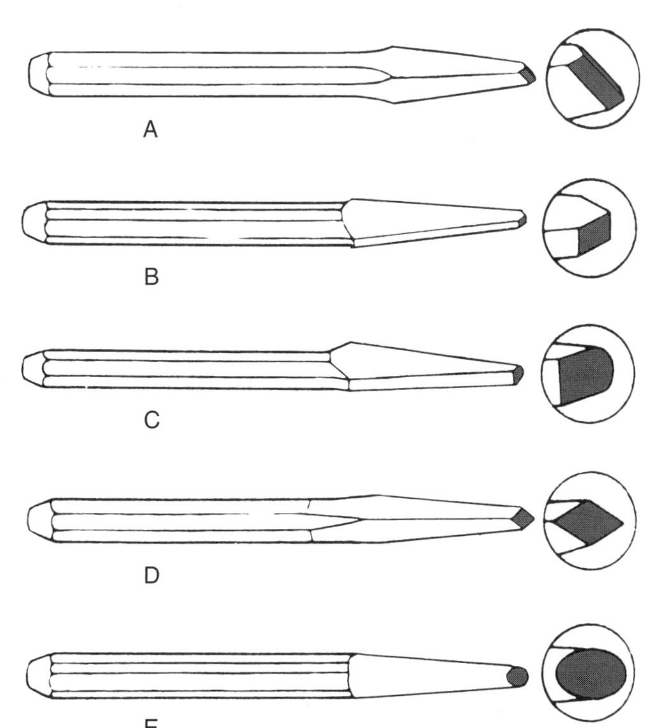

Name ______________________________

Identify the different types of pliers shown here.

26. Diagonal cutting pliers. 26. B
27. Interlocking joint pliers. 27. D
28. Combination slip-joint pliers. 28. A
29. Brake pliers. 29. G
30. Locking pliers. 30. E
31. Long nose pliers. 31. C
32. Snap ring pliers. 32. F

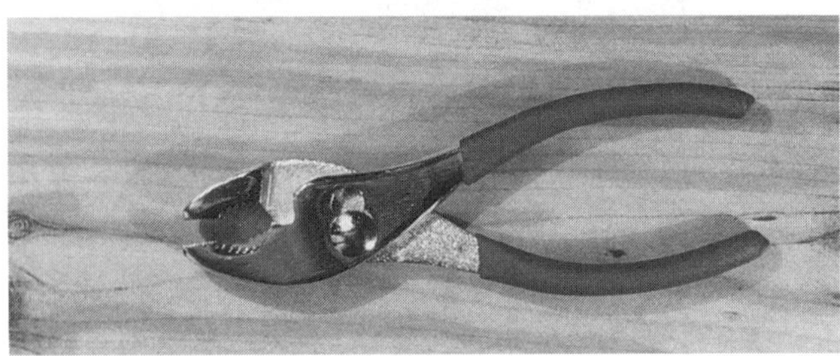

A

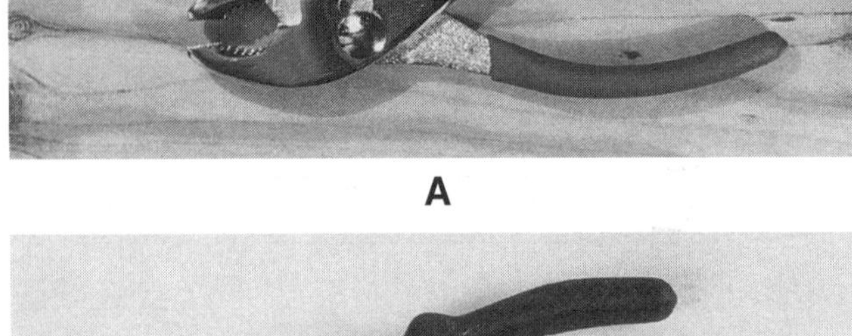

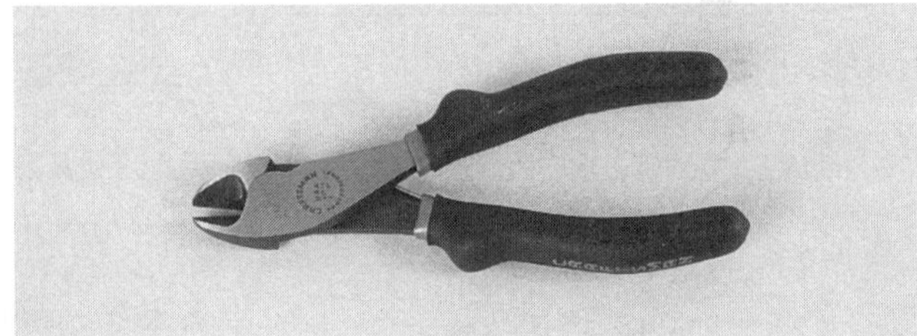

B

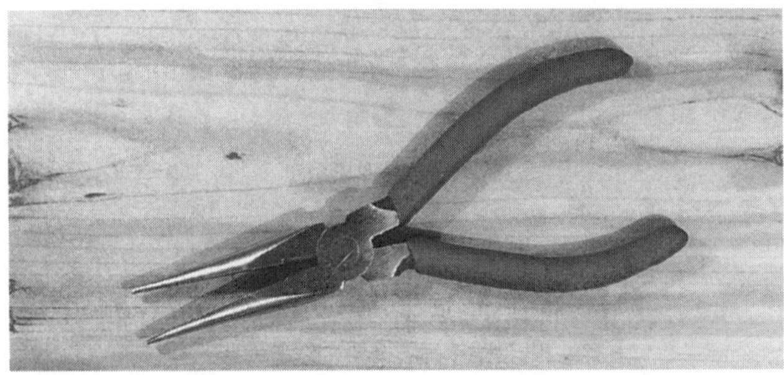

C

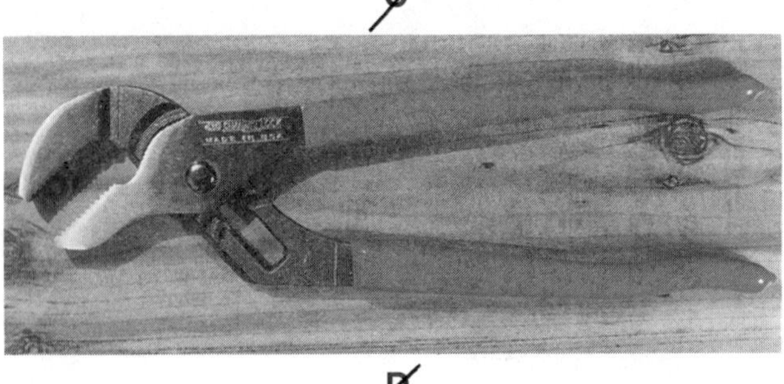

D

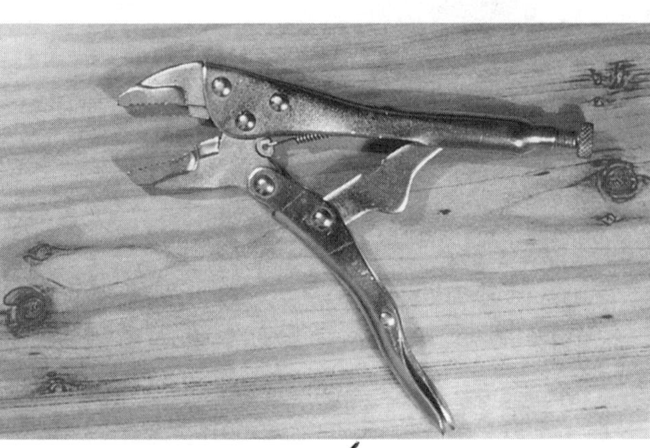

E

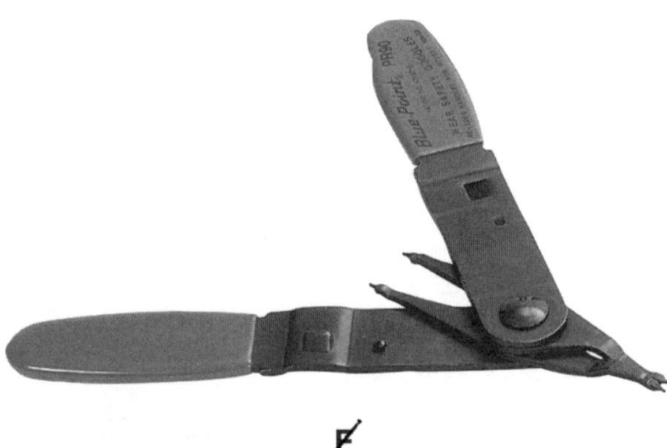

F

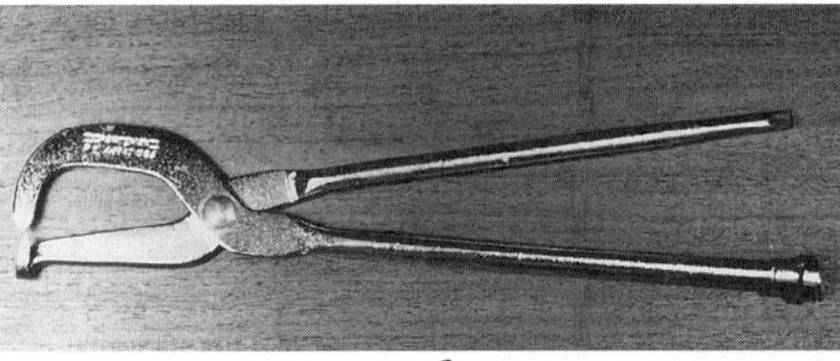

G

Name ______________________________

Identify the cleaning tools used in automobile repair.

33. Flexible carbon scraper. 33. C
34. Rigid carbon scrapers. 34. A
35. Putty knives. 35. E
36. General-purpose scrapers. 36. D
37. Gasket scraper. 37. B

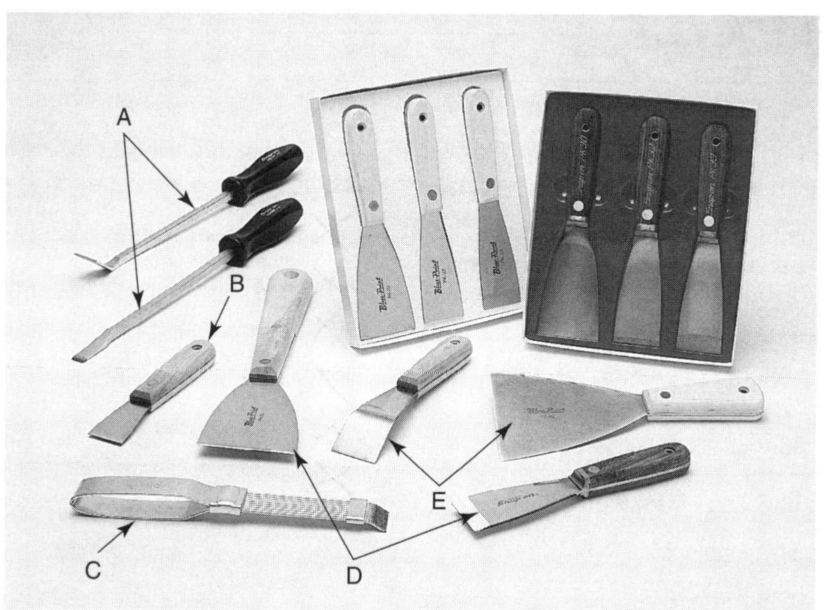

Completion

38. A wrench's size is determined by the width of its ______. 38. OPENING
39. Used with a ratchet handle, ______ greatly reduce the time needed to remove nuts and bolts. 39. SOCKETS
40. The size of a screwdriver is determined by the size of its ______. 40. BLADE
41. If there is any danger of damaging the surface of a component, a(n) ______ hammer should be used. 41. SOFT-FACE
42. The drill ______ is mounted in an electric drill and does the actual cutting. 42. BIT
43. ______ wrenches are designed for loosening and tightening nuts and bolts quickly. 43. SPEED
44. A magnetic ______ tool can be used to remove items from restricted areas. 44. RETRIEVING
45. Rosin core solder is used for ______ (electrical, non-electrical) repairs. 45. NON-ELECTRICAL
46. Acid core solder is used for ______ (electrical, non-electrical) repairs. 46. ELECTRICAL
47. ______ are used to enlarge or smooth holes. 47. REAMERS

Name ______________________________

Short Answer

48. Explain why a hammer with a loose head should never be used.

THE HAMMER HEAD MIGHT COME OFF AND HIT SOMEONE

49. Describe the preferred method of filing.

PUSH DOWN GOING FORWARD AND LIGHTLY ON THE BACK STROK

Matching

Place the procedures described in the right column in their correct order. Place the corresponding letter in the blank.

50. Because these pliers can be opened wider at the hinge, they are used for gripping large-diameter components.
51. Can be adjusted to several different sizes, permitting the jaws of the pliers to remain approximately parallel.
52. Used for cutting wire and removing cotter pins.
53. Used to remove snap rings from various parts.
54. Used for gripping small objects.
55. Used to hold parts together and to remove broken studs.

(A) Diagonal cutting pliers.
(B) Combination slip-joint pliers.
(C) Long nose pliers.
(D) Interlocking joint pliers.
(E) Locking pliers.
(F) Snap ring pliers.

50. D
51. B
52. A
53. F
54. C
55. E

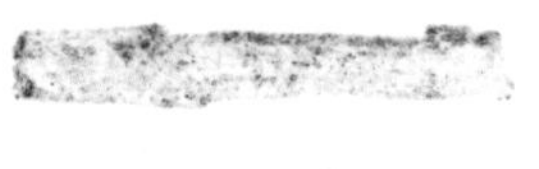

Chapter 4

Fasteners, Seals, and Gaskets

Name ______________________________

Date ______________ Instructor ______________

Score ______ Textbook pages 47–58

After studying the chapter in the text and completing this section of the workbook, you will be able to:

- ❑ List the various types of fasteners used in the automobile.
- ❑ Determine which fastener is appropriate for a specific job.
- ❑ Explain how to select and measure a bolt.
- ❑ Describe the different methods of repairing threads.
- ❑ Select the appropriate seal for a specific job.
- ❑ Describe the various lubricants and sealers used in an automobile and list their applications.
- ❑ Demonstrate the steps in preparing a new gasket for installation.

Multiple Choice

1. Which of the following is a type of key used in automotive design?
   (A) Woodruff key.
   (B) Square key.
   (C) Gib-head key.
   (D) All of the above.

   1. D

2. RTV sealants should be used _____.
   (A) in place of a head gasket
   (B) on the rear main bearing cap to prevent leaks
   (C) on carburetors
   (D) on automatic transmissions

   2. B

3. Adhesives are used to _____.
   (A) secure external moldings and emblems
   (B) hold weatherstripping in place
   (C) attach interior trim pieces
   (D) All of the above.

   3. D

Name ______________________________

4. Which of the following statements about the Teflon sealing ring is *not* true? — 4. C
   (A) It has an interlocking feature.
   (B) It can conform to irregularities.
   (C) Metal particles can become embedded in the sealing side, reducing its effectiveness as a seal.
   (D) It is distinguished by an angle cut.
5. Before installing any new gasket, _____. — 5. C
   (A) silicone sealer must be applied to the old gasket
   (B) all old gasket material must be removed from the mating surfaces
   (C) Both A and B.
   (D) None of the above.

Identification

Identify the following types of machine screw heads.

6. Clutch head. — 6. D
7. Truss head. — 7. A
8. Hex slotted head. — 8. H
9. Cross recessed flat head. — 9. G
10. Oval head. — 10. B
11. Fillister head. — 11. E
12. Pan head. — 12. F
13. Flat slotted. — 13. C

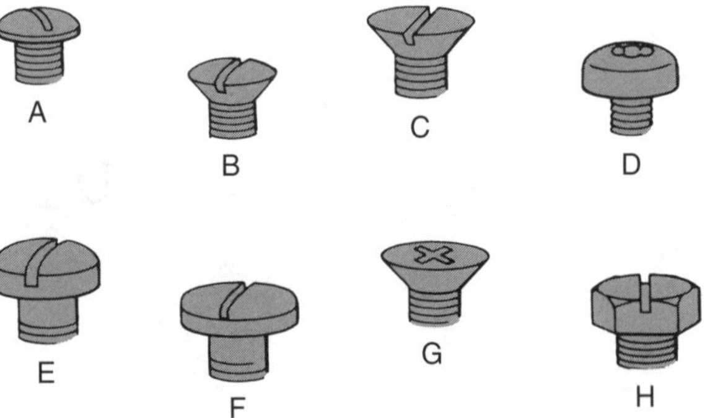

14. Indicate which of the following refers to the bolt size. — 14. A

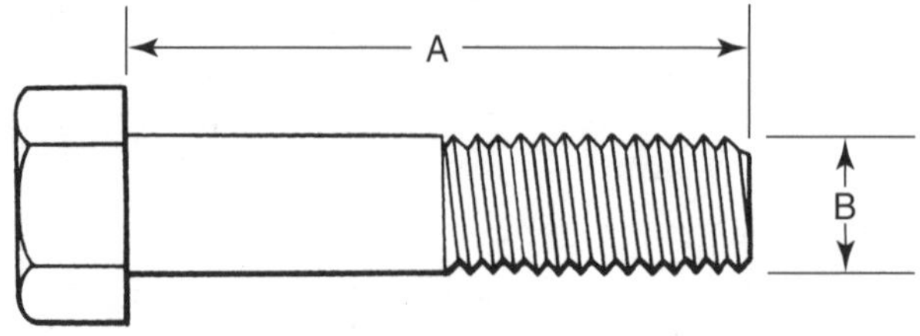

Name ______________________

What wrench size should be used on the bolts shown below?

15. 3/4

16. 13mm

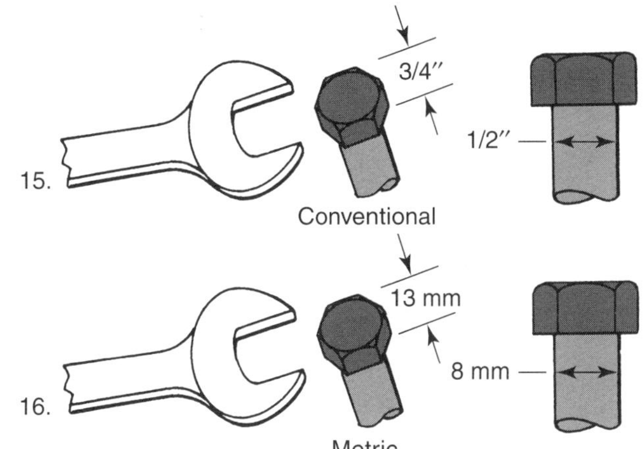

Identify the types of nuts illustrated below.

17. Slotted. 17. A

18. Lock. 18. K

19. Wing. 19. L

20. Panel. 20. I

21. Castle. 21. C

22. Specialty. 22. M

23. Acorn. 23. J

24. Serrated. 24. D

25. Flanged. 25. F

26. Single thread. 26. H

27. Spring. 27. G

28. Weld. 28. E

29. Hex plain. 29. B

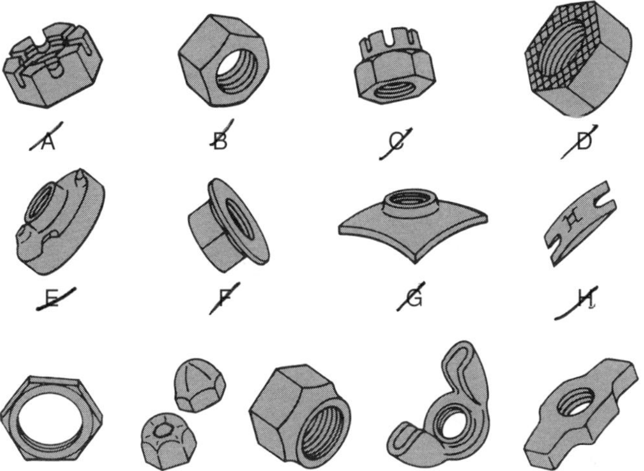

Name ______________________________

Identify the following types of washers.

30. Spring or lock washer. 30. A
31. Tooth-type lock washer. 31. C
32. Typical flat washer. 32. B

A

B

C

Identify the following types of sheet metal screws.

33. Countersunk flat head. 33. E
34. Round head. 34. A
35. Truss head. 35. C
36. Pan head. 36. B
37. Countersunk oval head. 37. D

A B C D E

Identify the various types of pins shown below.

38. Spring pin. 38. F
39. Cotter pin. 39. A
40. Dowel pin. 40. B
41. Quick-lock pin. 41. D
42. Clevis pin. 42. E
43. Grooved pin. 43. H
44. Taper pin. 44. G
45. Spring locking pin. 45. C

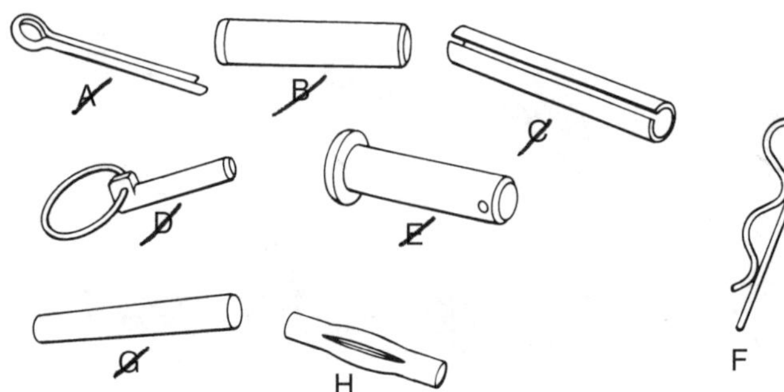

Name ____________________

Identify the snap rings shown below.

46. External hole type. 46. C

47. Internal hole type. 47. B

48. Internal prong type. 48. A

49. External "E" type. 49. D

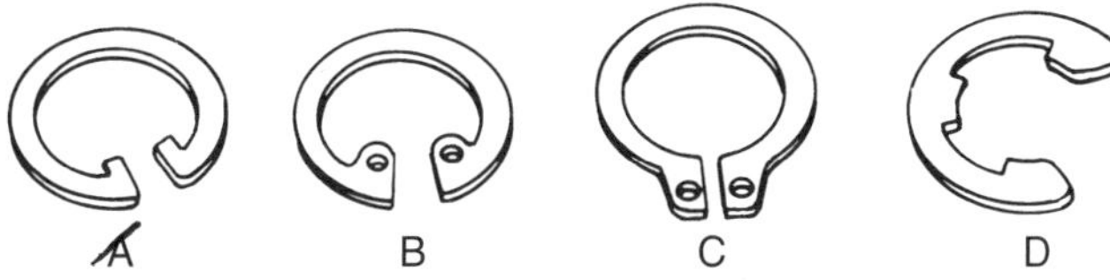

Decipher the markings that might appear on an SAE bolt.

50. Stands for unified screw thread standard. 50. C

51. Length. 51. F

52. Bolt size (diameter). 52. A

53. Coarse. 53. D

54. Number of threads per inch. 54. B

55. Fit symbol. 55. E

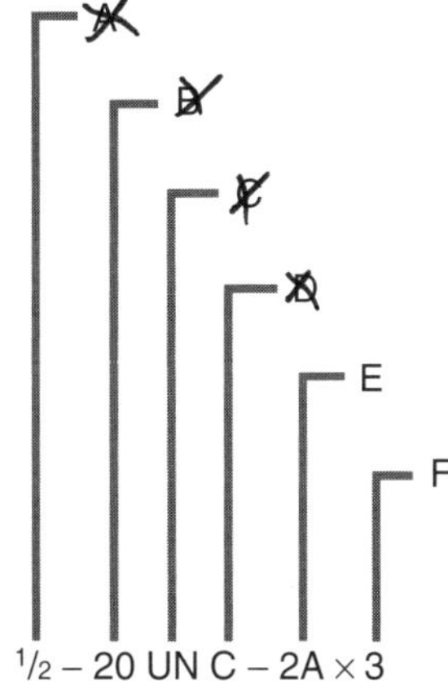

Name ______________________________

Decipher the markings that might appear on a metric bolt.

56. Strength (property class). — 56. F

57. Diameter (mm). — 57. B

58. Pitch (mm). — 58. C

59. Length. — 59. E

60. ISO metric thread. — 60. A

61. Fit symbol. — 61. D

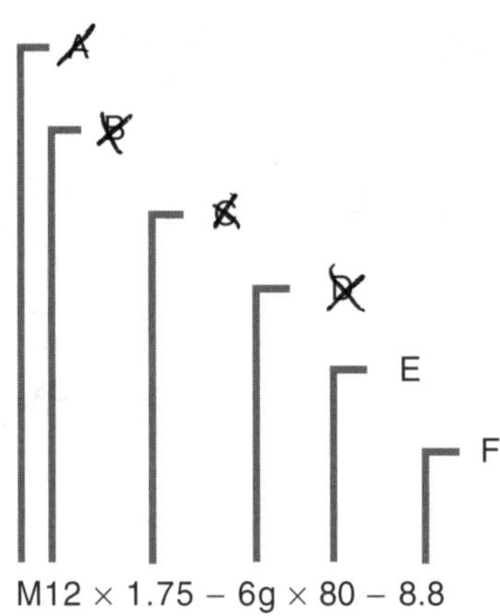

Completion

62. A(n) _____ has threads at each end and has no head. — 62. STUD

63. Torque-to-yield bolts are tightened until they are stretched beyond their _____ limit. — 63. ELASTIC

64. In order to measure the number of threads per inch, or pitch if metric, a special _____ should be used. — 64. GAUGE

65. When internal or external threads are stripped, often they can be repaired by means of a _____ and _____ or a heli-coil. — 65. STANDARD SCREW & TAPPED HOLE

66. When replacing metric bolts, increasing numbers indicate _____ (increasing, decreasing) strength. — 66. INCREASING

67. A(n) _____ sealer is similar to RTV, but it can cure in the absence of air. — 67. ANAEROBIC

68. The purpose of any _____ is to prevent a liquid from going where it is not wanted. — 68. SEAL

69. _____-_____ are used where there is no axial or rotational movement. — 69. O-RINGS

70. A(n) _____ _____ seal is used where there is only axial movement like a disc brake caliper. — 70. SQUARE-CUT

71. _____ rings are used where there is axial and rotational movement. — 71. SNAP

Name ______________________

72. The _____ seal prevents oil or lubricant from leaking while the shaft turns and prevents dirt from entering into the lubricant.

72. SHAFT

73. A(n) _____ compensates for small irregularities between two flat metal surfaces.

73. GASKET.

74. If a cylinder head is warped _____ of an inch or more, the head must be machined.

74. .006"

75. If more than 0.030″ must be removed from a cylinder head, the remaining cylinder head on a V-type engine and intake manifold must also be resurfaced. If this is not done, the bolt holes and passages will not _____.

75. AILGN

Short Answer

76. List four types of information you need to know when ordering threaded fasteners.

SIZE

THREADS PER INCH

COARSE

LENGTH

77. What is the difference between a cap screw and a machine screw?

MACHINE SCREW IS SPICIC SIZE

78. What is the procedure for removing a broken bolt?

DRILL THE BOLT 1/2 THE DIAMETER

HAMMER THE TAP

USE WRENCH OR RATCHET TO REMOVE

79. What is the most common cause of gasket failure?

OVER TIGHTENING BOLTS

80. Should a gasket be reused? Explain your answer.

NO IT WONT HAVE A TIGHT SEAL

Chapter 5
Measuring Instruments

Name ____________________

Date ____________ Instructor ____________

Score ______ Textbook pages 59–64

After studying the chapter in the text and completing this section of the workbook, you will be able to:
- ❑ List the different types of measuring instruments used when servicing automobiles.
- ❑ Explain how to read a micrometer.
- ❑ State the purpose of telescoping gauges.
- ❑ Demonstrate how to read a Vernier caliper.

Multiple Choice

1. Which of the following is an instrument used to take linear measurements? 1. ____________
   (A) Vernier caliper.
   (B) Micrometer.
   (C) Dial gauge.
   (D) Feeler gauge.
2. To read the micrometer, multiply the number of vertical divisions visible on the sleeve by _____. 2. ____________
   (A) 5
   (B) 10
   (C) 25
   (D) 100
3. A Vernier caliper is a measuring device capable of measuring to within _____. 3. ____________
   (A) 0.01″
   (B) 0.001″
   (C) 0.0001″
   (D) 0.00001″

Name ______________________

4. A feeler gauge consists of _____. 4. ______________
   (A) an assortment of steel strips of graduated thicknesses
   (B) springs
   (C) dials
   (D) None of the above.

Identification

Identify the parts indicated on the conventional micrometer below.

5. Friction stop. 5. ______________

6. Anvil. 6. ______________

7. Spindle. 7. ______________

8. Spindle lock. 8. ______________

9. Thimble. 9. ______________

10. Sleeve. 10. ______________

11. Frame. 11. ______________

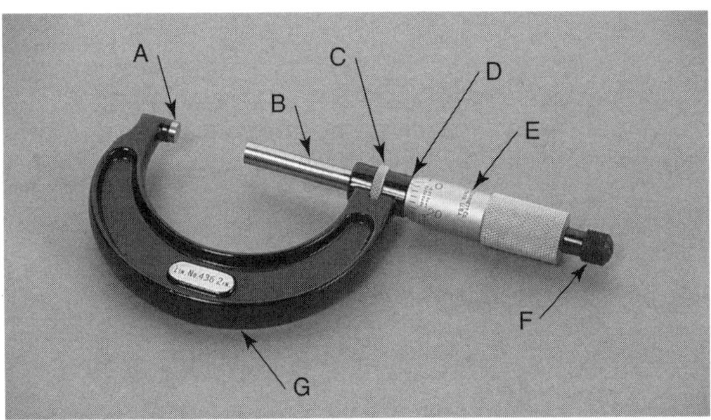

Identify the parts of the dial gauge at the top of the next page.

12. Dial face. 12. ______________

13. Shank. 13. ______________

14. Contact. 14. ______________

15. Bezel. 15. ______________

16. Pointer. 16. ______________

17. Graduations. 17. ______________

18. Increments. 18. ______________

19. Stem. 19. ______________

Name ______________________

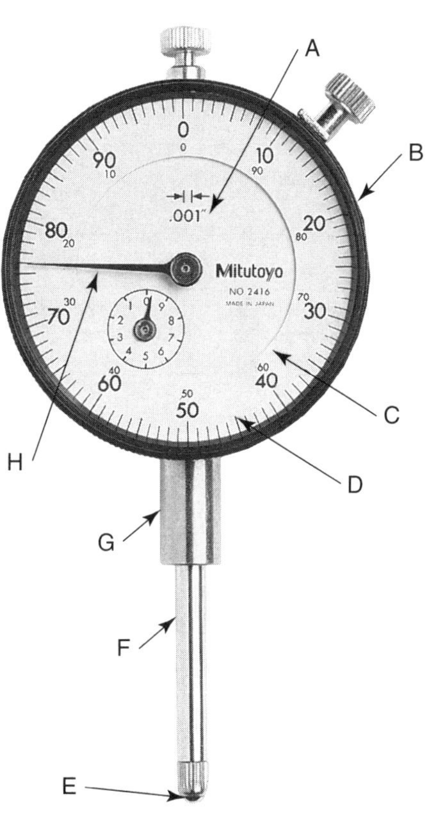

Completion

20. The _____ micrometer is used for measuring the inside diameter of a cylinder. 20. ______________

21. The _____ micrometer is designed to measure the outside diameter of cylindrical forms and the thickness of materials. 21. ______________

22. ____ gauges are used to duplicate inner dimensions. A micrometer is then used to measure the gauge. 22. ______________

23. _____ gauges are used extensively for measuring the backlash of gears and the end play of shafts. 23. ______________

Short Answer

24. What is the reading on this conventional micrometer?

____

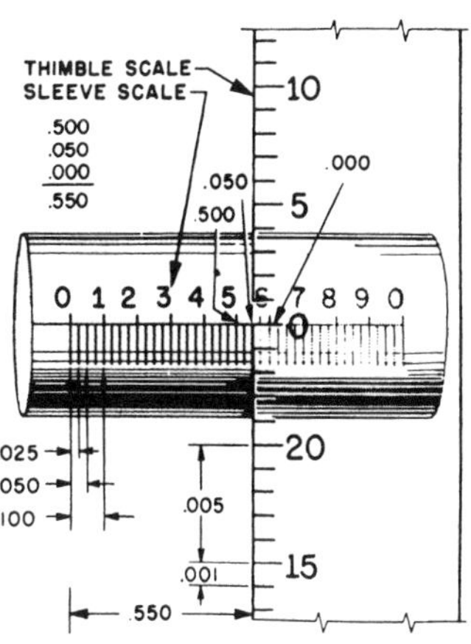

Name ______________________________

25. When using a micrometer, why should you take care *not* to turn the thimble too tight?

____

____

26. What is the reading on this metric micrometer scale?

____

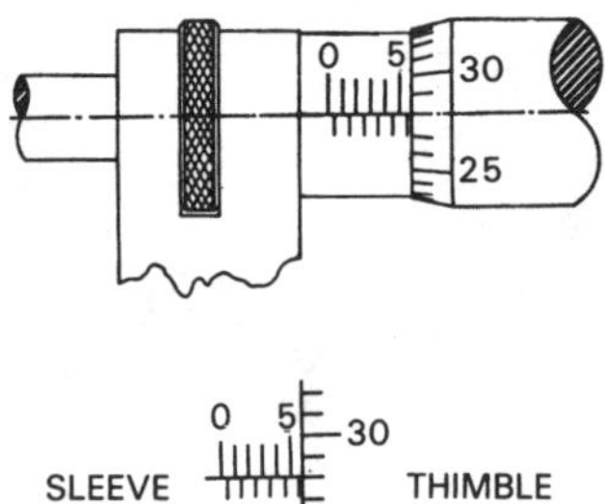

SLEEVE 0 5 30 25 THIMBLE

27. What is the reading on this Vernier caliper?

____

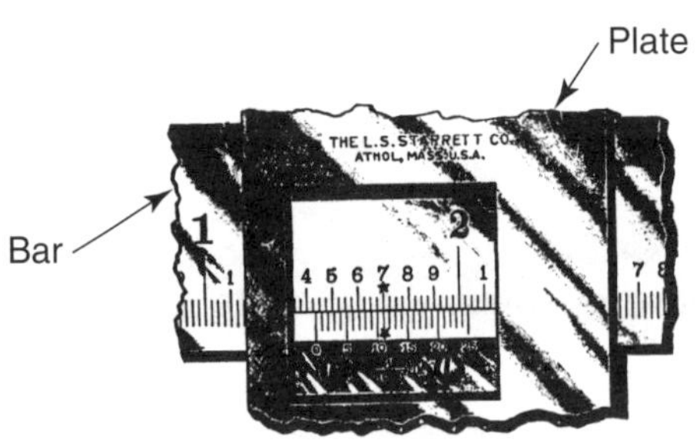

28. What is being checked with the dial indicator shown below?

____

____

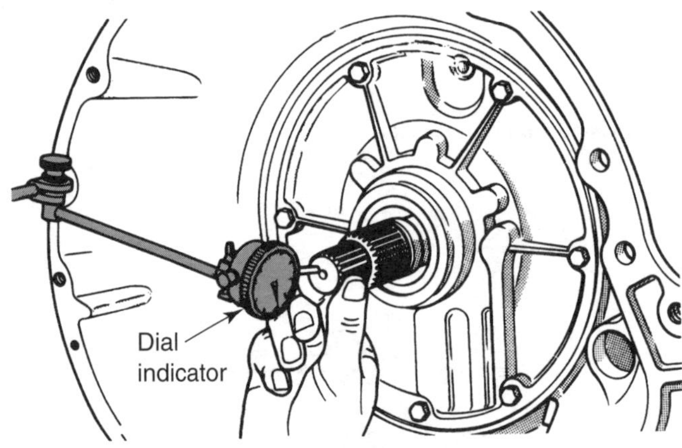

29. Explain how to use a feeler gauge and describe when it would be used.

____

____

____

Chapter 6

Meters, Testers, and Analyzers

Name ______________________

Date ____________ Instructor ____________

Score ______ Textbook pages 65–72

After studying the chapter in the text and completing this section of the workbook, you will be able to:

- ❑ List the basic instruments used for electrical systems testing.
- ❑ Explain how voltmeter and ammeter leads must be hooked up to an electrical circuit.
- ❑ State tests that are possible with a battery fast charger/tester.
- ❑ Name and describe a broad range of engine analyzers.

Multiple Choice

1. Which of the following would an automotive technician use to test electrical systems? 1. ____________
   (A) Vacuum gauge.
   (B) Cylinder leakage tester.
   (C) Ammeter.
   (D) Infrared exhaust analyzer.

2. Which of the following would an automotive technician use for internal engine troubleshooting? 2. ____________
   (A) Voltmeter.
   (B) Compression tester.
   (C) Alternator-regulator tester.
   (D) Ohmmeter.

3. The tachometer is designed to measure the _____. 3. ____________
   (A) speed of a rotating part
   (B) inductance produced by an electrical component
   (C) temperature of engine parts
   (D) specific gravity of electrolyte

Name ______________________

4. Five-gas analyzers can be used to measure each of the following except:
   (A) hydrocarbons
   (B) nitrogen
   (C) carbon dioxide
   (D) carbon monoxide

4. ______________________

5. Which of the following allows the technician to visually observe and measure the instantaneous voltage in an electrical circuit?
   (A) Ammeter.
   (B) Oscilloscope.
   (C) Scan tool.
   (D) All of the above.

5. ______________________

Identification

Identify the two test instruments shown below.

6. Multimeter. 6. ______________________
7. Scan tool. 7. ______________________

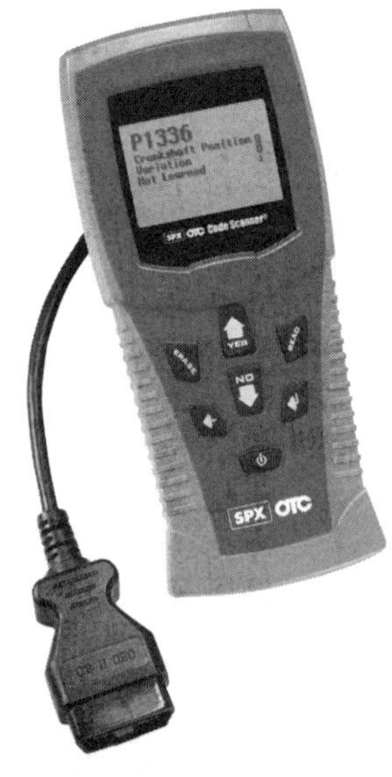

A

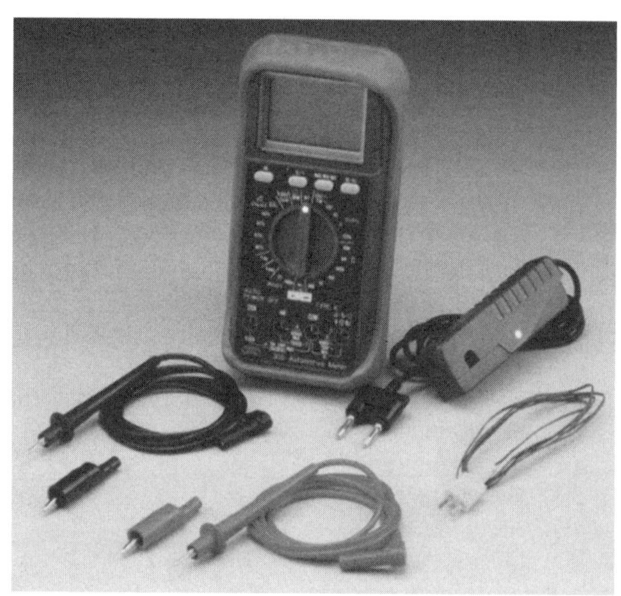

B

Completion

8. The schematic below shows how to hook up a(n) ______ across a circuit.

8. ______________________

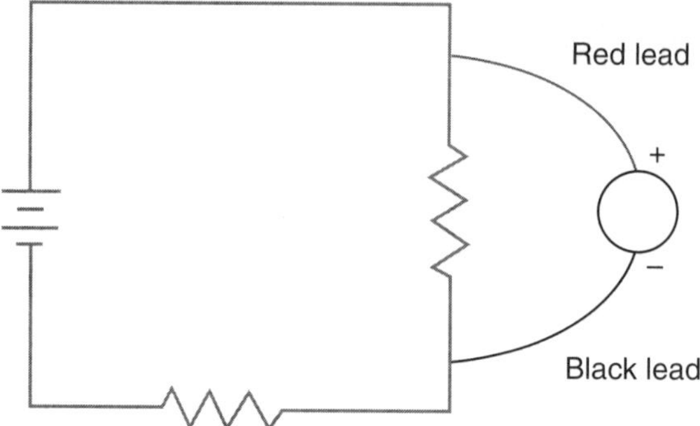

Name ______________________________

9. The schematic below shows how to hook up a(n) ______ in the circuit. 9. ______________________________

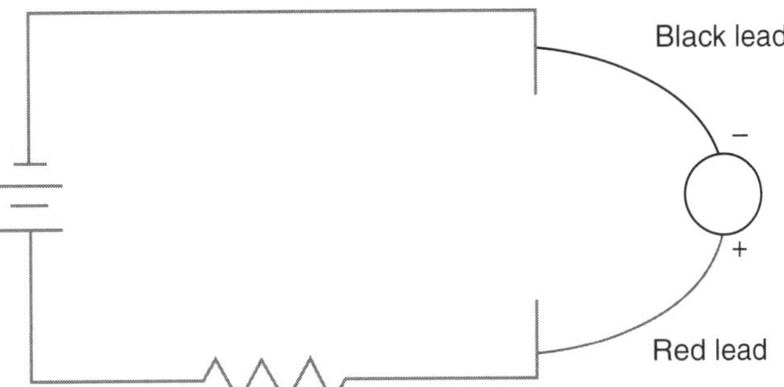

10. The schematic drawing below shows how to hook up a(n) ______. 10. ______________________________

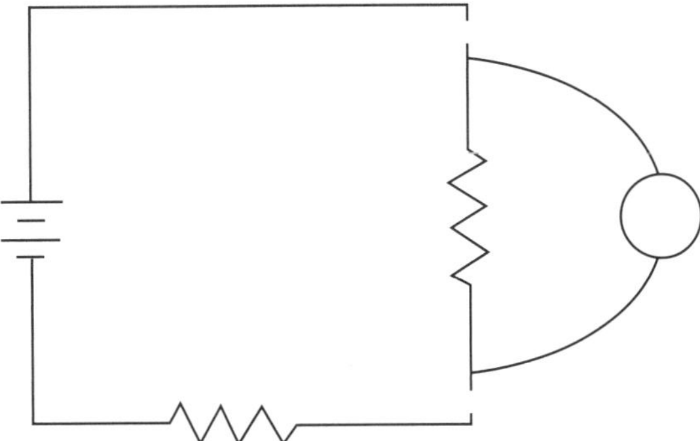

11. The ______ is designed to indicate the speed of a rotating part in revolutions per minute (rpm) as in measuring the speed of the engine. 11. ______________________________

12. A ______ ______ is used to retrieve diagnostic trouble codes from a vehicle's computer system. 12. ______________________________

13. A timing light is used to check ______ timing. 13. ______________________________

14. ______ gas analyzers provide information that can be used to determine air-fuel ratio. 14. ______________________________

Short Answer

15. List the two types of meters used most often in automotive service work.

____

____

Name ______________________________

16. Describe what the technician is doing in the photo below.

____

____

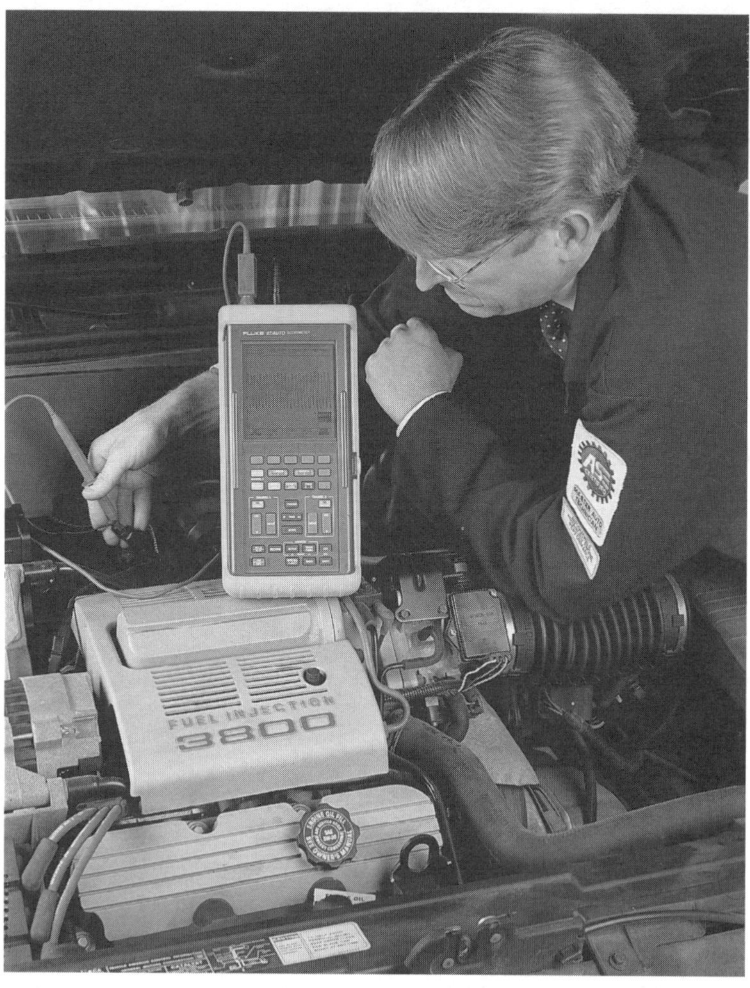

17. Explain why the scan tool is one of the most important diagnostic tools used by the automotive technician.

____

____

____

____

____

____

Matching

Match the term in the right column with its description in the left column. Place the corresponding letter in the blank.

18. Used to measure voltage.	(A) Ammeter.	18. ______
19. Used to measure resistance.	(B) Voltmeter.	19. ______
20. Used to measure current.	(C) Ohmmeter.	20. ______

Chapter 7
Engine Fundamentals

Name ______________________________

Date ______________ Instructor ______________

Score ______ Textbook pages 73–84

After studying the chapter in the text and completing this section of the workbook, you will be able to:
- ❑ Differentiate between various engine types.
- ❑ Describe the construction and operation of the major engine components.
- ❑ List the sequence of events in two- and four-cycle engine operation.

Multiple Choice

1. The ______ internal combustion engine has been refined to such a degree that it has almost complete dominance of the automotive field.
   (A) free piston
   (B) rotary combustion
   (C) four-cycle, reciprocating
   (D) gas turbine

1. C

2. Which of the following is ordinarily the most intricate piece of metal in the automobile?
   (A) Engine block.
   (B) Cylinder head.
   (C) Crankshaft.
   (D) Pistons.

2. A

3. The pistons move ______ in the engine cylinders.
   (A) side-to-side
   (B) diagonally
   (C) up-and-down
   (D) None of the above.

3. C or A

4. In an I-head engine, both valves are located ______ the piston.
   (A) under
   (B) above
   (C) on the side of
   (D) None of the above.

4. B

Name ______________________________

5. Most automobile engines operate on a _____ cycle.
   (A) four-stroke
   (B) three-stroke
   (C) two-stroke
   (D) one-stroke

5. A

6. In a two-stroke engine, the _____ acts like a valve in controlling the filling and emptying of the cylinder.
   (A) piston
   (B) lifter
   (C) camshaft
   (D) crankshaft

6. A

Identification

Identify the parts indicated on this water-cooled engine.

7. Return heater hose. — 7. C
8. Thermostat. — 8. A
9. Radiator drain petcock. — 9. E
10. Heater hose. — 10. B
11. Radiator cap. — 11. H
12. Radiator. — 12. F
13. Water pump. — 13. G
14. Lower radiator hose. — 14. D
15. Bypass hose. — 15. I
16. Overflow hose. — 16. J

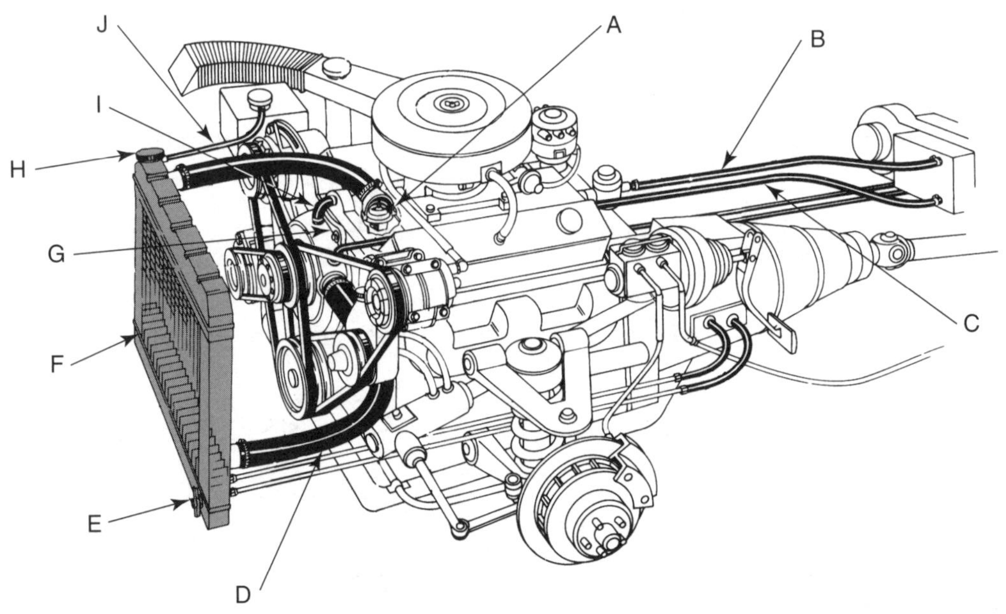

Name ____________________

Identify the cylinder arrangement in the engine blocks shown below.

17. Opposed. 17. C
18. In-line. 18. A
19. V-type. 19. B

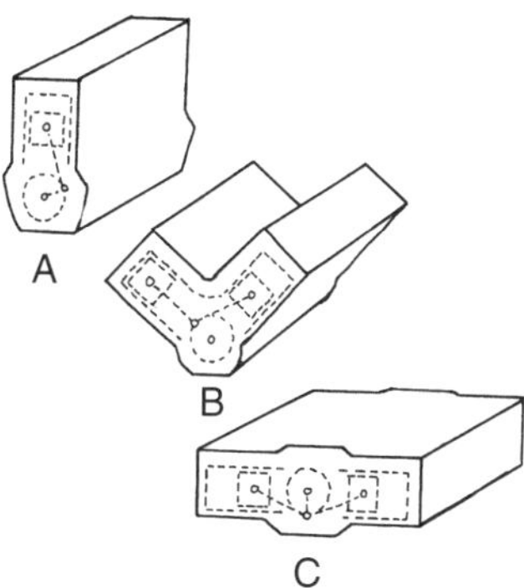

Identify the parts of the piston below.

20. Head. 20. A
21. Ring grooves. 21. C
22. Lands. 22. F
23. Cut provides clearance from counterweights when piston is at BDC. 23. D
24. Skirt. 24. E
25. Indentations that provide clearance for valves. 25. B

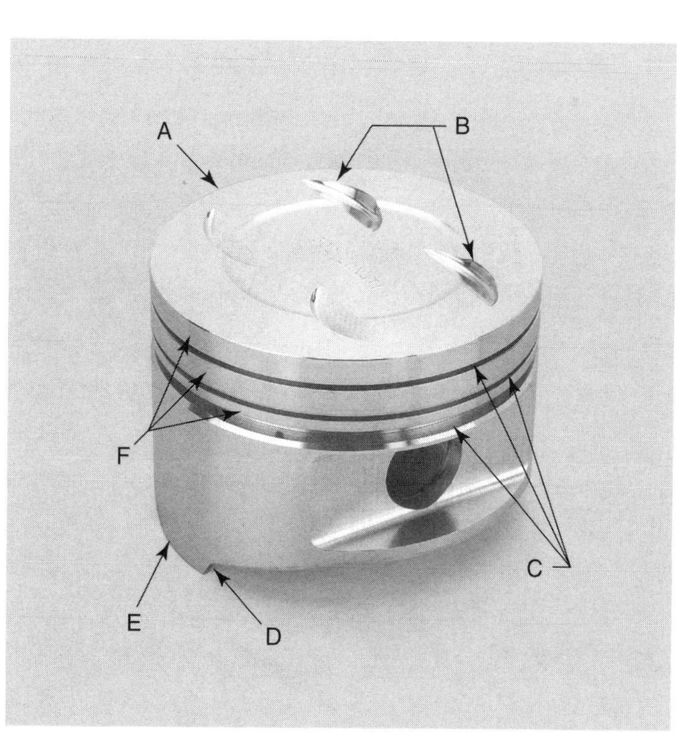

Name ______________________________

Identify the parts indicated on this illustration.

26. Head gasket. — 26. B
27. Cylinder block. — 27. C
28. Cylinder head. — 28. A

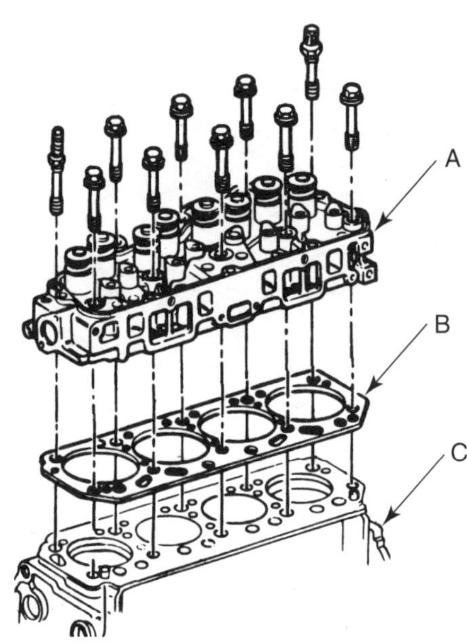

Identify the parts indicated on the diagram below.

29. Belt tensioner. — 29. B
30. Timing belt. — 30. C
31. Camshaft pulley. — 31. A
32. Crankshaft pulley. — 32. D

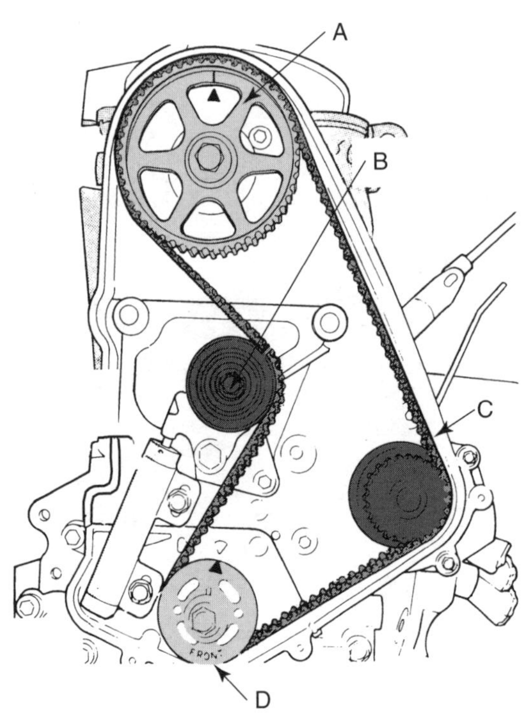

Name ______________________

Identify the combustion chamber shapes shown below.

33. "Hemi" or hemispherical. 33. B

34. Wedge. 34. A

A

B

Completion

35. All internal combustion engines burn fuel _____ their cylinders. 35. WITHIN

36. The _____ _____ link the pistons to the crankshaft. 36. CONNECTING ROD

37. The _____ opens the valves at the appropriate times in the combustion cycle. 37. CAMSHAFT

38. A(n) _____ transmits the action of the cam to the valve or push rod. 38. LOBE

39. The _____-shaped combustion chamber is an efficient design used in most engines. 39. V

40. The _____ chamber is the space within the cylinder above the piston where the burning of the air-fuel mixture occurs. 40. COMBUSTION

Short Answer

41. List seven design requirements that are considered desirable in an automobile engine.

EASE OF STARTING

RELIABILITY

POWER

RESPONSIVENESS

ECONOMY IN FUEL, OIL, AND REPAIRS

EASE OF HANDLING

QUIET OPERATION

Name ______________________________

42. List the eight basic components in a four-cycle automotive engine.

ENGINE BLOCK

CRANKSHAFT

PISTONS

PISTONS RINGS

CONNECTING RODS

PISTON PIN

CYLINDE HEAD

VALVE TRAIN

43. What is the purpose of the piston rings?

TO SEAL THE COMBUSTION CHAMBER

44. Describe the sequence of events in the following diagrams of this four-cycle engine.

(A) PISTON HEAD MOVES DOWN TAKEING IN AIR AND FUEL

(B) PISTON MOVES UP WITH INTENCE COMPRESON, ~~[illegible]~~ AND BEFOR IT REACHES THE TOP & A SPARK

(C) AIR/FUEL AND IGNITES FORCEING THE PISTON DOWN

(D) ~~BEFOR~~ ~~IT~~ ~~ONE~~ ONCE AROUND THE EXSAUST VALE IS OPEND

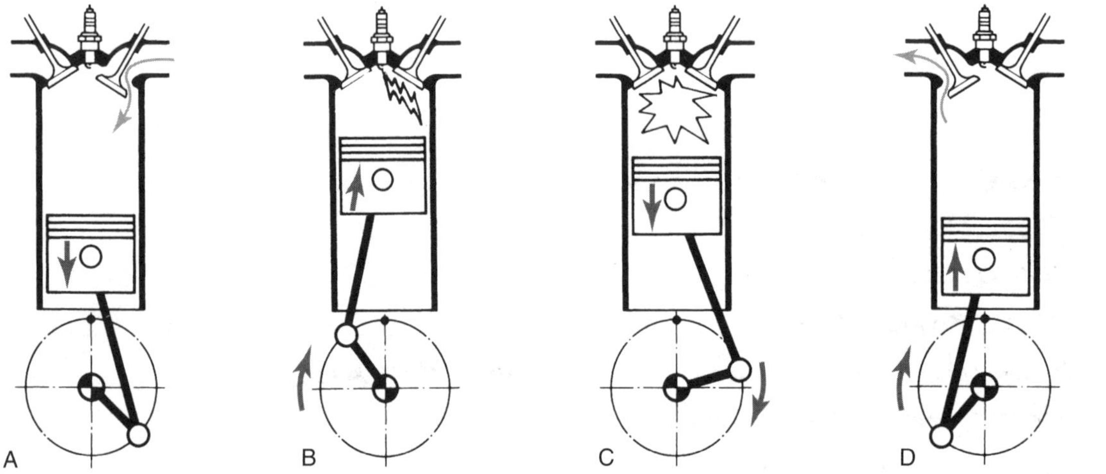

A B C D

Name ______________________

45. Describe the sequence of events in the following diagram of this two-cycle diesel engine.

(A) Piston at BDC. The intake ports are uncoverd and the blower forces air into the cylinder

(B) As the piston moves upward, the ports are closed. The air is compressed, causing the temp of the air to increase

(C) Fuel is injected into the cylinder. The temp of the compressed air ignites the fuel mixture (no spark plug)

(D) Explosion forces the piston down. The exhaust valve starts to open and the exhaust gases escape

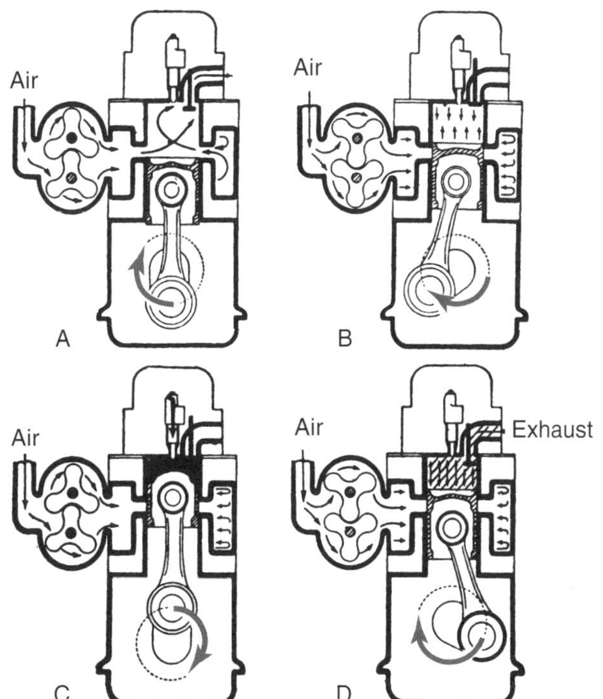

Chapter 8

Measuring Engine Performance

Name ______________________________

Date ______________ Instructor ______________

Score ______ Textbook pages 85–92

After studying the chapter in the text and completing this section of the workbook, you will be able to:

- ❑ Define work, inertia, energy, torque, and friction.
- ❑ Explain the different types of measurable horsepower.
- ❑ Determine the compression ratio of an engine.

Multiple Choice

1. Inertia is the force that causes an object to remain _____. 1. ______________
   - (A) stationary, unless acted upon by an external force
   - (B) in motion once that object is in motion, unless the object is acted on by an external force.
   - (C) Both A and B.
   - (D) None of the above.
2. A piston at TDC is an example of _____. 2. ______________
   - (A) potential energy
   - (B) kinetic energy
   - (C) torque
   - (D) friction
3. After a certain engine speed is reached, the volumetric efficiency _____. 3. ______________
   - (A) drops rapidly
   - (B) increases rapidly
   - (C) increases gradually
   - (D) remains the same
4. The diameter of an engine cylinder is referred to as the _____. 4. ______________
   - (A) displacement
   - (B) bore
   - (C) stroke
   - (D) compression

Name ______________________________

5. Engine horsepower ratings have dropped since 1972 because of _____. 5. ______________________
   (A) the extra "plumbing" that has been installed to reduce exhaust emissions
   (B) quoting net horsepower ratings instead of gross horsepower ratings
   (C) quoting gross horsepower ratings instead of net horsepower ratings
   (D) Both A and B.

Identification

The graph below shows percentages of where the power goes on a normally aspirated engine. Indicate where this power goes in the space provided.

6. In power train. 6. ______________________
7. To propel vehicle. 7. ______________________
8. In cooling water, air, and oil. 8. ______________________
9. In engine friction. 9. ______________________
10. In exhaust gas. 10. ______________________

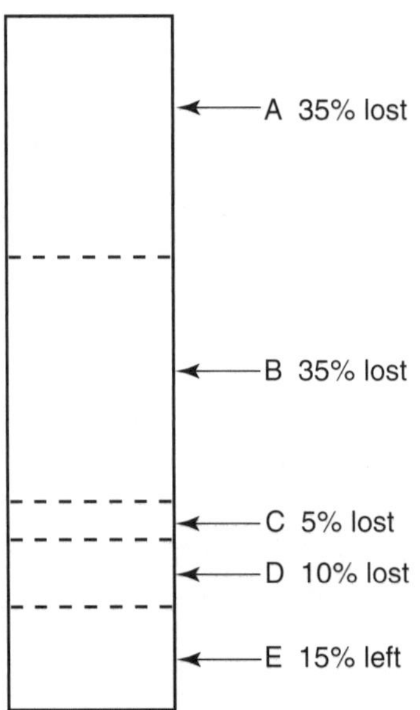

Completion

11. _____ is the turning or twisting force on an object. 11. ______________________
12. _____ is the resistance between two bodies in contact with each other, or separated only by a lubricant. 12. ______________________
13. The ratio of the amount of charge actually taken in per cycle to a complete charge is known as the _____ efficiency. 13. ______________________
14. The ratio of the heat equivalent of work done in an engine to the total heat supplied is referred to as its _____ efficiency. 14. ______________________

Name ______________________________

15. _____ _____ is the power that is available for propelling the vehicle. It is the power developed within the cylinder (indicated horsepower) less the power that remains after the effects of friction and the power that is required to drive the fan, water pump, oil pump, and generator.

15. ______________________________

16. Friction horsepower is the power to overcome the friction within the _____.

16. ______________________________

17. Look at the diagrams below. The compression ratio is equal to the volume of _____ (A,B) divided by _____ (A,B).

17. ______________________________

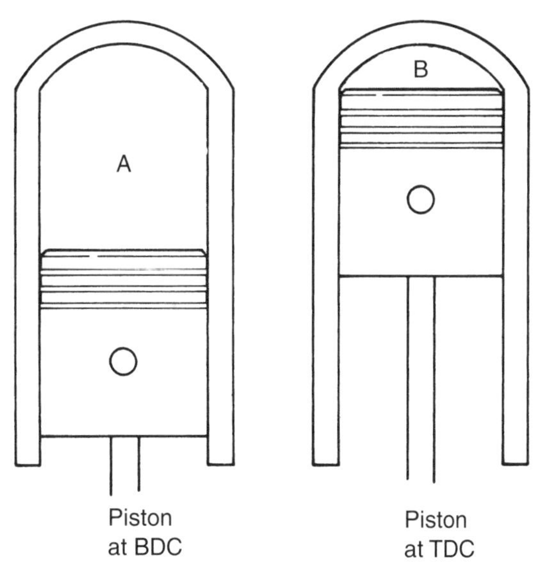

Short Answer

18. If a 5 lb. weight is lifted 2 ft., how much work is performed in foot pounds?

____

19. How many horsepower would be required to raise a weight of 2000 lb. a distance of 60 ft. in two minutes?

____

20. Name the type of energy illustrated below.

____

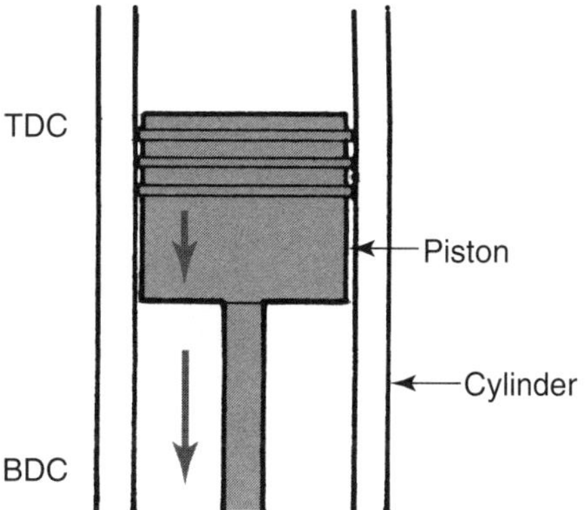

Name ______________________________

21. In the following formula, what do the letters represent?

    Displacement = A x S x N

    A = ______________________________

    S = ______________________________

    N = ______________________________

22. How is the compression ratio of an engine calculated?

    ____

    ____

23. In the formula for rated horsepower, what do the following letters represent?

    N = ______________________________

    B = ______________________________

24. In the formula for indicated horsepower, what do the following letters represent?

    P = ______________________________

    L = ______________________________

    A = ______________________________

    N = ______________________________

    K = ______________________________

25. List six ways the horsepower of an engine can be increased.

    ____

    ____

    ____

    ____

    ____

    ____

26. Explain why installation of a turbocharger is one of the most effective methods of increasing the output of an engine.

    ____

    ____

    ____

    ____

Chapter 9

Engine Top End Construction

Name ______________________________

Date ______________ Instructor ______________

Score _____ Textbook pages 93–106

After studying the chapter in the text and completing this section of the workbook, you will be able to:

- ❑ Identify engine top end components.
- ❑ Describe cylinder head variations.
- ❑ Describe the function of intake and exhaust manifolds.
- ❑ Explain the importance of cylinder head gaskets.
- ❑ Describe the function of the camshaft and explain how the shape of the cams affect engine operation.
- ❑ Explain the construction and operation of poppet valves.

Multiple Choice

1. If a cylinder head gasket is not sealing properly, _____.
   (A) engine performance will improve
   (B) engine performance will suffer
   (C) engine performance will be unaffected
   (D) None of the above.

   1. ______________________

2. Most camshafts have _____ cams as there are cylinders.
   (A) the same number of
   (B) twice as many
   (C) three times as many
   (D) four times as many

   2. ______________________

3. Exhaust valves are usually made of heat-resistant _____.
   (A) iron
   (B) copper
   (C) alloy steel
   (D) None of the above.

   3. ______________________

Name ______________________________

4. Valve seals prevent _____ from entering the valve guide. 4. ______________________
   (A) water
   (B) oil
   (C) fuel
   (D) air

Identification

Identify the typical engine top end components shown below.

5. Valve. 5. ______________________
6. Valve guide. 6. ______________________
7. Valve seal and valve spring seat assembly. 7. ______________________
8. Camshaft oil seal. 8. ______________________
9. Hydraulic lash adjuster. 9. ______________________
10. Camshaft bearing caps. 10. ______________________
11. Head gasket. 11. ______________________
12. Valve spring. 12. ______________________
13. Valve retaining locks. 13. ______________________
14. Roller follower. 14. ______________________
15. Plug. 15. ______________________
16. Cylinder head. 16. ______________________
17. Valve spring retainer. 17. ______________________
18. Camshaft. 18. ______________________

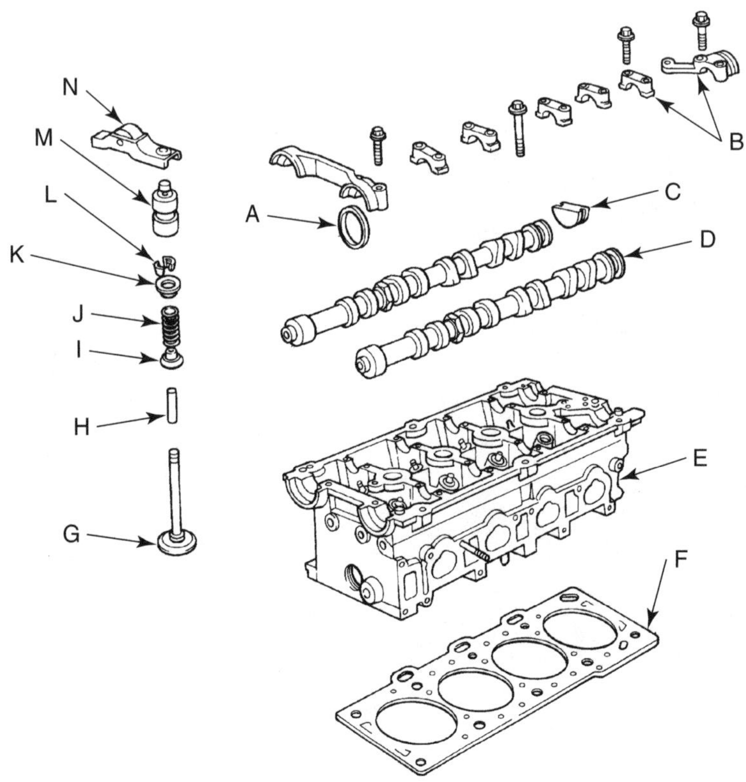

Name ______________________________

Identify the parts indicated on the valve train below.

19. Intake valve. 19. ______________________
20. Exhaust valve. 20. ______________________
21. Cylinder head. 21. ______________________
22. Valve spring. 22. ______________________
23. Camshaft. 23. ______________________
24. Cam. 24. ______________________
25. Rocker arms. 25. ______________________
26. Push rods. 26. ______________________
27. Lifter. 27. ______________________

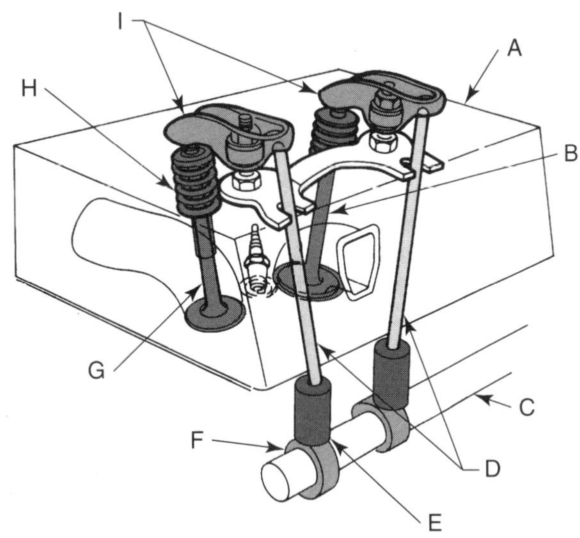

Identify the items indicated on the valve shown below.

28. Valve margin. 28. ______________________
29. Stem. 29. ______________________
30. Valve face. 30. ______________________
31. Fillet. 31. ______________________
32. Head. 32. ______________________

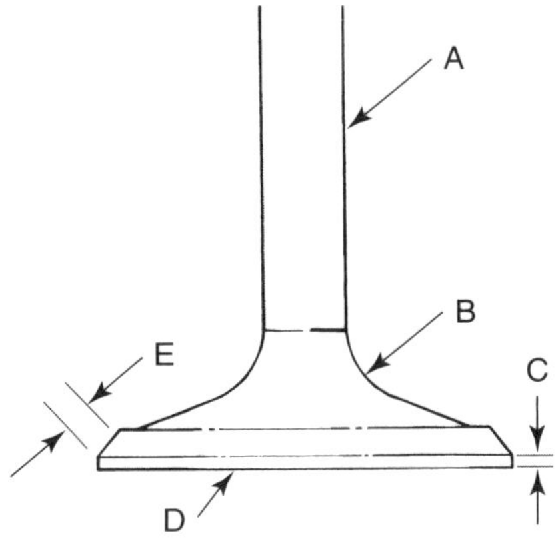

Name ______________________________

Identify the parts indicated on the hydraulic valve lifter shown below.

33. Spring. 33. ______________
34. Ball retainer. 34. ______________
35. Lock ring. 35. ______________
36. Push rod cup. 36. ______________
37. Body. 37. ______________
38. Metering disc. 38. ______________
39. Ball. 39. ______________
40. Plunger. 40. ______________

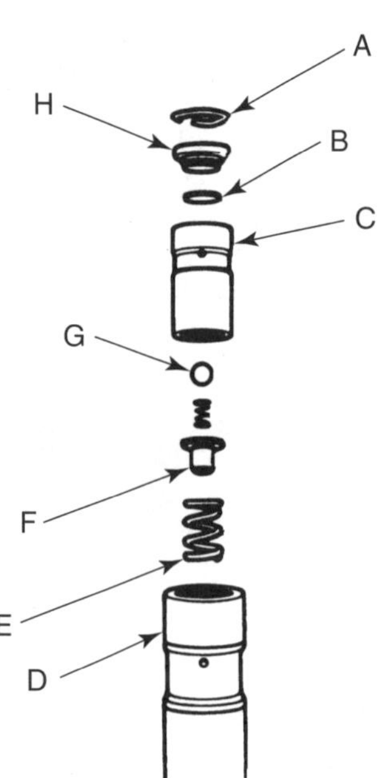

Completion

41. The _____ _____ is mounted on the top of the engine block and forms the top section of the combustion chamber. 41. ______________

42. The _____ manifold routes air or an air/fuel mixture from the throttle body or carburetor to the cylinder head valve ports. 42. ______________

43. A(n) _____ manifold routes exhaust from the cylinder head exhaust ports to the exhaust system. 43. ______________

44. In a car's engine, the _____ open and close the valves of the engine as they rotate. 44. ______________

45. Anything that reduces the _____ area between the valve and the cylinder head will hamper the transfer of heat from the valve. 45. ______________

Name ____________________

46. The _____ _____ is a device in the valve system that transmits the action of the cam to the valve or the push rod. 46. ____________________

47. _____ _____ change the direction of the cam's lifting motion. 47. ____________________

48. _____ _____ use cylindrical rods that transfer the motion of the lifters to the rocker arms. 48. ____________________

49. Variable valve timing systems can alter valve timing in relation to engine _____. 49. ____________________

Short Answer

50. List the three major components of the engine top end.

____

____

____

51. List the four components of the valve train.

____

____

____

____

52. Why is an overhead camshaft more efficient than a camshaft located in the engine block?

____

____

____

53. In valve cooling, how does the heat of combustion flow?

____

____

____

Chapter 10
Engine Bottom End Construction

Name ______________________________

Date ______________ Instructor ______________

Score ______ Textbook pages 107–122

After studying the chapter in the text and completing this section of the workbook, you will be able to:

- ❑ Identify engine bottom end components.
- ❑ Describe crankshaft constructions.
- ❑ Describe the purpose of connecting rods.
- ❑ Describe piston and piston ring variations.
- ❑ Explain the operation of poppet valves.
- ❑ Describe various components designed to minimize engine vibration.
- ❑ Explain the purpose of engine bearings and identify the types of bearings used in a modern engine.

Multiple Choice

1. Engine block distortion may occur from _____. 1. ______________________
   (A) incorrect placement of the metal masses around the cylinders
   (B) expansion and contraction due to the heat of operation
   (C) excessive mechanical stresses
   (D) All of the above.

2. Without special balance weights or counterweights on the crankshaft, severe vibration would result from _____. 2. ______________________
   (A) weight of reciprocating parts and rotating parts
   (B) inertial force of reciprocating parts
   (C) combustion pressures and variations in torque
   (D) All of the above.

3. _____ balance of the crankshaft is obtained with the weight distributed equally in all directions from the center of the crankshaft while it is at rest. 3. ______________________
   (A) Static
   (B) Dynamic
   (C) Direct
   (D) Rotating

Name ______________________________

4. _____ is now preferred as a material for pistons.
   (A) Iron
   (B) Silicon
   (C) Aluminum alloy
   (D) Copper alloy

4. ______________________________

5. Latest developments in the design of piston rings tend to _____.
   (A) reduce emissions
   (B) reduce oil consumption
   (C) improve engine durability
   (D) All of the above.

5. ______________________________

Identification

Identify the items indicated on the illustration below.

6. Camshaft. 6. ______________________________
7. Bearings. 7. ______________________________
8. Crankshaft. 8. ______________________________
9. Connecting rod. 9. ______________________________
10. Engine block. 10. ______________________________
11. Bearings. 11. ______________________________
12. Connecting rod cap. 12. ______________________________
13. Piston. 13. ______________________________
14. Bearing caps. 14. ______________________________
15. Bearings. 15. ______________________________

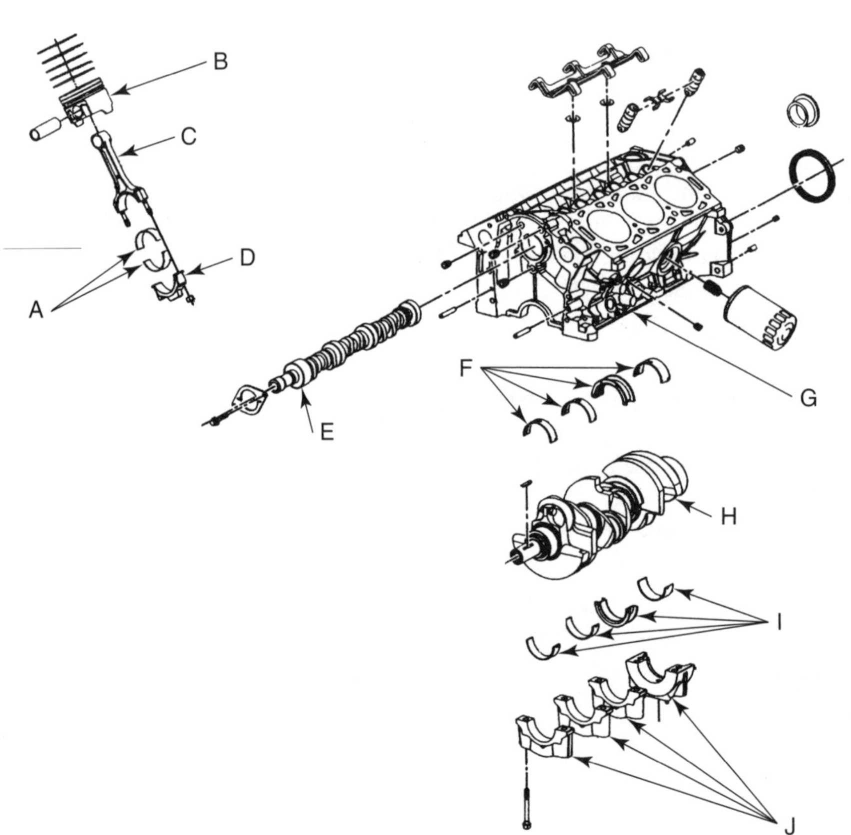

Name ____________________

Identify the items indicated on the illustration below.

16. Retainer. 16. ____________________
17. Piston. 17. ____________________
18. Connecting rod. 18. ____________________
19. Piston pin. 19. ____________________

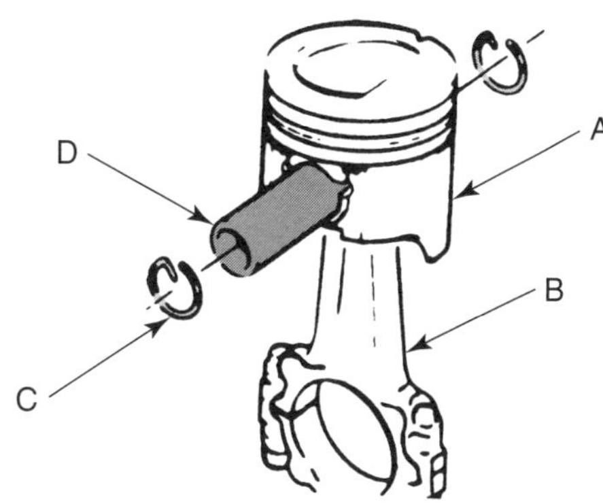

Identify the items indicated on the precision insert bearing below.

20. Precision bearing. 20. ____________________
21. Connecting rod. 21. ____________________
22. Tang. 22. ____________________
23. Notch. 23. ____________________
24. Notch. 24. ____________________
25. Rod cap. 25. ____________________

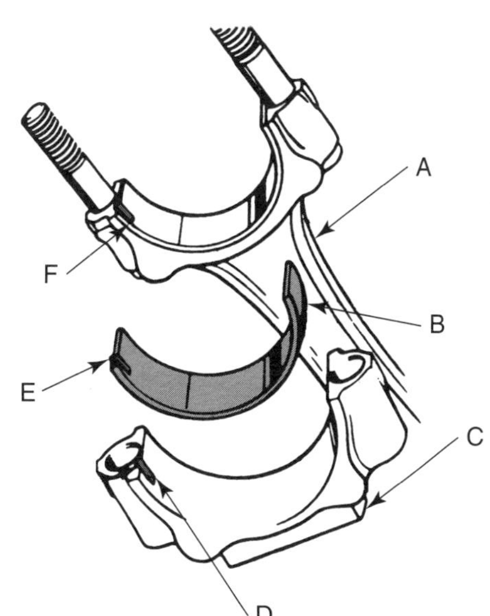

Name ______________________________

Identify the items indicated on the illustration below.

26. Lower main bearing. 26. ______________________
27. Engine block. 27. ______________________
28. Lower thrust bearing. 28. ______________________
29. Lower main bearing. 29. ______________________
30. Upper thrust bearing. 30. ______________________
31. Crankshaft. 31. ______________________
32. Upper main bearing. 32. ______________________
33. Upper main bearing. 33. ______________________
34. Rear main seal. 34. ______________________
35. Main bearing caps. 35. ______________________

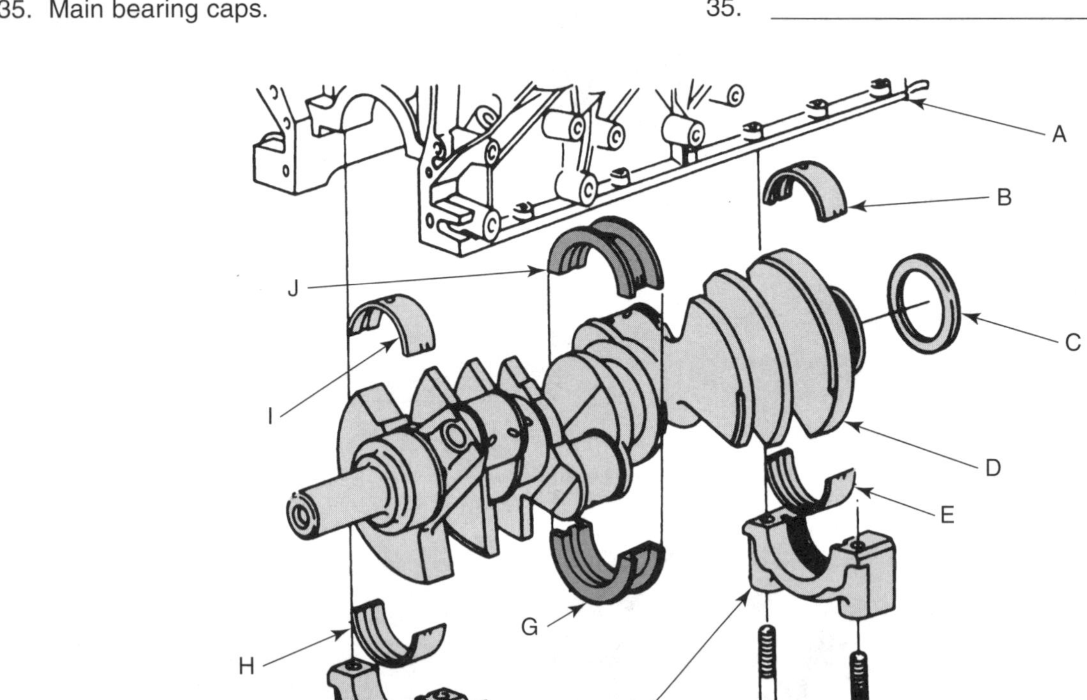

Completion

36. The _____ _____ is an intricate metal casting that contains the cylinders, pistons, connecting rods, crankshaft, and in some cases, the camshaft. 36. ______________________

37. The number of _____ used to support the crankshaft will depend on the number of cylinders in the engine and the design of the engine. 37. ______________________

38. _____ offset the weight of the piston and rod. 38. ______________________

39. _____ _____ add mass to the end of the crankshaft opposite the flywheel to minimize crankshaft twist. 39. ______________________

40. _____ _____ connect the upper end of the connecting rod to the piston. 40. ______________________

Name ______________________

41. The purpose of the _____ is to help the engine idle smoothly by carrying the pistons through parts of the operating cycle when power is not being produced.
42. While different firing orders are used, the general idea of an inline engine firing order is to fire cylinders as nearly as possible at _____ ends of the crankshaft.
43. The purpose of any _____ _____ is to provide a surface of dissimilar metal for the moving parts to rotate on, reducing friction.
44. A _____ rear main seal is the most commonly used in modern engines.

41. ______________________

42. ______________________

43. ______________________

44. ______________________

Short Answer

45. What components make up the engine bottom end?

____

____

____

46. Why are piston skirts impregnated with silicon?

____

____

47. The modern method of connecting the piston to the connecting rod involves what is known as an interference fit. Explain how this is achieved.

____

____

48. List the two types of antifriction bearings that have been used in automobile engines.

____

____

Chapter 11

Engine Removal, Disassembly, and Cleaning

Name ______________________________

Date ________________ Instructor ________________

Score_______ Textbook pages 123–130

After studying the chapter in the text and completing this section of the workbook, you will be able to:

- ❑ Describe how an engine is removed from a vehicle.
- ❑ Explain the basic steps for engine disassembly.
- ❑ Describe the various methods used to clean engine parts during and after disassembly.

Multiple Choice

1. Immediately after removal, _____.
   (A) mount the engine on an engine stand
   (B) lower the engine to the ground and support it on wood blocks
   (C) suspend the engine with a hoist or crane before beginning work
   (D) Either A or B.

1. ______________________________

2. If the timing belt, gear, or chain cover is stuck, _____ to remove it.
   (A) tap it lightly with a soft-faced hammer
   (B) strike it firmly with a hammer
   (C) pry between the mating surfaces
   (D) None of the above.

2. ______________________________

3. Parts made of _____ should be cleaned with special detergents at lower temperatures than used on other metals.
   (A) iron
   (B) aluminum
   (C) steel
   (D) Both A and C.

3. ______________________________

Name ______________________________

4. Which of the following cleaning methods uses high-frequency vibrations introduced into a liquid? 4. ______________________
   (A) Jet method.
   (B) Blasting.
   (C) Ultrasonic.
   (D) Hot tank method.

Identification

Identify the items that must be removed or disconnected before engine removal from the diagram shown at the top of the next page.

5. Disconnect battery cables. 5. ______________________
6. Drain radiator. 6. ______________________
7. Discharge A/C. 7. ______________________
8. Remove/Install air cleaner assembly. 8. ______________________
9. Remove/Install battery and tray. 9. ______________________
10. Remove/Install integrated relay controller, cooling fan, radiator, and shroud. 10. ______________________
11. Remove/Install engine NVH bracket to shock tower. 11. ______________________
12. Disconnect/Connect evaporative emission line. 12. ______________________
13. Disconnect/Connect upper radiator hose. 13. ______________________
14. Disconnect/Connect starter brace. 14. ______________________
15. Disconnect/Connect lower radiator hose. 15. ______________________
16. Disconnect/Connect exhaust manifold at pipe. 16. ______________________
17. Disconnect/Connect power steering pump lines. 17. ______________________
18. Disconnect/Connect fuel lines. 18. ______________________
19. Disconnect/Connect vacuum lines. 19. ______________________
20. Disconnect/Connect exhaust manifold at pipe. 20. ______________________
21. Disconnect/Connect ground strap. 21. ______________________
22. Disconnect/Connect heater lines. 22. ______________________
23. Disconnect/Connect accelerator cable linkage, throttle valve linkage, speed control cable. 23. ______________________
24. Disconnect/Connect alternator wiring. 24. ______________________
25. Disconnect/Connect A/C clutch wiring. 25. ______________________
26. Disconnect/Connect EGO sensor wiring. 26. ______________________

Name ______________________________

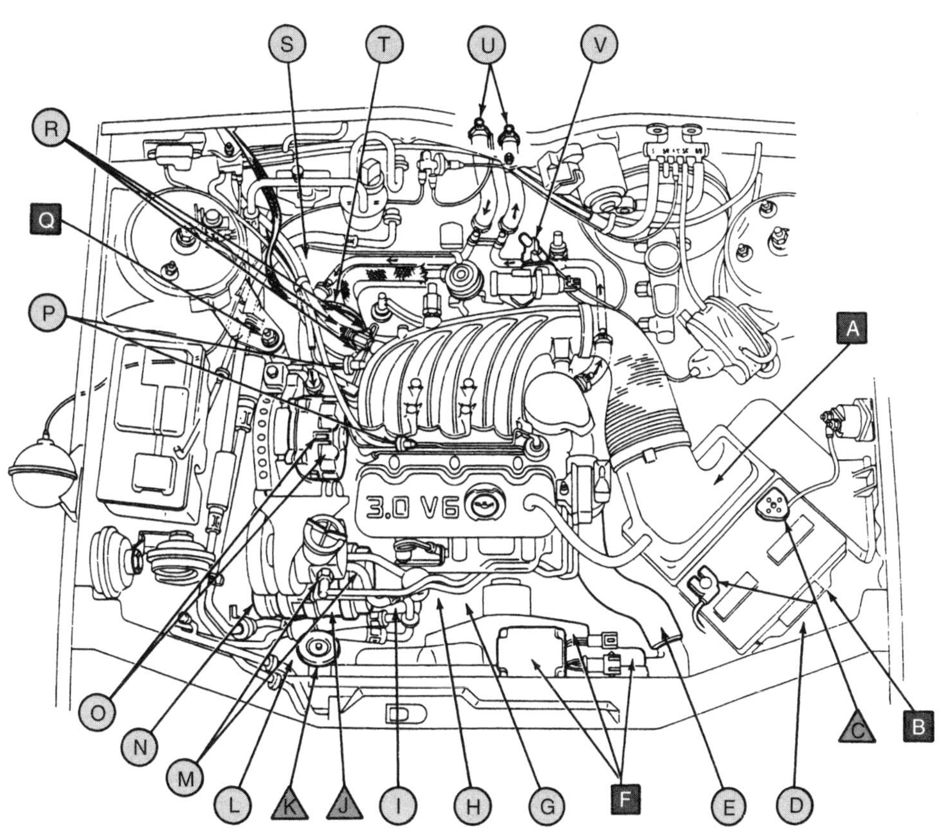

Completion

27. When removing a valve cover, take care not to damage the _____ surfaces. 27. ______________________

28. Blasting with _____ beads is a method used for cleaning automotive parts. 28. ______________________

29. Before cleaning a cylinder block or a cylinder head, remove the _____ _____ plugs. 29. ______________________

Short Answer

30. Why is it necessary to refer to an appropriate service manual when removing an engine?

____

____

31. Why should you never pry against the mating surfaces of the cylinder head or engine block?

____

____

Chapter 12

Engine Top End Service

Name ____________________

Date ______________ Instructor ______________

Score_______ Textbook pages 131–150

After studying the chapter in the text and completing this section of the workbook, you will be able to:

- ❑ Identify the procedures involved in engine top end service.
- ❑ Explain how to disassemble and service a cylinder head.
- ❑ Describe valve and valve operating mechanism service.
- ❑ Explain how to properly torque cylinder head bolts.

Multiple Choice

1. Trying to remove a mushroomed valve from the cylinder head _____.
   (A) should be done with force
   (B) may damage the valve guides
   (C) will not harm the valve guide
   (D) None of the above.

   1. ____________________

2. If a 0.006″ feeler gauge can be placed between a straightedge and a cylinder head, the head is _____.
   (A) warped and must be machined
   (B) warped and must be replaced
   (C) in good condition
   (D) None of the above.

   2. ____________________

3. Before any measurement is made, the valve stem must be _____.
   (A) cleaned
   (B) oiled
   (C) polished
   (D) Both A and C.

   3. ____________________

Name ______________________________

4. If the valve stem is scored, pitted, bent, or worn more than 0.002″, the valve should be _____.
   (A) repaired
   (B) reconditioned
   (C) discarded
   (D) None of the above.

4. ______________________________

5. Which of the following could cause valve lifters to stick if it is wedged between the plunger and cylinder?
   (A) A speck of dust.
   (B) A fleck of carbon.
   (C) A fine thread of lint from a wiping cloth.
   (D) All of the above.

5. ______________________________

6. If a push rod is bent or warped, it must be _____.
   (A) repaired
   (B) straightened
   (C) replaced
   (D) Both A and B.

6. ______________________________

7. If the bottom of any lifter is not _____, a new set of lifters and a camshaft are required.
   (A) convex
   (B) concave
   (C) flat
   (D) None of the above.

7. ______________________________

Identification

Identify the points to check for wear on a valve.

8. Valve face angle. 8. ______________________________

9. This line parallel with valve head. 9. ______________________________

10. Diameter. 10. ______________________________

11. Check for bent stem. 11. ______________________________

12. Minimum dimension. 12. ______________________________

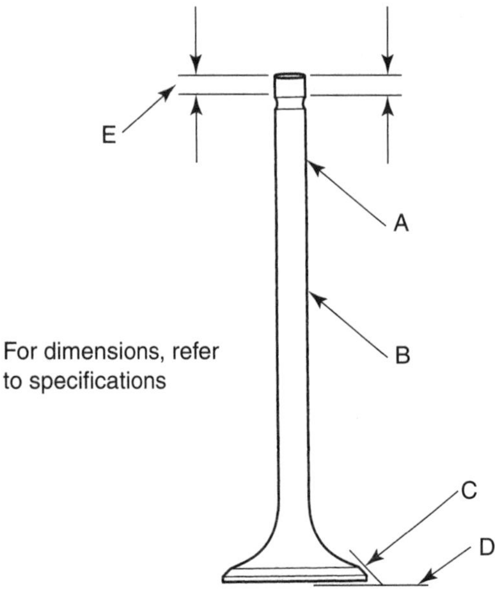

Name ________________________________

Identify the points to check on a valve train that are prone to wear.

13. Valve key. 13. ____________________
14. Spring seat. 14. ____________________
15. Camshaft. 15. ____________________
16. Rocker arm. 16. ____________________
17. Valve stem. 17. ____________________
18. Tappet. 18. ____________________
19. Guide. 19. ____________________
20. Rocker arm shaft. 20. ____________________
21. Adjusting screw. 21. ____________________
22. Seat. 22. ____________________
23. Spring retainer. 23. ____________________
24. Push rod. 24. ____________________
25. Face. 25. ____________________
26. Spring. 26. ____________________

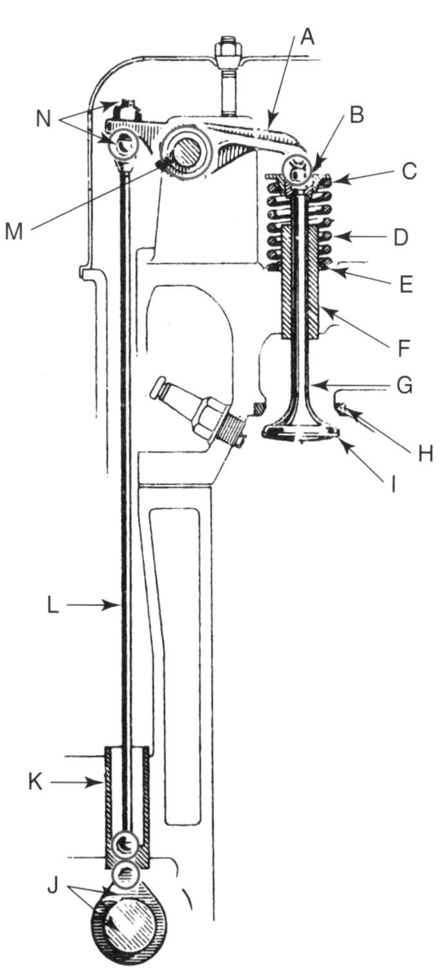

Name ______________________________

Identify the various types of wear that may be found when inspecting a timing belt.

27. Abnormal wear (fluffy strand). 27. ______________________
28. Peeling. 28. ______________________
29. Rubber exposed. 29. ______________________
30. Peeling. 30. ______________________
31. Cracks. 31. ______________________
32. Tooth missing and canvas fiber exposed. 32. ______________________
33. Rounded edge. 33. ______________________

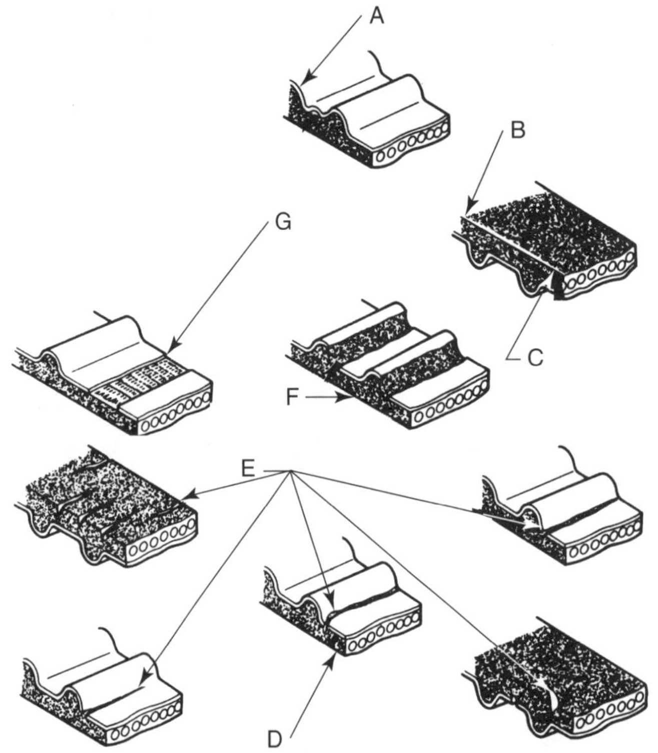

Completion

34. _____ involves attaching strong magnets to the cylinder head and then shaking a fine iron powder on the head. The powder will accumulate along any cracks in the head. 34. ______________________

35. The valve _____ must be perfectly round so the valve face can close squarely on the seat. 35. ______________________

36. _____ can recondition the guide if wear is less than 0.006″. 36. ______________________

37. Valve _____ must be square, or the pressure will be directed to one area of the valve face. 37. ______________________

38. When engine oil decomposes, a _____ can form that collects on the plunger and in the cylinder, causing sticking. 38. ______________________

39. Adjustment of mechanical lifter clearance is made with a _____ _____. 39. ______________________

Name ______________________________

40. In the diagram below, the difference between line A and line B is the amount of _____.

40. ______________________________

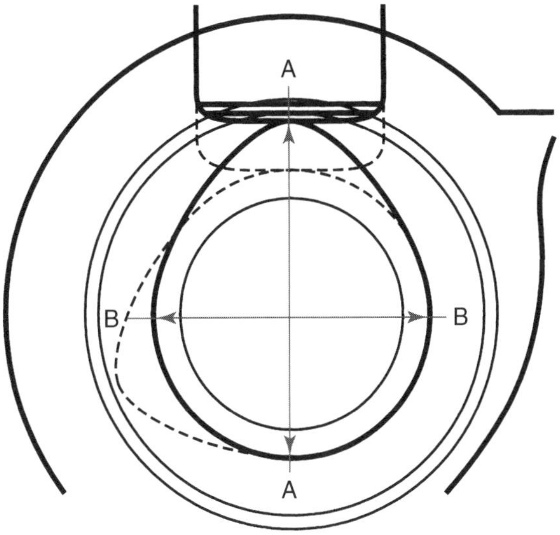

41. The timing belt should be replaced during a _____ job.

41. ______________________________

Short Answer

42. What does engine top end service involve?

____

____

43. What does cylinder head service consist of?

____

____

____

____

44. What would happen if a push rod on an overhead valve engine became warped or bent?

____

____

____

45. Why should a thread compound be used on cylinder head bolts, especially those used with aluminum cylinder heads and blocks?

____

____

____

Chapter 13

Engine Bottom End Service

Name ______________________

Date ______________ Instructor ______________

Score_______ Textbook pages 151–176

After studying the chapter in the text and completing this section of the workbook, you will be able to:

- ❑ Identify the procedures involved in engine bottom end service.
- ❑ Explain how to inspect and service an engine block.
- ❑ Describe procedures for inspecting and servicing crankshafts.
- ❑ Describe piston, piston ring, connecting rod, and piston pin service.
- ❑ Explain the importance of engine balancing.

Multiple Choice

1. The starting point for engine bottom end reconditioning is the _____.
   (A) pistons
   (B) crankshaft
   (C) engine block
   (D) None of the above.

1. ______________________

2. The greatest amount of wear in a cylinder occurs at the _____ of the cylinder.
   (A) top
   (B) side
   (C) bottom
   (D) None of the above.

2. ______________________

3. The desired cylinder wall finish is a _____.
   (A) mirror surface
   (B) pattern of diagonal crosshatch scratches
   (C) pattern of parallel longitudinal scratches
   (D) None of the above.

3. ______________________

Name ____________________

4. Lubrication grooves are sometimes added to the bearing design to help _____.
   (A) distribute oil over a wider area of the journals
   (B) route oil to other oil passages in the engine block
   (C) distribute oil evenly over the flange of the thrust bearing
   (D) All of the above.

4. ____________________

5. Which piston ring needs more gap clearance at the ends and more sidewise clearance in the piston grooves?
   (A) Top.
   (B) Middle.
   (C) Bottom.
   (D) It does not matter.

5. ____________________

Identification

Identify the bearings shown below.

6. Precision insert bearing. 6. ____________________
7. Precision insert thrust bearing. 7. ____________________

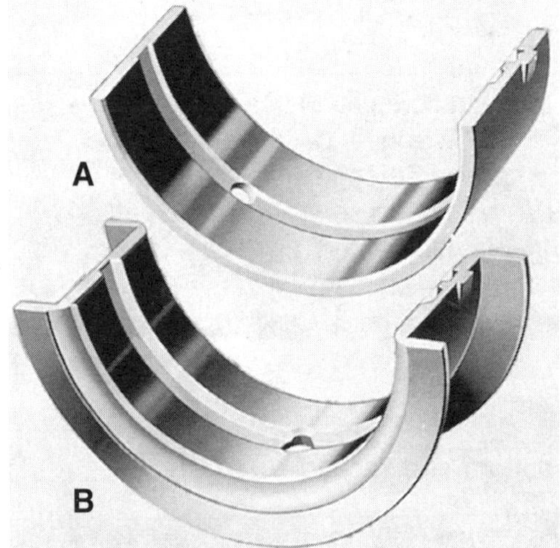

Identify the items indicated on the typical thrust bearing shown below.

8. Height. 8. ____________________
9. Machined flanges. 9. ____________________
10. Bearing made to exact size. 10. ____________________
11. Steel or bronze back. 11. ____________________

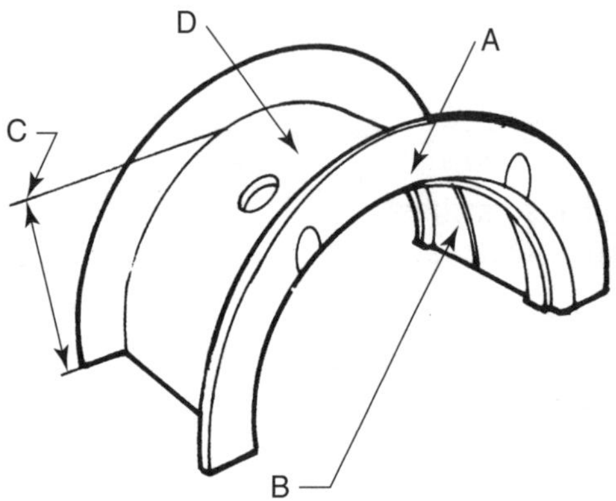

Name ______________________________

Identify the parts indicated on the bearings below.

12. Oil holes. 12. ______________________
13. Oil groove. 13. ______________________
14. Oil groove. 14. ______________________
15. Oil holes 15. ______________________
16. Thrust bearing. 16. ______________________

Completion

17. Look at the diagrams below. A cylinder block can be repaired with a metallic plastic in the _____ (shaded, unshaded) areas only. 17. ______________________

Typical for 4-cylinder engine

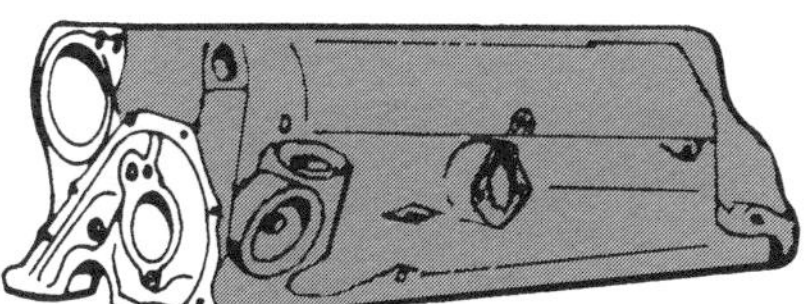

Front and left side

Typical for V-8 engine

Front and left side

Front and left side view 3.8 L engine

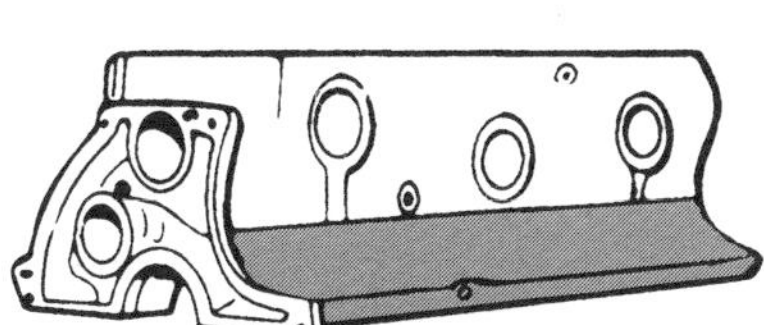

Rear and right side

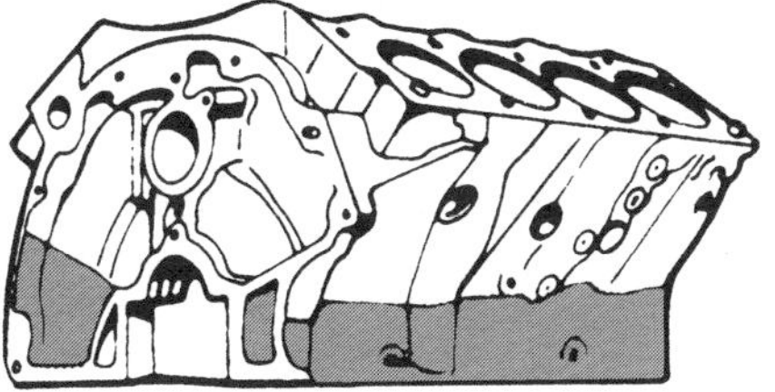

Rear and right side

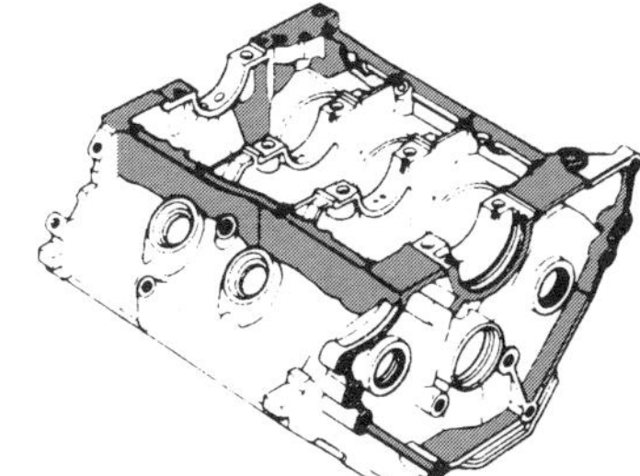

Rear and right side view 3.8 L engine

Colored areas may be repaired with metallic plastic

Note: The metallic plastic must not be applied around bolt holes or bores in the cylinder block. Maintain a minimum 3.1 mm (5/16-inch) gap between sealer and any such cylinder block holes.

Name ______________________________

18. Usually, a cracked cylinder head is _____ (repaired, replaced). 18. ______________________

19. Refer to the diagram below. The difference between line A and line B is the amount the cylinder is _____-_____-_____. The difference in measurement between line C and line D is the amount of ____ in the cylinder. Line E will be the original _____ of the cylinder, as the piston rings do not travel that far down. 19. ______________________

____

____

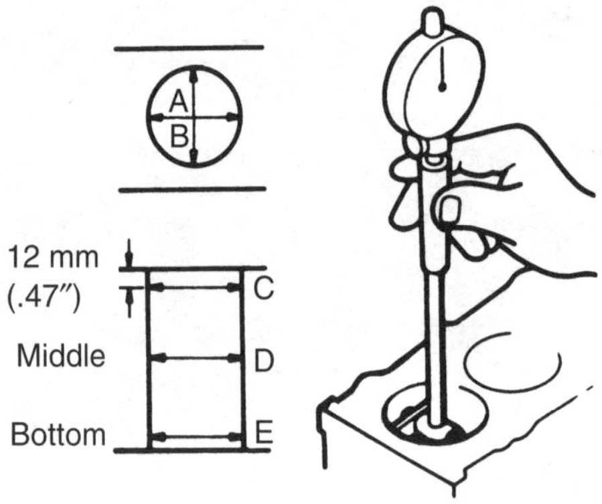

20. If a _____ _____ is bent or is out of alignment, it will tend to wear the crankpin journal in a tapered fashion. 20. ______________________

21. The first step in bearing removal is to remove the _____ from the cylinder. 21. ______________________

22. Bearing _____ should not be tightened completely until all the bearing inserts are in position. 22. ______________________

23. _____ is the escape of combustion pressure past the piston rings and into the crankcase. 23. ______________________

24. Oil _____ occurs when oil passes upward into the cylinder. 24. ______________________

25. When installing piston rings in a rebuilt engine without boring the cylinders, plain _____ _____ rings are often preferred. 25. ______________________

26. If the piston pin is not parallel with the crankshaft, every force on the piston will cause it to slide endwise on the piston pin, causing piston _____, which is a knock created by the piston. 26. ______________________

27. Fitting piston _____ is one of the most delicate operations encountered in automobile repair work. 27. ______________________

Name ____________________

Short Answer

28. What is being done in the illustration below?

____

____

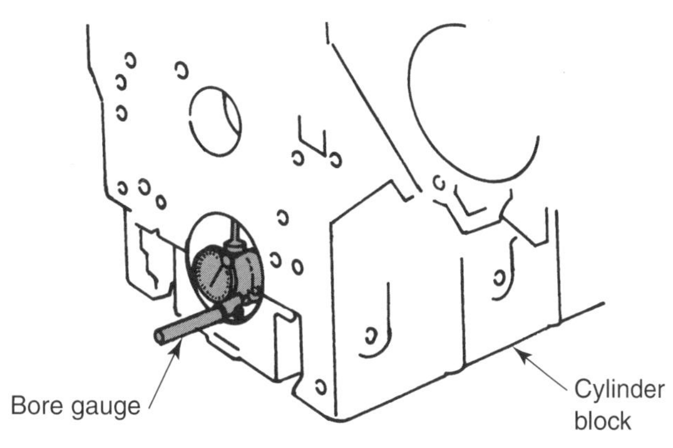

29. Describe the procedures being performed below.

A. ____________________

B. ____________________

C. ____________________

D. ____________________

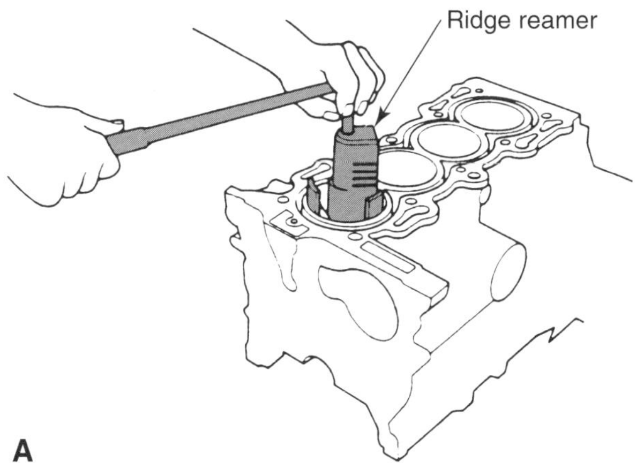

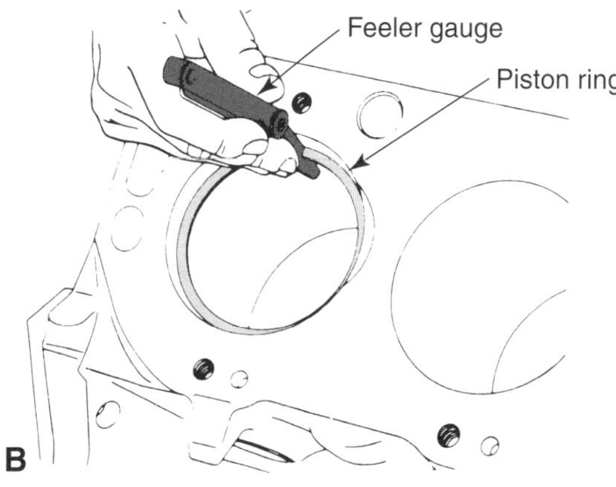

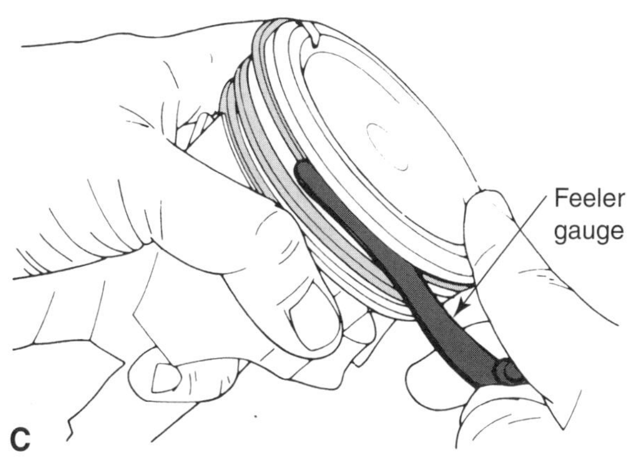

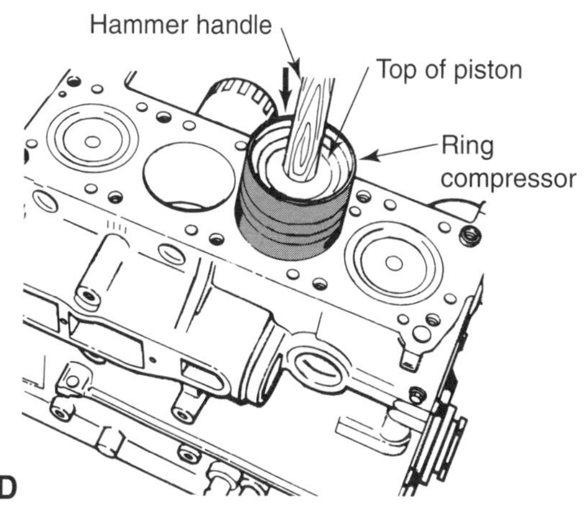

Name ______________________________

30. Why must piston ring gaps be staggered when the rings are installed on the piston?

____

31. Why do piston pins have an interference fit in the upper end of the rod?

____

____

32. Why is it important that all rotating and reciprocating parts of an engine are precision balanced?

____

____

____

Chapter 14
Engine Lubrication

Name ______________________________

Date ______________ Instructor ______________

Score_______ Textbook pages 177–186

After studying the chapter in the text and completing this section of the workbook, you will be able to:
- ❑ Explain how a lubricating system operates.
- ❑ State the purpose of lubrication.
- ❑ List the properties of engine oil.
- ❑ Select the proper engine oil for a specific engine.

Multiple Choice

1. In areas where there are seasonal changes or extreme temperature differences between the morning and afternoon, which type of oil should be used?
   (A) Straight weight oil.
   (B) Multi-viscosity or multi-weight oil.
   (C) Either A or B.
   (D) None of the above.

   1. B

2. Which of the following is the only group responsible for testing the viscosity of oil?
   (A) American Society for Testing Materials (ASTM).
   (B) American Petroleum Institute (API).
   (C) Society of Automotive Engineers (SAE).
   (D) None of the above.

   2. B

3. Which of the following additives have the ability to coat metal surfaces with a strong and slippery film that prevents direct metal-to-metal contact?
   (A) Foam inhibitors.
   (B) Antiwear additives.
   (C) Viscosity index improvers.
   (D) Oxidation inhibitors.

   3. B

Name ______________________

4. Which of the following additives are used to prevent sludge and varnish deposits?
   (A) Detergent-dispersant additives.
   (B) Corrosion and rust inhibitors.
   (C) Antiwear additives.
   (D) Pour point depressants.

4. A

5. When making oil changes, use _____ oil and make the prescribed oil changes.
   (A) nondetergent
   (B) low-viscosity
   (C) SA
   (D) None of the above.

5. D

Identification

Identify the parts indicated on the diagram below.

6. Drain plug. 6. B
7. Oil filter. 7. C
8. Drain. 8. A

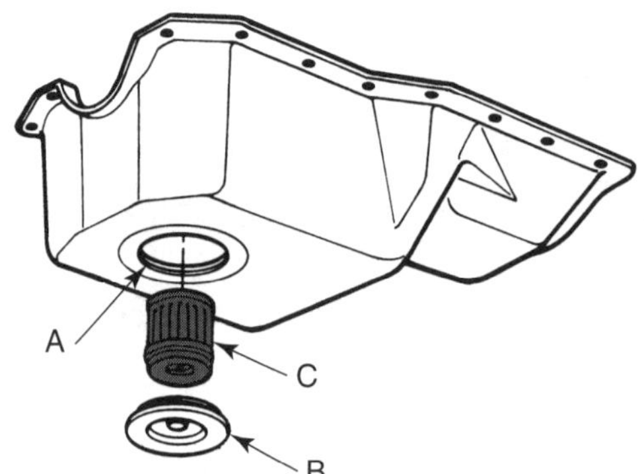

Identify the parts indicated on the illustration at the top of the next page.

9. Oil pump. 9. E
10. Oil pick-up screen. 10. F
11. Main oil gallery. 11. A
12. Oil filter. 12. C
13. Filter feed gallery. 13. D
14. Filter bypass valve. 14. B

Name ______________________________

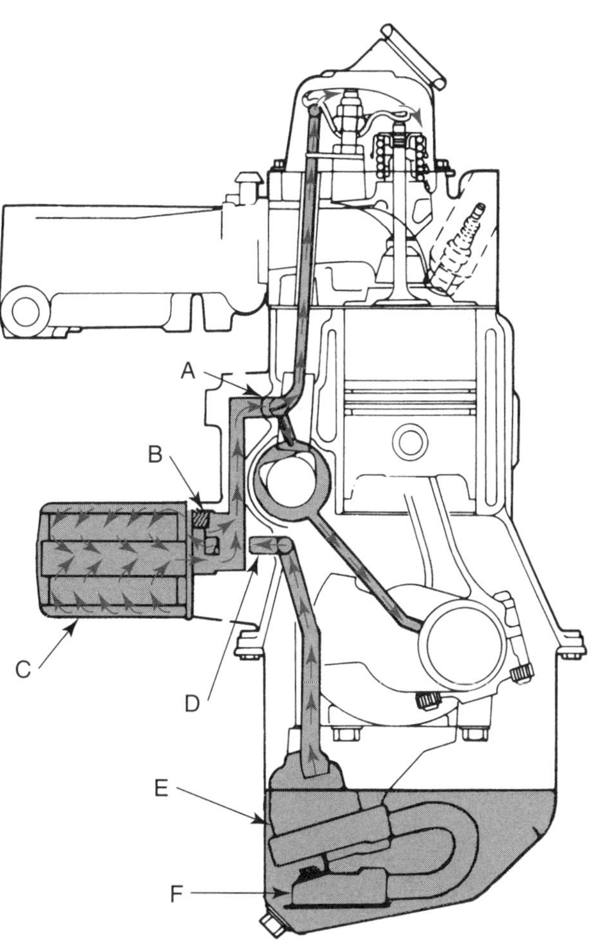

Identify the types of oil pumps shown below.

15. Rotor type. 15. A

16. Gear type. 16. B

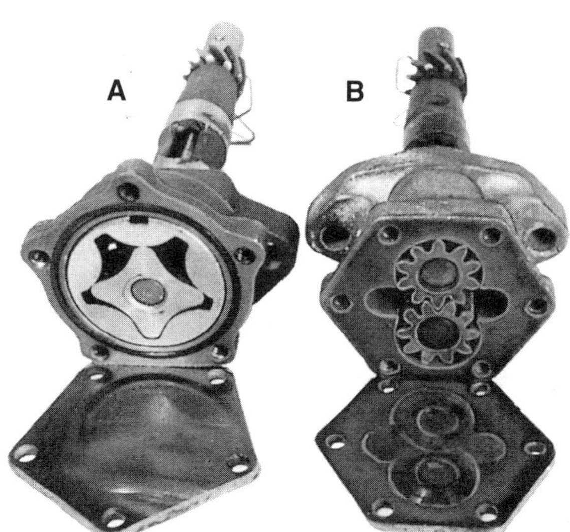

Name ______________________________

Identify the parts indicated below.

17. Retainer cap. 17. D
18. Spring. 18. E
19. Cotter pin. 19. B
20. Oil pump assembly. 20. A
21. Relief valve. 21. C

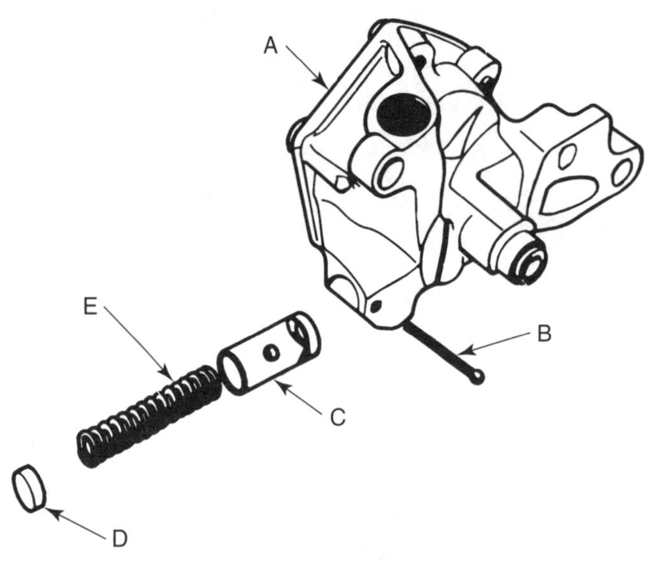

Identify the parts indicated on the PCV system shown below.

22. Air cleaner. 22. B
23. PCV valve. 23. D
24. Throttle body. 24. A
25. Air intake. 25. C
26. Combustion chamber. 26. E
27. Blow-by gases. 27. F
28. Crankcase inlet cleaner. 28. G

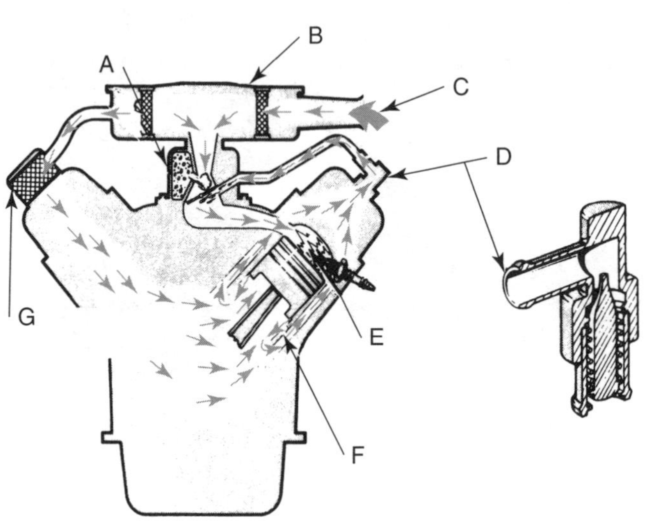

Name ______________________

Completion

29. A _____ (high, low) numerical viscosity oil is needed in cold weather, or the engine will have difficulty turning over due to the resistance of the thick oil. A _____ (high, low) numerical viscosity oil is needed in hot weather, or the oil will thin out and not provide enough protection for the engine components.

29. LOW/HIGH

30. Some connecting rods have oil passages drilled lengthwise to carry oil to the _____ _____.

30. PISTON PIN

31. The connecting rods in some engines have a spurt hole drilled in them on one side. A squirt of oil shoots out on the _____ _____ when the hole aligns with the oil passage in the crankshaft.

31. CYLINDER WALLS

32. The oil pressure _____ _____ in a simple spring-loaded valve which relieves excess pressure in the circulating system by bypassing the excess oil back to the sump.

32. RELIEF VALVE

33. An accumulation of _____ on an oil pick-up screen will stop the flow of oil, causing the engine to seize.

33. SLUDGE

Short Answer

34. List four tasks lubricating oil performs in an automobile engine.

LUBRICATES THE MOVING PARTS

SEALS BETWEEN THE PISTON RINGS AND THE CYLINDER WALL

CARRIES HEAT AWAY FROM ENGINE PARTS

CARRIES CONTAMINATION AWAY FROM MOVING PARTS

35. List and describe the two classifications manufacturers generally use for engine oil change recommendations.

SEVERE CONDITIONS - SHORT TRIPS, TOWING, EXCESSIVE IDLING, DRIVEING IN DUSTY AREAS

NORMAL DRIVING - TRIPS 10 MILES OR MORE, NO PULLING TRAILERS, NO DUST

Chapter 15

Engine Cooling Systems

Name ______________________________

Date ______________ Instructor ______________

Score_______ Textbook pages 187–206

After studying the chapter in the text and completing this section of the workbook, you will be able to:

- ❑ List components of the cooling system.
- ❑ Explain how the cooling system operates.
- ❑ Describe how the components of the cooling system operate.

Multiple Choice

1. If a radiator hose has either soft spots or hard, brittle spots, the hose _____.
   (A) must be patched
   (B) must be replaced
   (C) can be used until a problem develops
   (D) None of the above.

   1. ______________________

2. To prevent injury, never remove the radiator cap when the coolant is _____.
   (A) hot
   (B) cool
   (C) frozen
   (D) None of the above.

   2. ______________________

3. The higher boiling point of _____ makes it a highly satisfactory coolant for use in both warm and cold weather.
   (A) water
   (B) oil
   (C) ethylene glycol
   (D) None of the above.

   3. ______________________

Name ______________________________

4. The most frequent cooling system complaints are _____. 4. ____________________
   (A) lack of oil and pressure
   (B) leakage of coolant and overheating
   (C) Both A and B.
   (D) None of the above.
5. Which of the following is a sure sign of coolant leakage? 5. ____________________
   (A) Grayish-white areas.
   (B) Rust stains.
   (C) Antifreeze dye stains.
   (D) All of the above.

Identification

Identify the parts indicated on the diagram below. Then draw arrows to indicate the cycle of the coolant through the cooling system.

6. Lower radiator tank. 6. ____________________
7. Thermostat. 7. ____________________
8. Water valve. 8. ____________________
9. Radiator. 9. ____________________
10. Hose to heater. 10. ____________________
11. Upper hose. 11. ____________________
12. Cylinder block water jackets. 12. ____________________
13. Heater core. 13. ____________________
14. Lower hose. 14. ____________________
15. Cylinder head water jacket. 15. ____________________
16. Return hose from heater. 16. ____________________

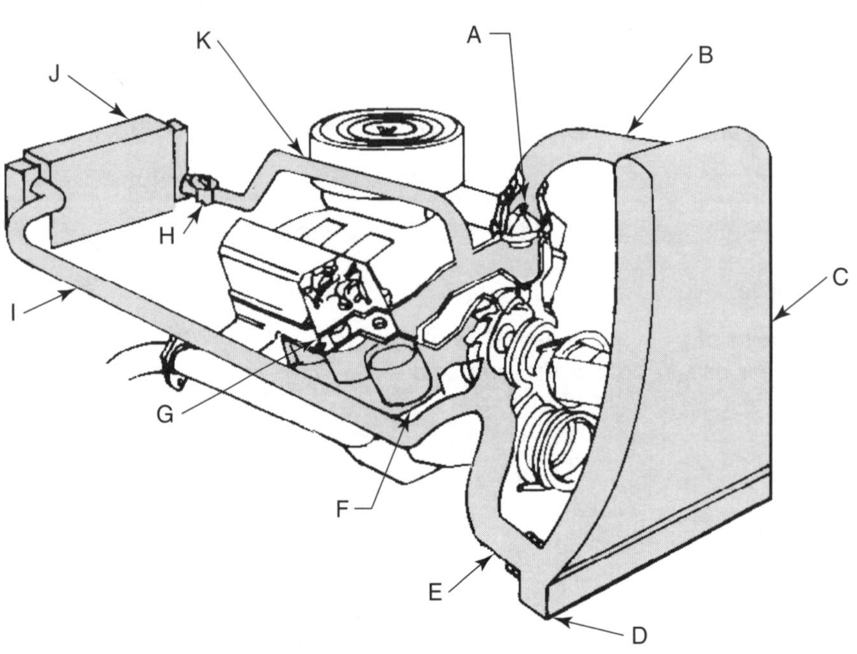

Name ______________________________

17–18. Using arrows, indicate where the belts on the following engines should be pressed to check whether they need to be tightened.

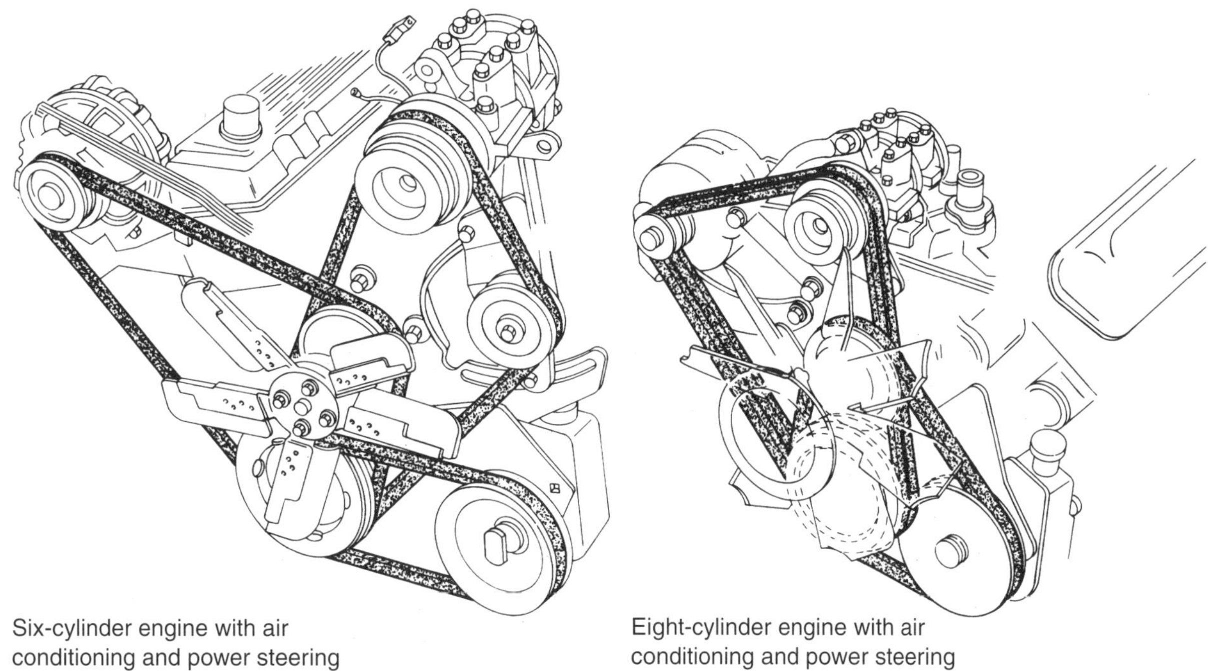

Six-cylinder engine with air conditioning and power steering

Eight-cylinder engine with air conditioning and power steering

Identify the types of hose clamps shown below.

19. Screw tower.	19.	______________
20. Worm drive.	20.	______________
21. Twin wire.	21.	______________
22. Spring or corbin.	22.	______________

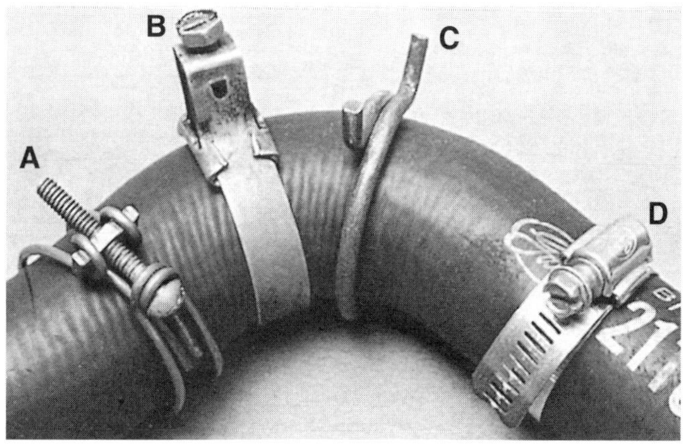

Name ______________________________

Identify the types of radiators shown below.

23. Cellular type. 23. ______________________

24. Tube type. 24. ______________________

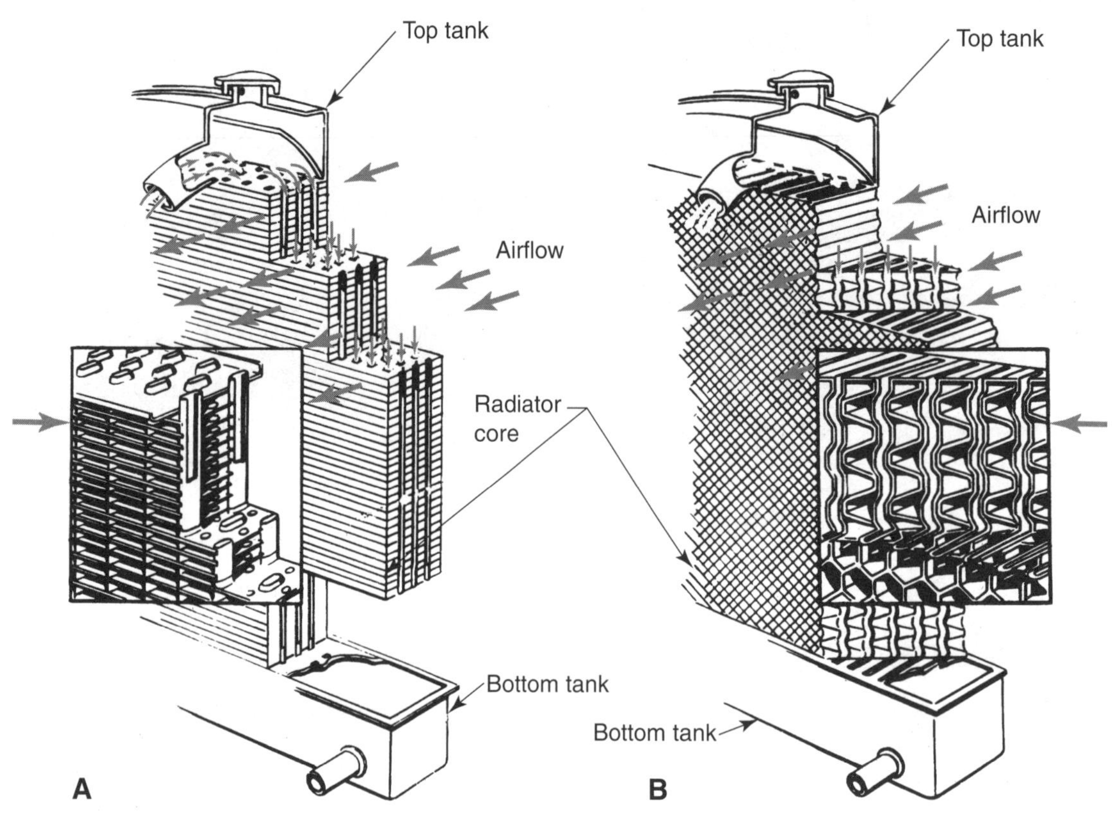

Identify the parts indicated on the diagram shown at the top of the next page.

25. Oil cooler. 25. ______________________

26. O-ring gasket. 26. ______________________

27. Washer. 27. ______________________

28. Radiator core. 28. ______________________

29. Outlet tank. 29. ______________________

30. Nut. 30. ______________________

31. Gasket. 31. ______________________

32. Inlet tank. 32. ______________________

33. O-ring gasket. 33. ______________________

Name ______________________________

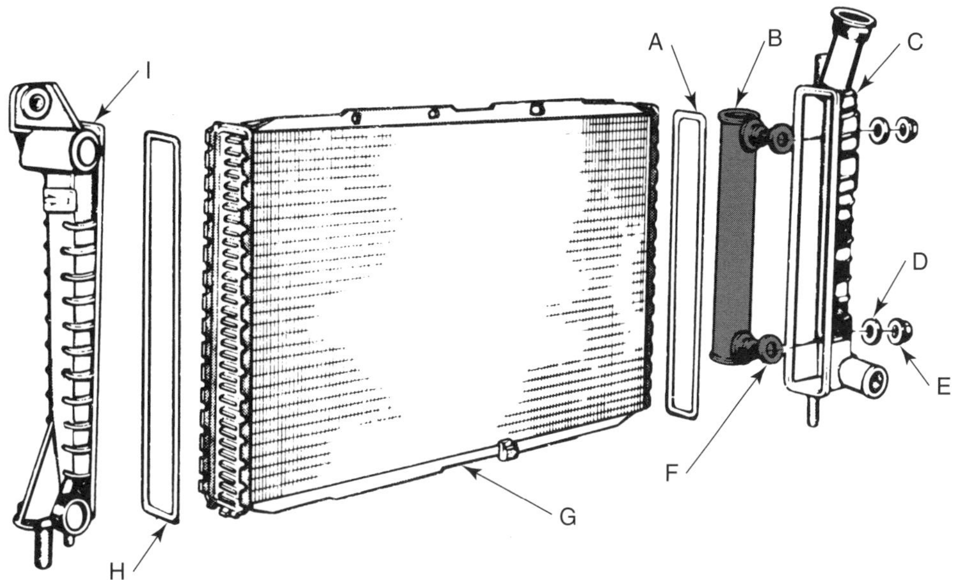

Which illustration shows vacuum relief and which shows pressure relief?

34. Vacuum relief. 34. ______________________

35. Pressure relief. 35. ______________________

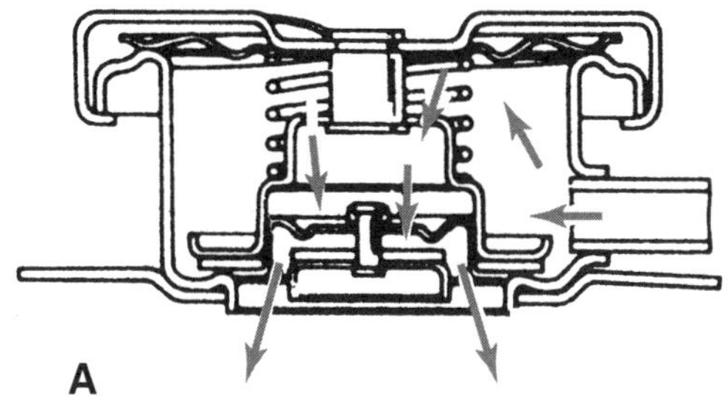

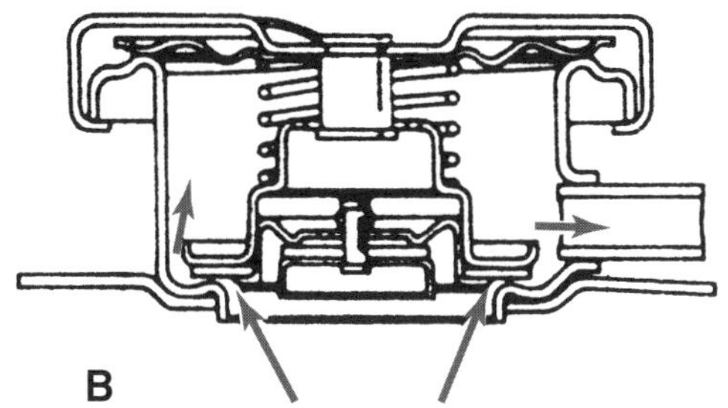

Identify the parts indicated on the illustration below.

36. Shroud with air conditioning. 36. ______________________

37. Radiator. 37. ______________________

38. Fan switch. 38. ______________________

39. Drain cock. 39. ______________________

40. Fan motor. 40. ______________________

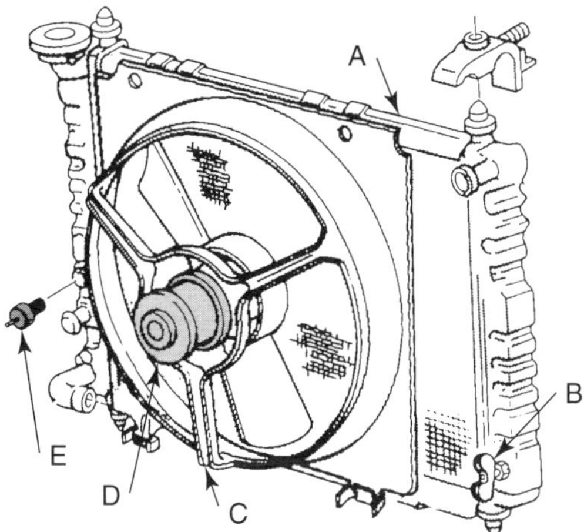

Name ______________________________

Identify the parts indicated on the engine thermostat shown below.

41. Flange seal. 41. ______________________

42. Coil spring. 42. ______________________

43. Frame. 43. ______________________

44. Wax-filled pellet. 44. ______________________

45. Thermostat valve. 45. ______________________

46. Flange. 46. ______________________

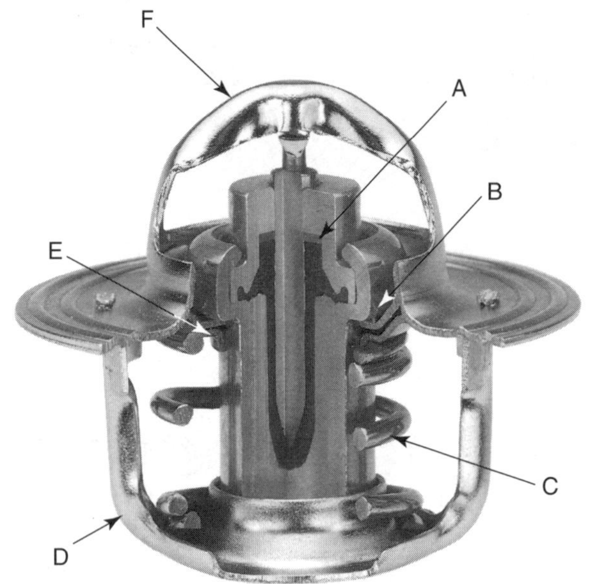

Completion

47. If an accumulation of rust and/or lime develops in the water jackets, heat from cylinders cannot be transferred to the coolant. This creates _____ _____ which can distort cylinder walls and valve seats. 47. ______________________

48. The _____ of the water pump force the coolant through the engine block. 48. ______________________

49. _____ (Older, Newer) belts have a banded design that show wear as they age. The _____ (older, newer) bandless design does not show wear as it ages, so it is extremely important to change this type of belt periodically even if the belt appears not worn. 49. ______________________

50. The _____ drive belt is a combination of a V-ribbed belt and a flat back belt. 50. ______________________

51. The _____ is a device designed to dissipate the heat that the coolant absorbs from the engine. 51. ______________________

52. A(n) _____ system connects a plastic tank to the radiator through a rubber tube. As the coolant becomes hot and expands, the coolant flows out of the radiator and into this plastic tank or reservoir. 52. ______________________

Name ______________________________

53. Today's radiator _____ is designed to seal the system so that it operates under 14-17 psi. 53. ______________________

54. A flexible fan blade flattens out as rpms _____ (increase, decrease). This reduces the amount of drag on the engine. 54. ______________________

55. The bimetal spring is sensitive to heat and controls the flow of _____ _____ to the fluid coupling, which governs fan speed. 55. ______________________

56. When an engine is cold, coolant circulates through the _____ _____ only. When the engine temperature rises, the thermostat opens and coolant flows through the upper radiator hose to the radiator. 56. ______________________

Short Answer

57. Which diagram below shows the correct installation of a V-ribbed belt?

____

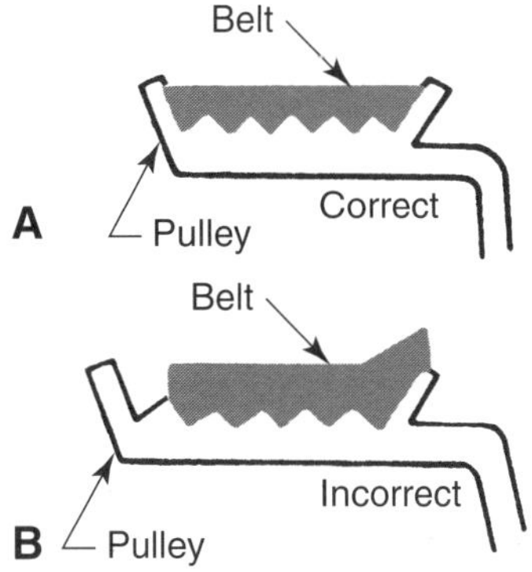

58. What do the cracks indicate on the V-ribbed belt below?

____

Chapter 16

Diesel and Other Engines

Name ______________________________

Date ______________ Instructor ______________

Score_______ Textbook pages 207–218

After studying the chapter in the text and completing this section of the workbook, you will be able to:

- ❑ List the different types of engines.
- ❑ Explain how a diesel engine works.
- ❑ Describe how the rotary engine operates.

Multiple Choice

1. The diesel engine _____. 1. ______________________
   (A) is heavier in structure than a gasoline engine
   (B) has no carburetor
   (C) is lighter in structure than a gasoline engine
   (D) Both A and B.

2. The most common type of diesel combustion chamber is the _____ chamber. 2. ______________________
   (A) precombustion
   (B) energy cell combustion
   (C) open combustion
   (D) turbulence combustion

3. In a Wankel engine, _____ percent of power goes to net HP. 3. ______________________
   (A) 1
   (B) 22
   (C) 67
   (D) 100

4. In a Wankel engine, all four cycles (intake, compression, power, and exhaust) take place in _____ revolution(s) of the rotor. 4. ______________________
   (A) one
   (B) two
   (C) three
   (D) four

Name ______________________________

5. Tests have shown reductions in hydrocarbon emissions from the Wankel engine of up to _____ percent when a thermal reactor has been used.
   (A) 10
   (B) 40
   (C) 90
   (D) 100

5. ______________________________

Identification

Identify the parts indicated on the following illustration.

6. Glow plug. 6. ______________________________
7. Injector. 7. ______________________________
8. Precombustion chamber. 8. ______________________________

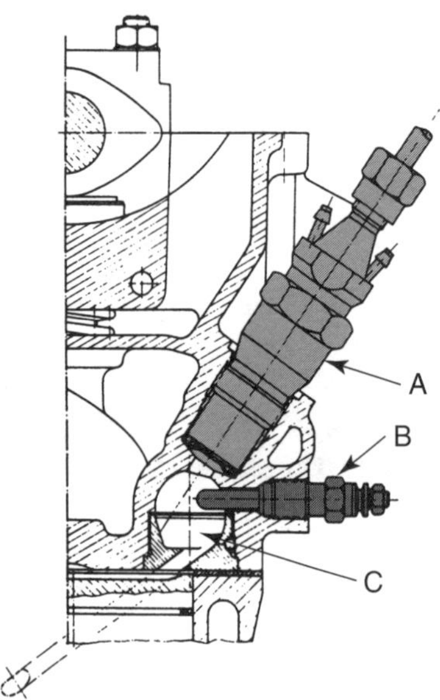

Identify the items on the Wankel-type rotary engine shown at the top of the next page.

9. Exhaust port. 9. ______________________________
10. Eccentric shaft. 10. ______________________________
11. Oil seals. 11. ______________________________
12. Apex seal. 12. ______________________________
13. Stationary gear (outer-toothed). 13. ______________________________
14. Side housing. 14. ______________________________
15. Intake port. 15. ______________________________
16. Rotor housing. 16. ______________________________
17. Rotor. 17. ______________________________
18. Side seals. 18. ______________________________
19. Internal gear (inner-toothed). 19. ______________________________
20. Spark plugs. 20. ______________________________

Name ______________________________

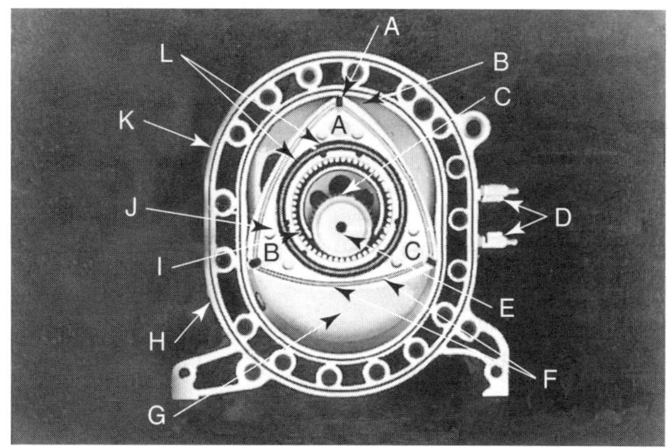

Refer to the diagrams below. Between what lobes does each cycle occur?

21. Intake _____ Compression _____ Power _____ Exhaust _____

22. Intake _____ Compression _____ Power _____ Exhaust _____

23. Intake _____ Compression _____ Power _____ Exhaust _____

24. Intake _____ Compression _____ Power _____ Exhaust _____

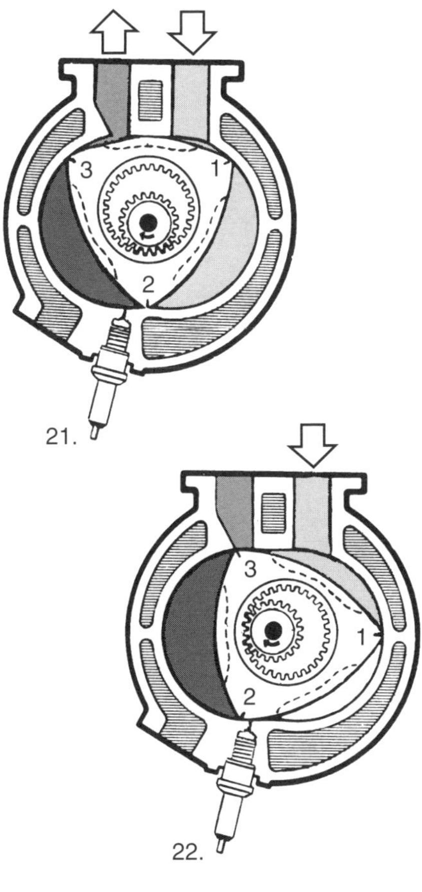

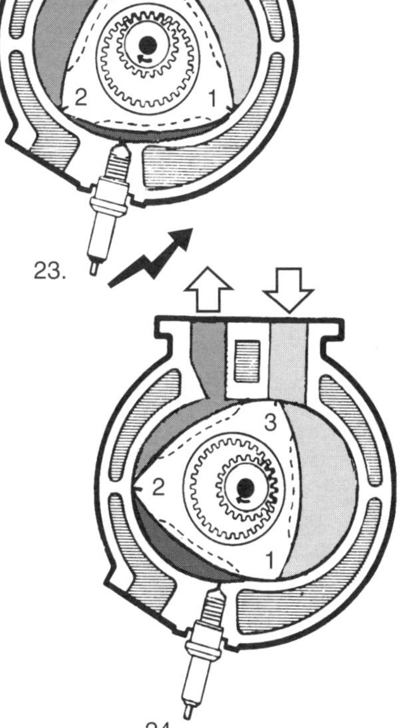

Name ______________________________

Completion

25. Since two-cycle engines are not as efficient as air pumps, it is necessary to force air into the cylinder and to force burned gases out of the cylinder by using a _____ or blower. 25. ______________________

26. The Wankel _____ is triangular in shape with slightly curved sides. It orbits eccentrically on a fixed gear in a housing that is shaped like a figure eight. 26. ______________________

27. Two spark plugs per chamber are used in the _____ engine. 27. ______________________

28. Most rotary engines do not require periodic _____ changes. 28. ______________________

29. A(n) _____-_____ engine uses unique valve timing and duration to help improve fuel economy and increase power. 29. ______________________

30. The top section of a variable-compression engine is called the _____. 30. ______________________

31. The chemical reaction that takes place in a fuel cell produces _____. 31. ______________________

Short Answer

32. What type of fuel injection is shown in this illustration?

____

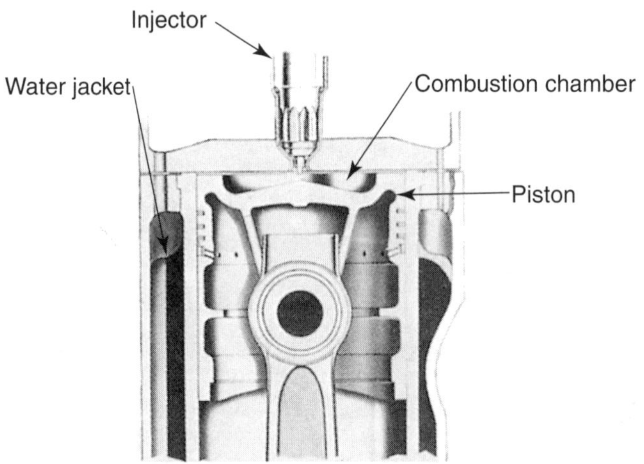

Name ______________________________

33. What type of combustion chamber is shown below?

____

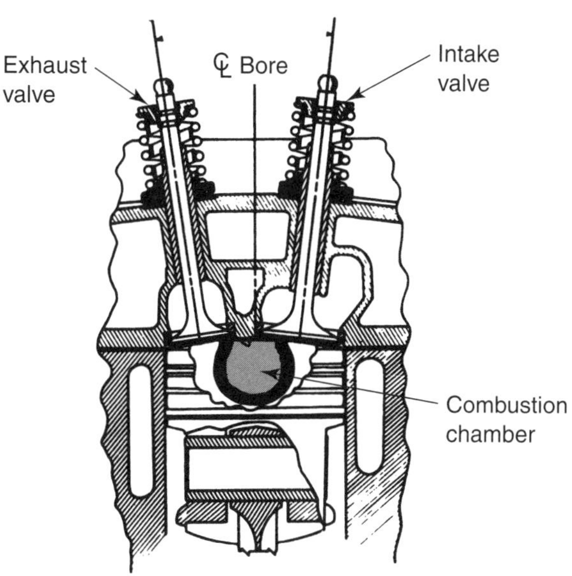

34. What type of combustion chamber is shown below?

____

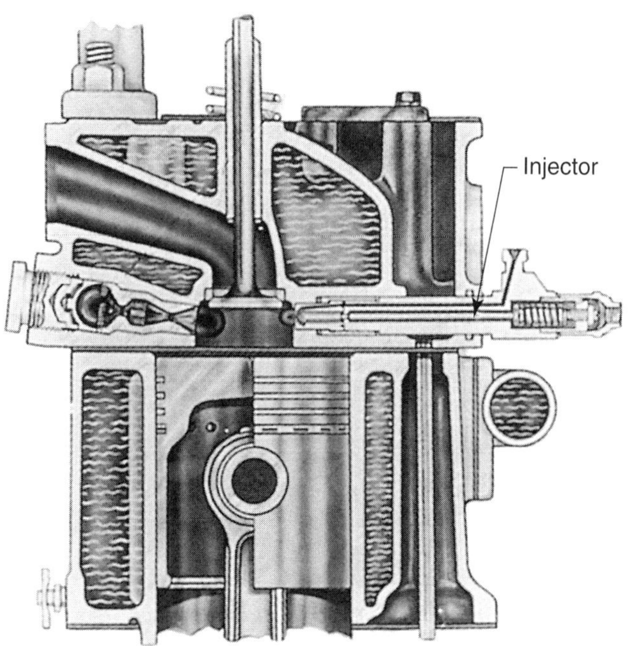

35. Explain the difference between a series hybrid and a parallel hybrid.

____

____

____

____

Name ____________________

Chapter 17

Fundamentals of Electricity, Magnetism, and Electronics

Name ______________________________

Date ______________ Instructor ______________

Score_______ Textbook pages 219–234

After studying the chapter in the text and completing this section of the workbook, you will be able to:

- ❑ Explain the makeup of matter in terms of the molecular theory.
- ❑ State the basics of the electron theory of electricity.
- ❑ Employ Ohm's law in troubleshooting electrical circuits.
- ❑ Describe the characteristics of series, parallel, and series-parallel circuits.
- ❑ Give the theory of permanent magnets and electromagnets.
- ❑ Explain the construction and operation of diodes, transistors, and silicon controlled rectifiers.
- ❑ Recognize the tremendous effect of electronics on automotive advances.

Multiple Choice

1. Electric current is the flow of _____.
   (A) electrons
   (B) protons
   (C) neutrons
   (D) None of the above.

1. A

2. In ______ circuits, the current passes from the power source to each device in turn, and then flows back to the other terminal of the battery.
   (A) parallel
   (B) series
   (C) series-parallel
   (D) None of the above.

2. A

3. Solid state means that a device _____.
   (A) is approved by the state
   (B) is very durable
   (C) has no moving parts other than electrons
   (D) None of the above.

3. C

Name ______________________

4. Semiconductors are designed to _____.
   (A) stop the flow of electrons
   (B) start the flow of electrons
   (C) control the amount of electron flow
   (D) All of the above.

4. D

5. A _____ is a solid state semiconductor that controls electron flow as its temperature or pressure changes.
   (A) diode
   (B) transistor
   (C) sensor
   (D) rectifier

5. B

Identification

Identify the items on the diagram below and indicate what charge, if any, each carries.

6. Proton (___+___ charge) 6. B
7. Electron (___–___ charge) 7. C
8. Neutron (___NO___ charge) 8. A

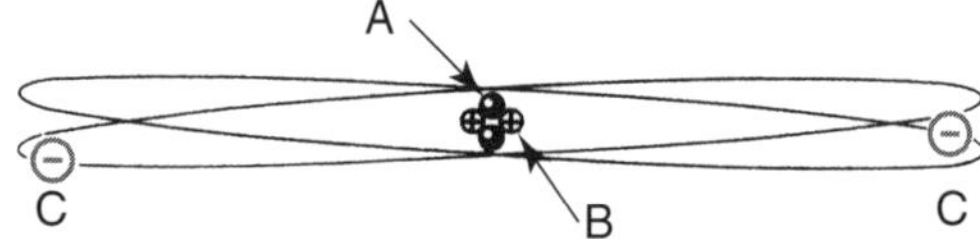

9. On the diagram below, indicate which are the north poles and which are the south poles by filling in the blanks.

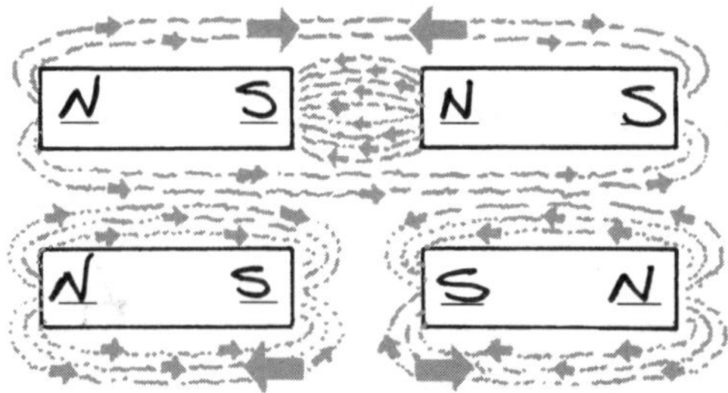

Identify the following transistor symbols.

10. NPN. 10. A
11. PNP. 11. B

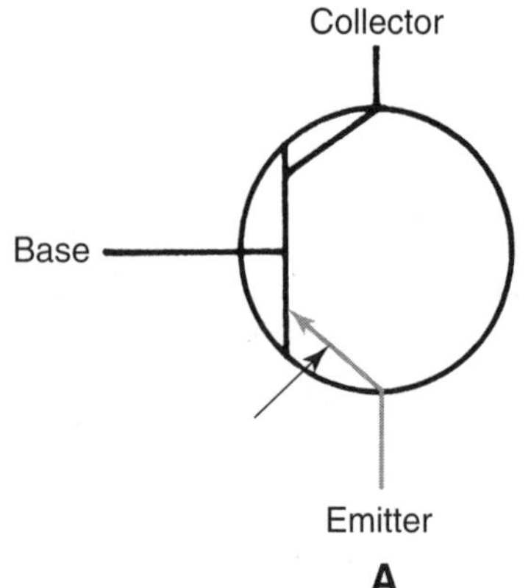

A

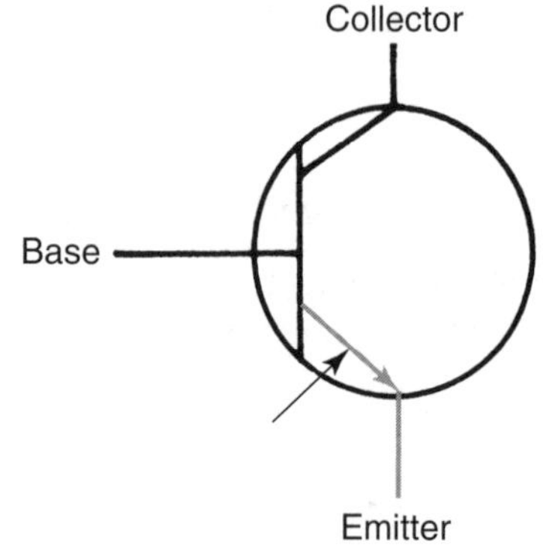

B

Name SIMILAR / OPPOSITE

Completion

12. One of the most important laws of electricity is as follows: Bodies with _____ (similar, opposite) charges repel each other. Bodies with _____ (similar, opposite) charges attract each other.
13. _____ _____ is the mathematical relationship between voltage, resistance, and current in an electrical circuit.
14. The decrease in voltage as current passes through a resistance is known as _____ _____.
15. All magnets have a magnetic field, which is evidenced by lines of force or _____ _____ around the magnet. The magnetic field is _____ (strongest, weakest) close to the magnet.
16. Lines of force leave a magnet or loop of wire at the _____ (north, south) pole and re-enter at the _____ (north, south) pole.
17. The attraction and repulsion of magnets form a fundamental law of magnetism: Like poles of magnets _____ (attract, repel) each other. Unlike poles _____ (attract, repel) each other.
18. A(n) _____ is a tubular core of wire with an air core. It is designed to produce a magnetic field.
19. _____ refers to any electrical component, assembly, circuit, or system that uses solid state devices.
20. When current flows through a diode, the diode is said to be _____ (reverse, forward) biased. When current flow is blocked by a diode, the diode is _____ (reverse, forward) biased.
21. _____ inverse voltage is the amount of voltage a diode can take in the reverse direction (reverse bias) without being damaged.
22. A(n) _____ is a solid state device used to switch and/or amplify the flow of electrons in a circuit.
23. A(n) _____ is a solid state semiconductor that controls electron flow as its temperature or pressure changes.

12. SIMILAR / OPPOSITE
13. OHM'S LAW
14. VOLTAGE DROP.
15. MAGNETIC FLUX / STRONGEST
16. NORTH / SOUTH
17. REPEL / ATTRACT
18. SOLENOID
19. ELECTRONICS
20. FORWARD / REVERSE
21. PEAK
22. TRANSISTOR
23. SENSOR

Short Answer

24. Briefly describe the electron theory.

EVERY THING IS MADE UP OF ATOMS AND AN ATOM CAN BE BROKEN DOWN INTO PROTONS, ELECTRONS, NEUTRONS

Name ______________________________

25. In the following equation, what do the letters represent?
    E= IR

    E = VOLTAGE IN VOLTS

    I = CURRENT IN AMPERES

    R = RESISTANCE IN OHMS

26. List the three general types of electrical circuits.

    SERIES CIRCUITS, PARALLEL CIRCUITS, SERIES-PARALLEL CIRCUITS

27. In which of the following illustrations would the current flow?

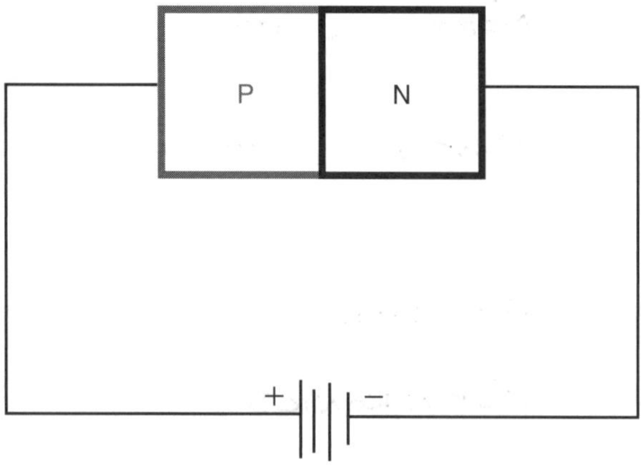

    ____

P N

\+ −

A

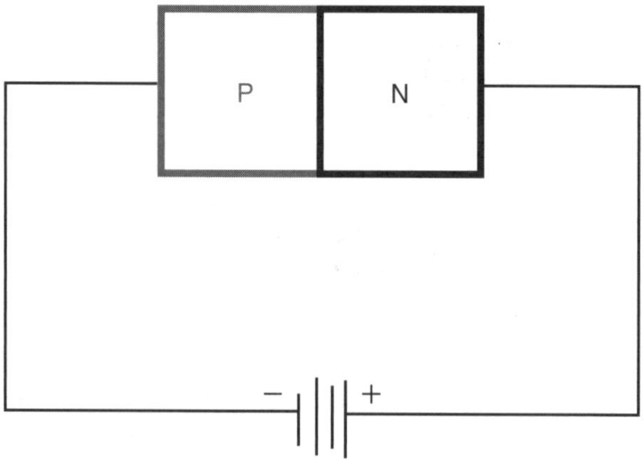

P N

− +

B

28. List the two transistor types and describe their differences.

    ____

    ____

29. List the three types of transistor leads (wires).

    ____

    ____

    ____

Chapter 18
Automotive Fuels

Name ______________________

Date ____________ Instructor ____________

Score _______ Textbook pages 235–242

After studying the chapter in the text and completing this section of the workbook, you will be able to:

- ❑ Describe detonation and preignition.
- ❑ List and explain the characteristics of various fuels.
- ❑ Compare various fuels, including alcohol, diesel fuel, and LP-Gas.

Multiple Choice

1. The fuel used in most automobiles and internal combustion engines is _____.
   (A) alcohol
   (B) benzol
   (C) gasoline
   (D) methanol

   1. GASOLINE

2. Detonation _____.
   (A) improves the performance of an engine
   (B) harms an engine and hinders its performance
   (C) keeps the engine running cool
   (D) has no effect on an engine

   2. ______________________

3. The ability of a fuel to resist knocking is measured by its ______.
   (A) octane rating
   (B) cetane rating
   (C) volatility
   (D) None of the above.

   3. OCTANE RATING

4. Which of the following fuels is made from farm products such as sugar cane, corn, and potatoes?
   (A) Methanol.
   (B) Ethanol.
   (C) Lead-free gasoline.
   (D) None of the above.

   4. ETHANOL

Name ____________________

5. Which grade of diesel fuel oil must be used in the winter?
   (A) Grade No. 1-D.
   (B) Grade No. 2-D.
   (C) Grade No. 4-D.
   (D) None of the above.

5. GRADE No. 1-D

Identification

Indicate what is illustrated in each of the following diagrams.

6. Detonation. — 6. B
7. Preignition. — 7. A
8. Normal combustion. — 8. C

A

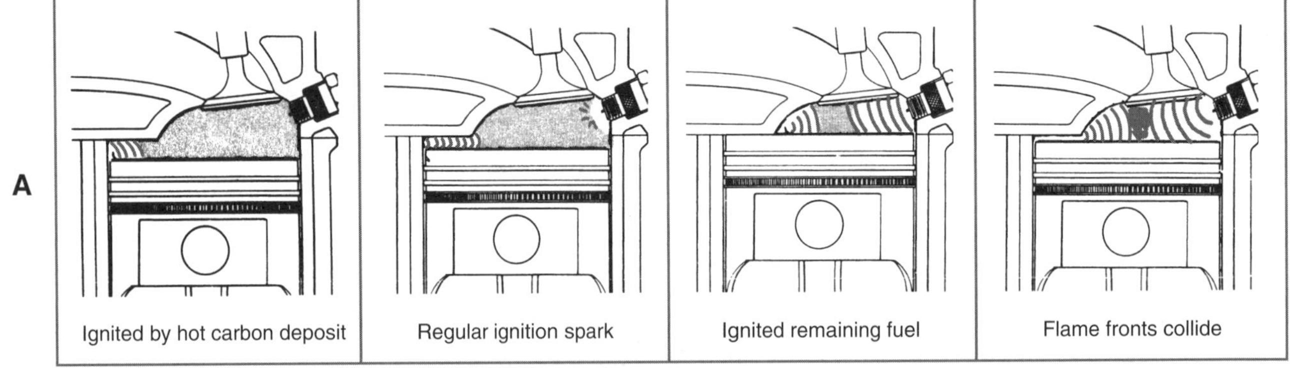

B

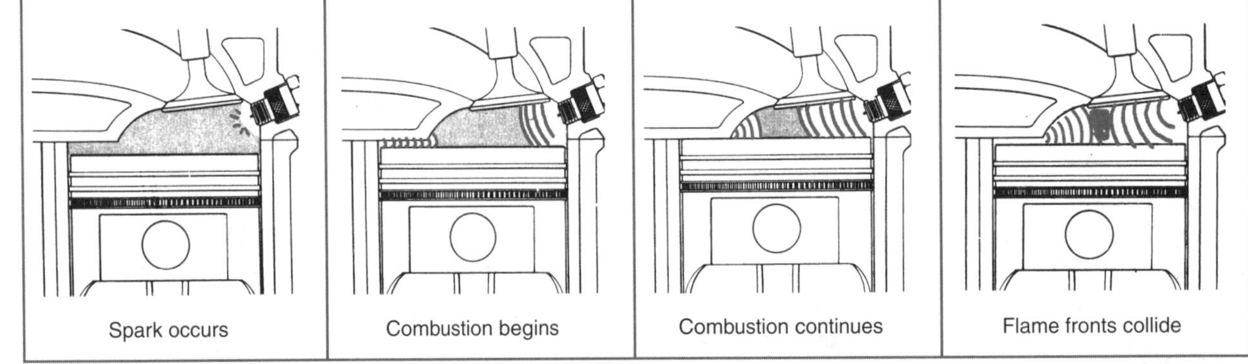

C

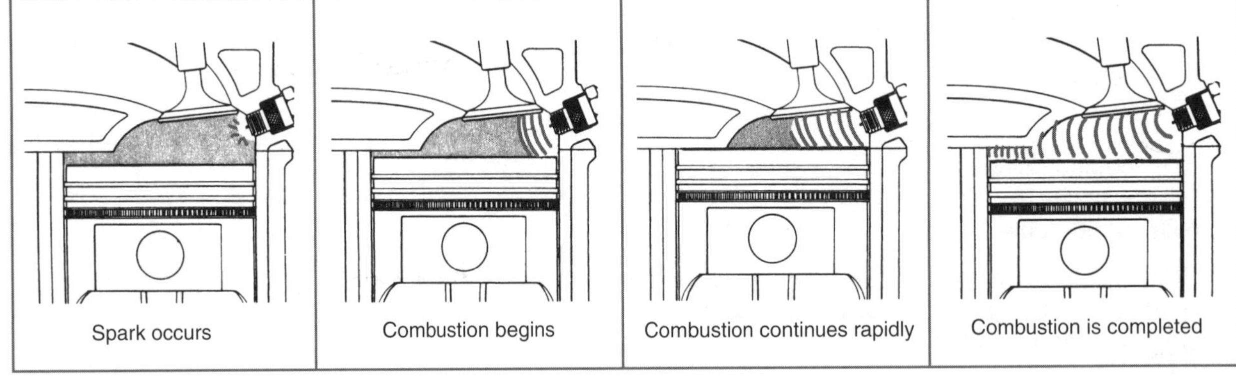

Name ______________________

Completion

9. Gasoline used for automobiles has a range of boiling points from approximately 100 °F to 400 °F. — 9. 100- 400

10. Both methanol and ethanol have a ______ (higher, lower) octane number than gasoline. — 10. LOWER

Short Answer

11. List the three stages of combustion.

FORMATION, HATCHING OUT, PROPAGATION

12. What can happen as a result of detonation?

THE UNBURND GASES MAY IGNITE SPONTANEOUSLY

13. List five causes of detonation.

LEAN AIR/FUEL MIXTURES
LOW OCTANE FUEL
IGNITION TIMING OVER-ADVANCED
LUGGING THE ENGINE
EXCESSIVE CARBON ACCUMULATIONS IN THE COMBUSTION CHAMBER

14. List six causes of preignition.

CARBON DEPOSITS THAT REMAIN INCANDESCENT
VALVES OPERATING AT HIGHER-THAN-NORMAL TEMPERATURE
HOT SPOTS CAUSED BY DEFECTS IN THE COOLING SYSTEM
SPARK PLUGS THAT RUN TOO HOT
SHARP EDGES IN THE COMBUSTION CHAMBER
DETONATION

Matching

Match the term in the right column with its description in the left column. Place the corresponding letter in the blank.

15. The vaporizing ability of a liquid. — 15. D
16. Rapidly combining fuel with oxygen to produce heat. — 16. C
17. Indicates too rapid burning or explosion of air/fuel mixture in engine cylinders. — 17. B
18. Ignition occurs earlier than intended. — 18. A

(A) Preignition.
(B) Detonation.
(C) Combustion.
(D) Volatility.

Chapter 19

Fuel Supply Systems, Intake Systems, Superchargers, and Turbochargers

Name ______________________

Date ____________ Instructor ____________

Score_______ Textbook pages 243–258

After studying the chapter in the text and completing this section of the workbook, you will be able to:

- ❑ List the different types of fuel pumps and gauges.
- ❑ Explain how mechanical and electrical fuel pumps operate.
- ❑ Explain the purpose of an intake system.
- ❑ Explain how to service an air cleaner.
- ❑ Describe various intake manifold designs.
- ❑ Describe turbocharger and wastegate operation.

Multiple Choice

1. If any part of a mechanical fuel pump is defective, the ____.
   (A) part must be replaced
   (B) entire pump must be replaced
   (C) part must be repaired
   (D) None of the above.

1. ______________________

2. A fuel filter is usually _____.
   (A) replaced every three months
   (B) replaced with a new filter once a year
   (C) replaced every five years
   (D) good for the life of the vehicle

2. ______________________

3. When cleaning a paper element or dry type air cleaner, _____.
   (A) soak it in water
   (B) soak it in gasoline
   (C) tap it against a hard, flat surface to shake loose the dirt and then direct compressed air at it to blow off any remaining dirt
   (D) None of the above.

3. ______________________

Name ______________________

4. Supercharges are used to _____. 4. ______
   (A) overcome friction losses in the intake system
   (B) aid in scavenging the cylinders of burnt gases
   (C) blow the combustible mixture into the cylinders of spark ignition engines
   (D) All of the above.

5. If the wastegate on a turbocharger remains in the closed position, _____. 5. ______
   (A) fuel consumption will be increased
   (B) fuel consumption will be decreased
   (C) detonation will result
   (D) Both A and C.

Identification

Identify the parts indicated on the electric roller type fuel pump shown below.

6. Pressure side. 6. B
7. Pressure limiter. 7. D
8. Non-return valve. 8. A
9. Motor armature. 9. C
10. Roller-cell pump. 10. F
11. Suction side. 11. E

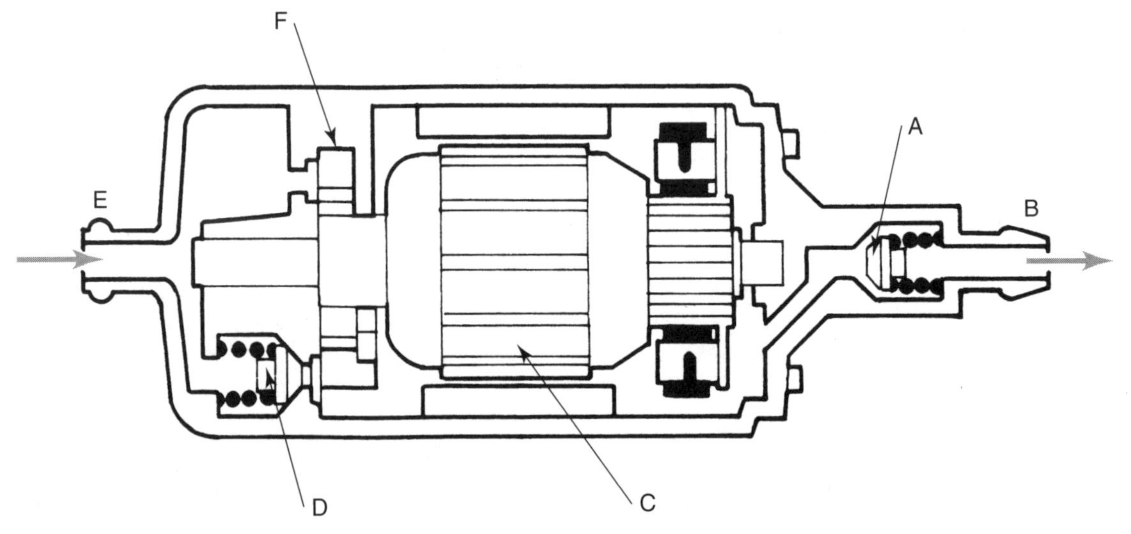

Identify the parts indicated on the fuel pump shown at the top of the next page.

12. Inlet valve. 12. B
13. Diaphragm spring. 13. H
14. Fuel pump chamber. 14. C
15. Rocker arm. 15. E
16. Outlet valve. 16. A
17. Fuel pump eccentric on camshaft. 17. F
18. Diaphragm. 18. D
19. Lever return spring. 19. G

Name ______________________________

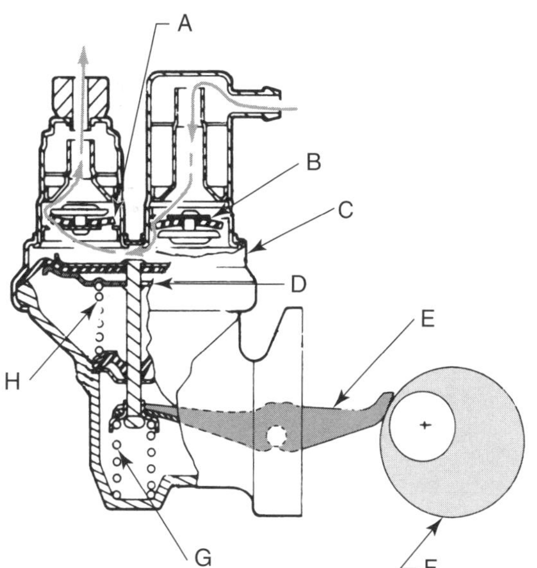

Identify the parts indicated on the diagram below.

20. Fuel lever sending unit assembly. 20. F

21. Body wiring harness. 21. A

22. Fuel tank. 22. C

23. Fuel supply line. 23. H

24. Fuel fill. 24. D

25. Vent line with rollover valve. 25. B

26. Fuel filter. 26. E

27. Fuel return line. 27. G

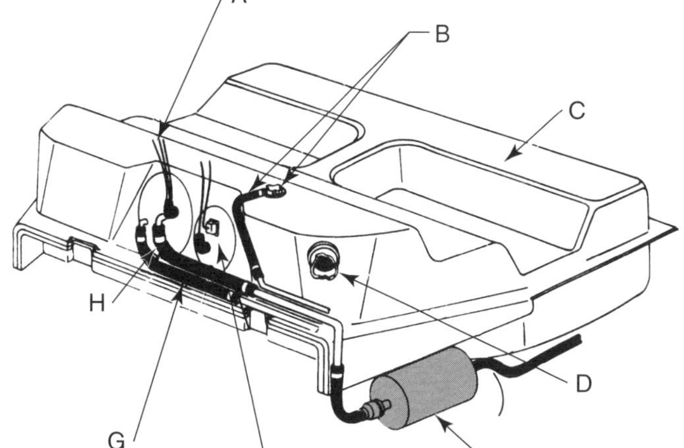

Name ______________________________

Identify the parts indicated on the crankcase breather element shown below.

28. Retainer. 28. B
29. Retainer clip. 29. D
30. Filter pack. 30. A
31. PCV hose. 31. E
32. Air cleaner shell. 32. C
33. Elbow. 33. F

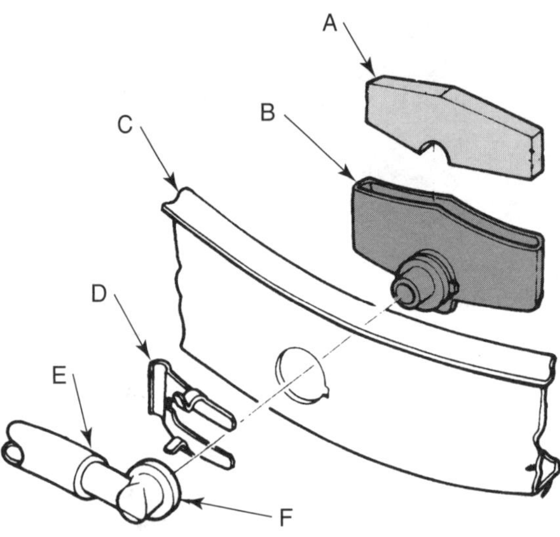

Using arrows on the diagram below, indicate the direction air flows during high vacuum conditions. In addition, identify the items indicated.

34. Combustion chamber. 34. E
35. Crankcase breather. 35. A
36. Air cleaner. 36. B
37. PCV valve. 37. D
38. Air intake. 38. C
39. Blowby gases. 39. F

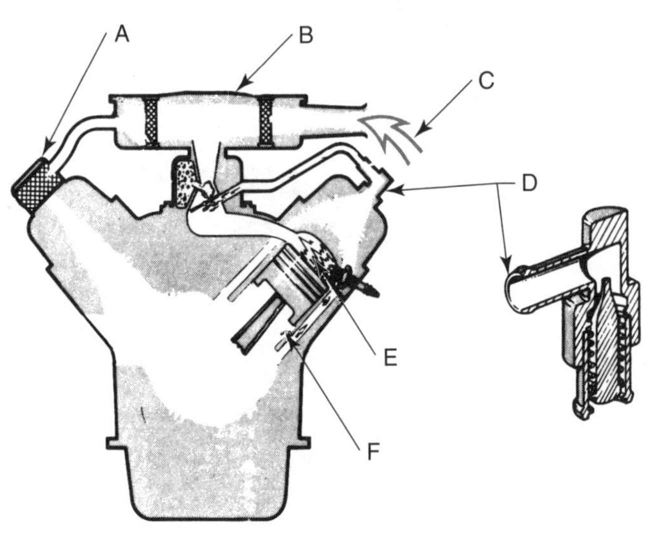

Name ______________________________

40. Using arrows, indicate the path air flows through the heated air intake system.

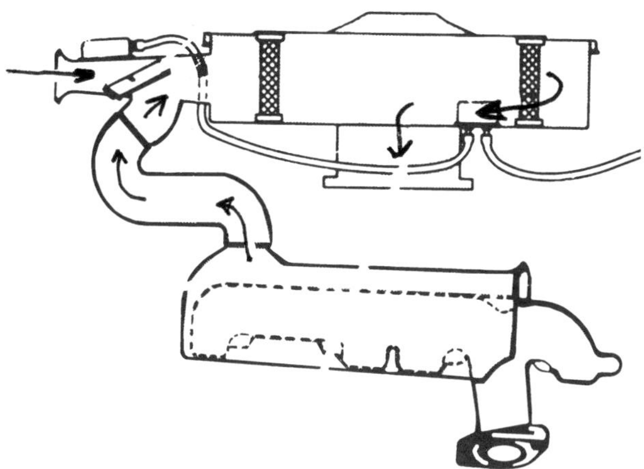

Identify the parts indicated in the photographs below.

41. Intake manifold. 41. ~~B~~ D
42. Intake ports of cylinder head. 42. B
43. Exhaust crossover passage. 43. G
44. Carburetor base. 44. F
45. Coolant passages. 45. A
46. Air-fuel mixture (to cylinders). 46. E
47. Where exhaust gases exit cylinder head when heat control valve is closed. 47. C

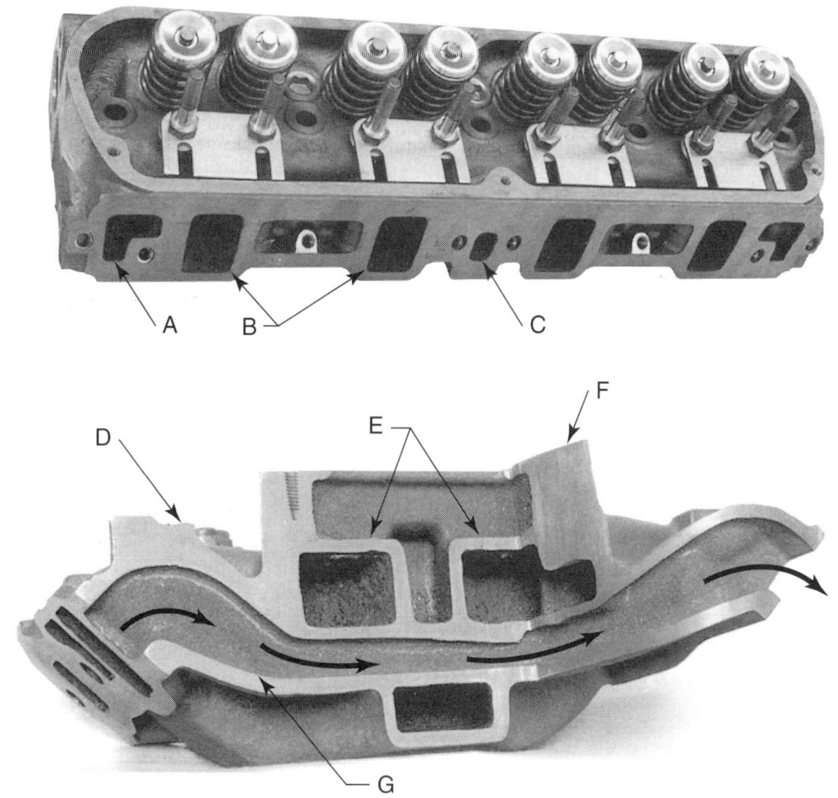

Name ________________________________

Identify the parts indicated on the turbo housing shown below.

48. Wastegate (inside). 48. C

49. Wastegate actuator. 49. A

50. Boost pressure hose (from compressor). 50. D

51. Rod. 51. B

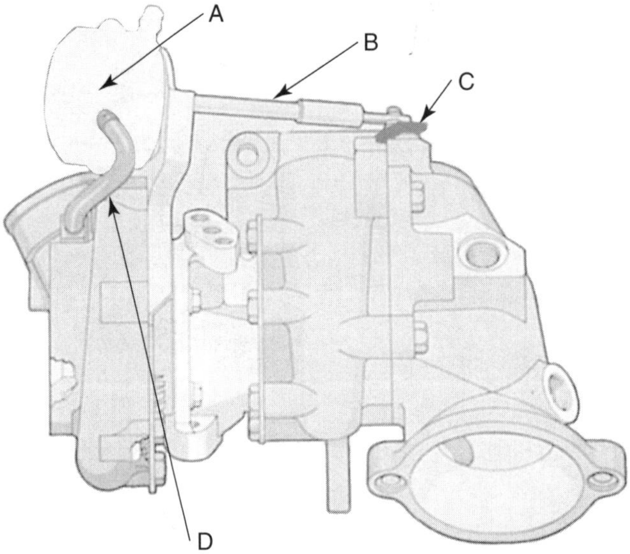

A

B

C

D

Completion

52. _____ fuel pumps are operated by means of a cam or eccentric on the camshaft of the engine. 52. MECHANICAL

53. _____ fuel pumps are energized by a built-in electric motor. 53. ELECTRIC

54. To ensure cleanliness, _____ filters are installed in the fuel line between the fuel pump and the injectors or the carburetor. 54. FUEL

55. The _____ _____ distributes air and fuel to the cylinders. 55. INTAKE SYSTEMS

56. While turbochargers and superchargers perform the same function, the _____ is driven by exhaust gases and the _____ is driven by belts or gears. 56. TURBOCHARGER, SUPERCHARGERS

Short Answer

57. List the four points where damage or wear will affect the performance of a fuel pump.

INLET VALVE, OUTLET VALVE, DIAPHRAGM SPRING, LEVER RETURN SPRING

Name ____________________

58. Indicate what is happening in each of the following diagrams.

(A) HOT AIR DELIVERY

(B) MODULATING HOT AND COLD AIR

(C) VALVE IS CLOSED TO BLOCK OFF HOT AIR, WHICH COULD CAUSE DETONATION

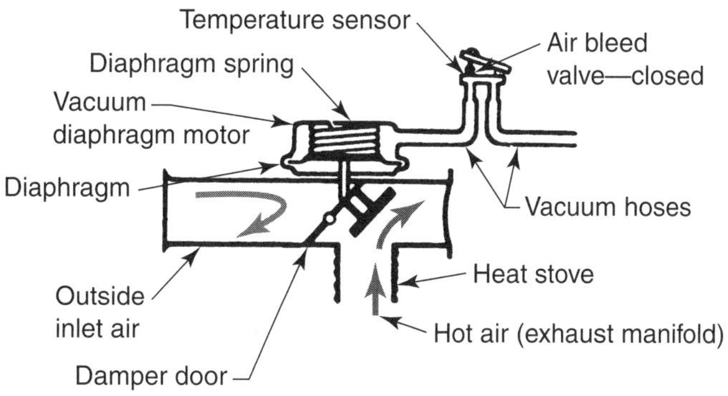

A

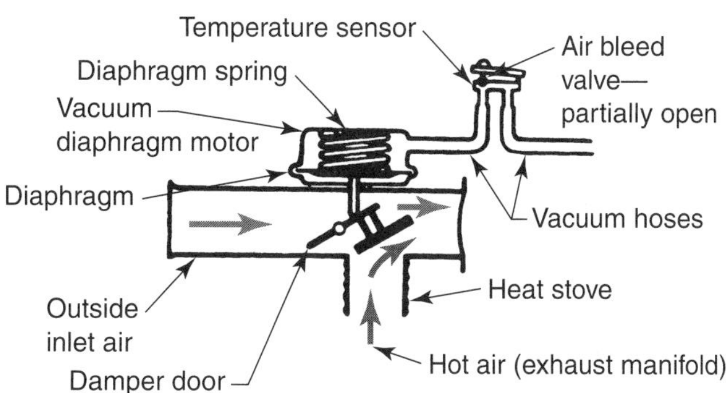

B

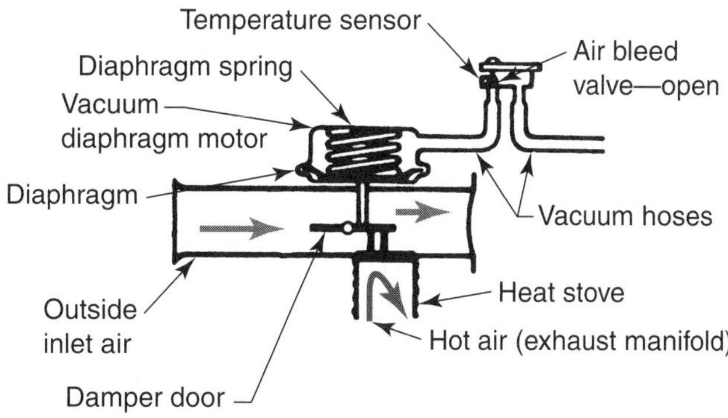

C

59. Explain why engine oil must be changed more frequently in a turbocharged engine than in a non-turbocharged engine.

THE TURBO HOUSING USES AN EXCESSIVE AMOUNT OF OIL

Chapter 20

Fuel Injection Systems

Name ______________________________

Date ______________ Instructor ______________

Score________ Textbook pages 259–274

After studying the chapter in the text and completing this section of the workbook, you will be able to:

- ❑ List the various types of fuel injection systems.
- ❑ Describe the three subgroups of an EFI system.
- ❑ Explain how the pressure regulator and fuel injector operate.
- ❑ Troubleshoot the fuel injection system.
- ❑ Tell why fuel pressure must be released and explain how it is released.

Multiple Choice

1. _____ injection is also referred to as throttle body injection (TBI).
   (A) Single-point
   (B) Multi-point
   (C) Direct fuel
   (D) None of the above.

1. ______________________________

2. The most common method of controlling the delivery of fuel to the injectors is _____ fuel injection.
   (A) mechanical
   (B) hydraulic
   (C) electronic
   (D) None of the above.

2. ______________________________

3. Which of the following sensors determines when the injector is energized?
   (A) Manifold absolute pressure sensor.
   (B) Crankshaft position sensor.
   (C) Oxygen sensor.
   (D) Throttle position sensor.

3. ______________________________

Name ______________________________

4. The mechanical fuel injection pump _____ the fuel at high pressure through the spray nozzle.
   (A) times
   (B) meters
   (C) forces
   (D) All of the above.

4. ______________________________

5. Which of the following problems can result from a defective fuel injector?
   (A) Rough idle.
   (B) Hard starting.
   (C) Poor fuel economy and engine misfire.
   (D) All of the above.

5. ______________________________

Identification

Identify the parts indicated on the photograph below.

6. Pressure regulator. 6. C
7. Fuel injector nozzle. 7. E
8. Fuel hose. 8. A
9. Throttle body. 9. D
10. Electrical connection. 10. B

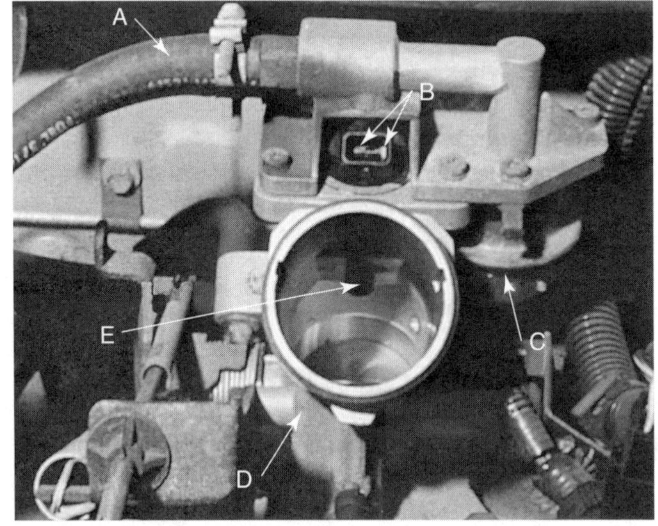

Identify the parts indicated on the diagram shown below.

11. Idle speed motor. 11. B
12. Fuel injectors. 12. A

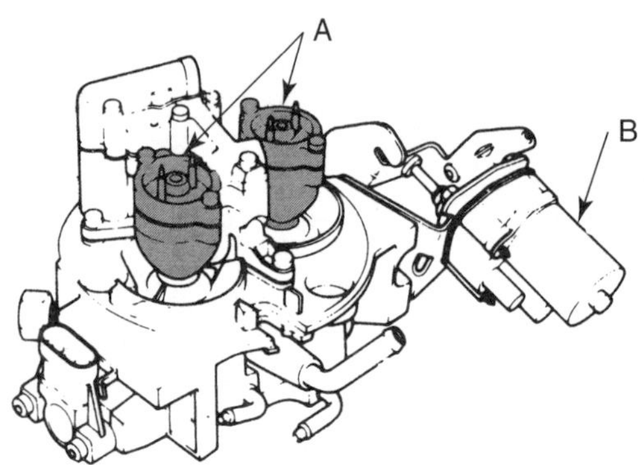

Name ______________________

Identify the parts indicated on the multi-point system shown below.

13. Fuel rail. 13. B

14. Fuel pressure regulator. 14. A

15. Fuel injectors. 15. C

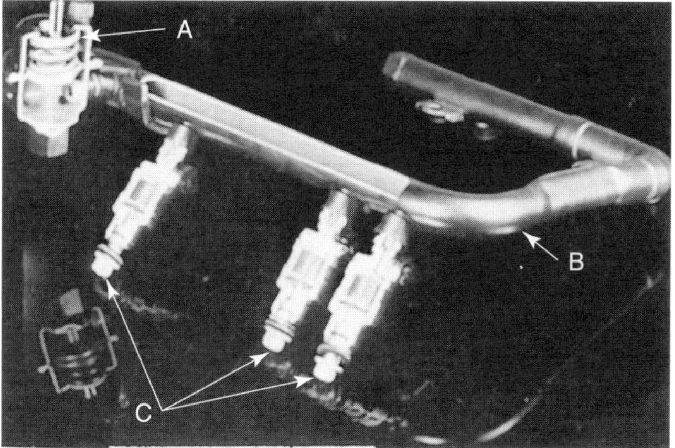

16. On the diagram below, use arrows to show the flow of fuel.

Regulated fuel path

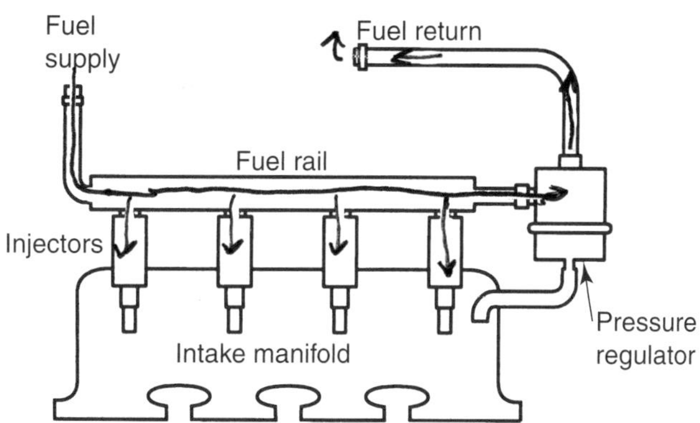

Identify the parts indicated on the diagram at the top of the next page.

17. Fuel filter. 17. C

18. O-ring. 18. E

19. Upper housing. 19. A

20. Gasket. 20. G

21. Diaphragm. 21. B

22. Fuel supply from tank. 22. D

23. Lower housing. 23. H

24. Fuel return to tank. 24. F

25. Tube engine vacuum reference. 25. L

26. Mounting plate. 26. I

27. Valve and seat assembly. 27. J

28. Spring. 28. K

Name ______________________________

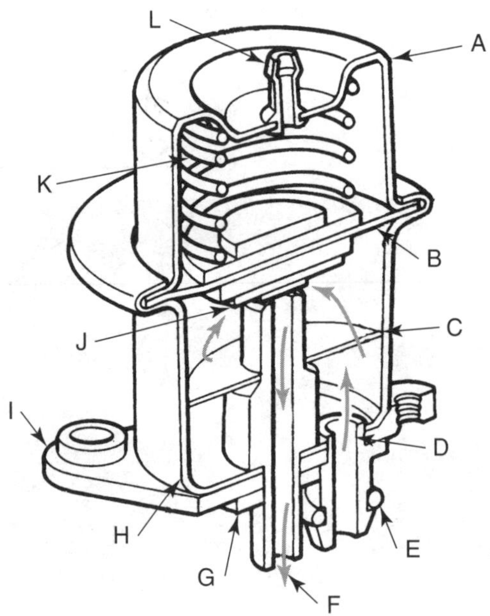

Identify the parts indicated on the fuel injector shown below.

29. Coil.	29.	I
30. Stainless steel needle or pintle.	30.	D
31. Rail O-ring.	31.	J
32. Integral filter.	32.	A
33. Washer.	33.	C
34. Manifold O-ring seal.	34.	G
35. Pintle protection cap.	35.	E
36. Electrical connector.	36.	B
37. Stainless steel body.	37.	F
38. Armature.	38.	H

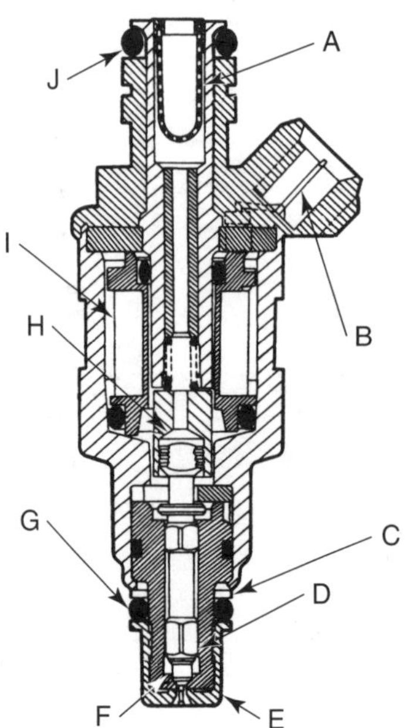

Name ______________________

Completion

39. In a(n) _____ injection system, fuel is sprayed continuously from the injectors. — 39. CONTINUOUS

40. The injectors in a(n) _____ injection system pulse on and off to control the amount of fuel entering the combustion chambers. — 40. INTERMITTENT

41. In the _____ injection system, there is generally an injector for each cylinder of the engine. — 41. SEQUENTIAL

42. The fuel pressure _____ keeps the fuel pressure at the injectors constant under all driving conditions. — 42. REGULATOR

43. In most cases, the _____ will trigger a malfunction indicator light (MIL) in the dashboard when a problem is detected in the fuel system and a diagnostic trouble code is stored. — 43. ECM

44. To quickly check the operation of a multi-point fuel injector, place a _____ against the body of the injector and listen for a clicking sound. — 44. STETHOSCOPE

45. The most common problem with a fuel injector is that the _____ in the nozzle become dirty and restrict fuel flow. — 45. NEEDLE OR PINTLE

46. If tests indicate a faulty injector, it must generally be _____. — 46. REPLACED

47. In _____ injection systems, the computer controls system pressure by regulating the output of the electric fuel pump. — 47. SEQUENTIAL

Short Answer

48. List nine advantages of fuel injection.

INCRASED POWER
HIGHER TORQUE
IMPROVED FUEL ECONOMY
QUICKER COLD WEATHER STARTING
FASTER WARMUP
NO NEED FOR MANIFOLD HEAT
LOWER INTAKE TEMPERATURES
[illegible]
[illegible]

49. Name three types of fuel injection systems.

CONTINUOUS INJECTION SYSTEM
INTERMITTENT INJECTION SYSTEM
SEQUENTIAL INJECTION SYSTEM

Name ______________________________

50. What is the first step in solving any fuel injection system problem?

USE A STETHOSCOPE TO FIND ANY CLING SOUNDS

51. What is being done in the photograph below?

TESTING THE FUEL PRESSURE

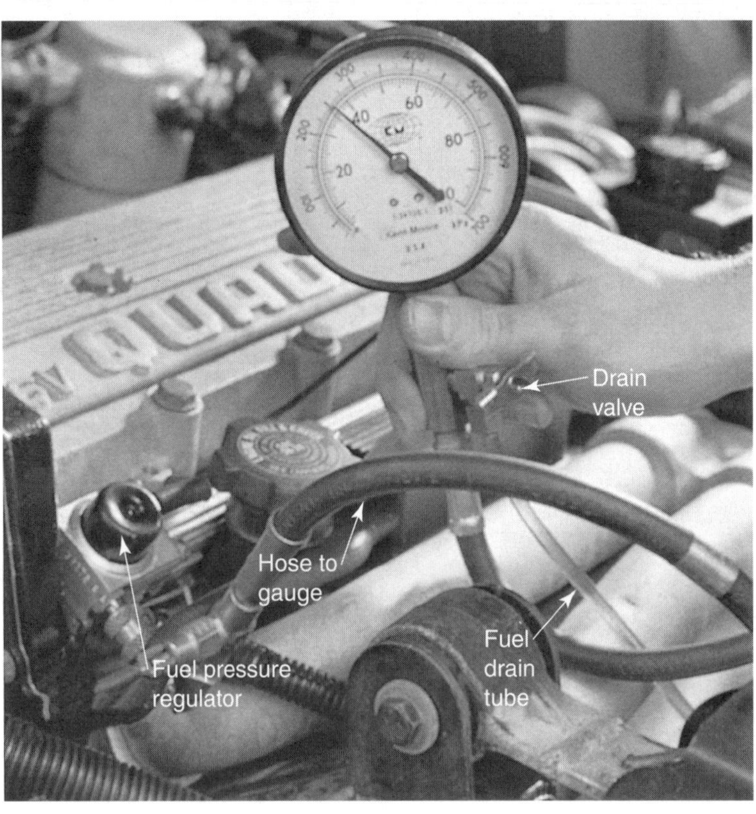

52. What can cause low fuel pressure?

BAD ~~JE~~ FUEL JETS, BAD SEAL ECT.

53. Why should you always relieve fuel pressure before disconnecting fuel lines in the fuel injection system?

SO YOU DONT GET GAS EVERYWHERE

54. List the two different methods of diesel fuel injection.

AIR INJECTION SYSTEM

MECHANICAL INJECTION SYSTEM

Chapter 21

Carburetor Fundamentals and Service

Name ______________________________

Date ________________ Instructor ________________

Score_______ Textbook pages 275–300

After studying the chapter in the text and completing this section of the workbook, you will be able to:

- ❑ State the purpose of the carburetor.
- ❑ List the circuits of the carburetor.
- ❑ Explain Bernoulli's Principle.
- ❑ Describe how each circuit of the carburetor works.
- ❑ Define what is meant by closed and open loop.
- ❑ Diagnose carburetor-related problems.
- ❑ Describe the procedure for adjusting carburetor idle speed and air/fuel mixture.

Multiple Choice

1. The best economy is obtained by a mix of 1 part gasoline to between _____ parts air.
   (A) 2 to 3
   (B) 16 to 17
   (C) 20 to 21
   (D) 51 to 52

   1. ______________________

2. If the carburetor float level is too low, _____.
   (A) not enough fuel will be supplied to the system
   (B) excessive fuel consumption will result
   (C) the engine will stall on turns
   (D) Both A and C.

   2. ______________________

3. A lean air-fuel mixture produces a high level of _____ in the exhaust.
   (A) nitrous oxides (NO_X)
   (B) hydrocarbons (HC)
   (C) carbon monoxide (CO)
   (D) All of the above.

   3. ______________________

Name ______________________________

4. A decal placed in the engine compartment provides the necessary information for _____. 4. ______________________
   (A) timing
   (B) idle speed
   (C) fuel mixture
   (D) All of the above.

5. Prior to adjusting the idle, make sure the _____. 5. ______________________
   (A) engine has reached its normal operating temperature
   (B) choke plate is open
   (C) choke plate is closed
   (D) Both A and B.

Identification

Identify the parts indicated on the diagram below.

6. Choke rod. 6. ______________________

7. Fast idle screw. 7. ______________________

8. Vacuum break rod. 8. ______________________

9. Thermostatic coil and rod. 9. ______________________

10. Choke valve. 10. ______________________

11. Secondary lockout lever. 11. ______________________

12. Fast idle cam. 12. ______________________

13. Choke coil lever. 13. ______________________

14. Fast idle cam follower. 14. ______________________

15. Unloader tang. 15. ______________________

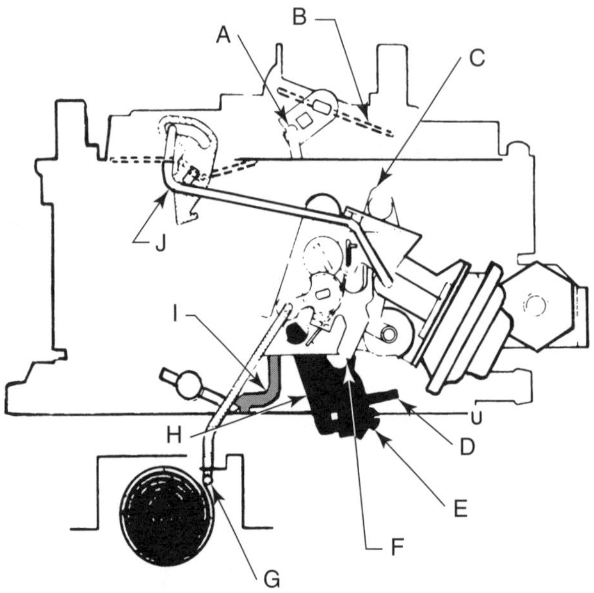

Name ______________________________

Identify the parts indicated on the float circuit below.

16. Float assembly. 16. ____________________
17. Fuel inlet fitting. 17. ____________________
18. Vent. 18. ____________________
19. Needle and seat assembly. 19. ____________________

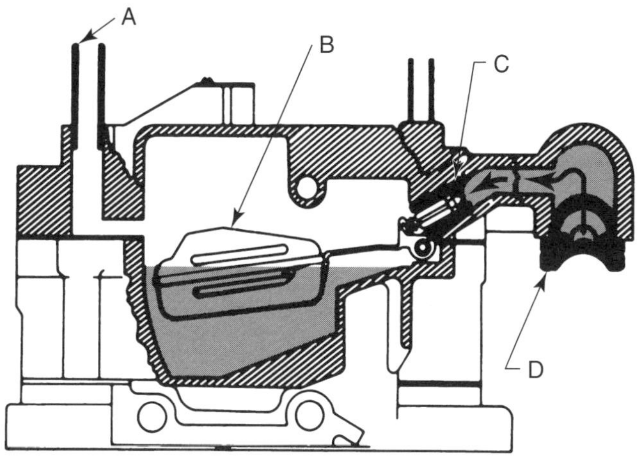

Identify the parts indicated on the idle circuit below.

20. Venturi cluster screws (2). 20. ____________________
21. Idle air bleed. 21. ____________________
22. Main metering rods (2). 22. ____________________
23. Main metering jets (2). 23. ____________________
24. Idle port. 24. ____________________
25. Idle fuel pick-up tube. 25. ____________________
26. Idle mixture adjustment screw. 26. ____________________
27. Transfer slot. 27. ____________________
28. Step-up piston. 28. ____________________
29. Idle restrictor. 29. ____________________

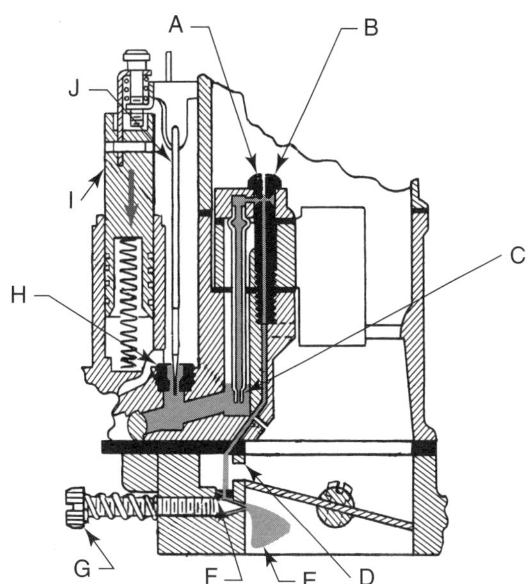

Name ______________________________

Identify the parts indicated on the main metering circuit below.

30. Plug-solenoid adjusting screw. 30. ____________________
31. Primary metering jet assembly. 31. ____________________
32. Solenoid plunger. 32. ____________________
33. Screw-solenoid adjusting (lean mixture). 33. ____________________
34. Pull-over enrichment fuel tube. 34. ____________________
35. Main well. 35. ____________________
36. Clean air inlet. 36. ____________________
37. Mixture control solenoid assembly. 37. ____________________
38. Air bleed valve assembly. 38. ____________________
39. Main well air bleeds. 39. ____________________
40. Pull-over enrichment discharge orifice. 40. ____________________
41. Rod-primary metering. 41. ____________________
42. Main venturi. 42. ____________________
43. Main discharge nozzle. 43. ____________________
44. Throttle valve. 44. ____________________
45. Boost venturi. 45. ____________________
46. Stop-rich mixture. 46. ____________________

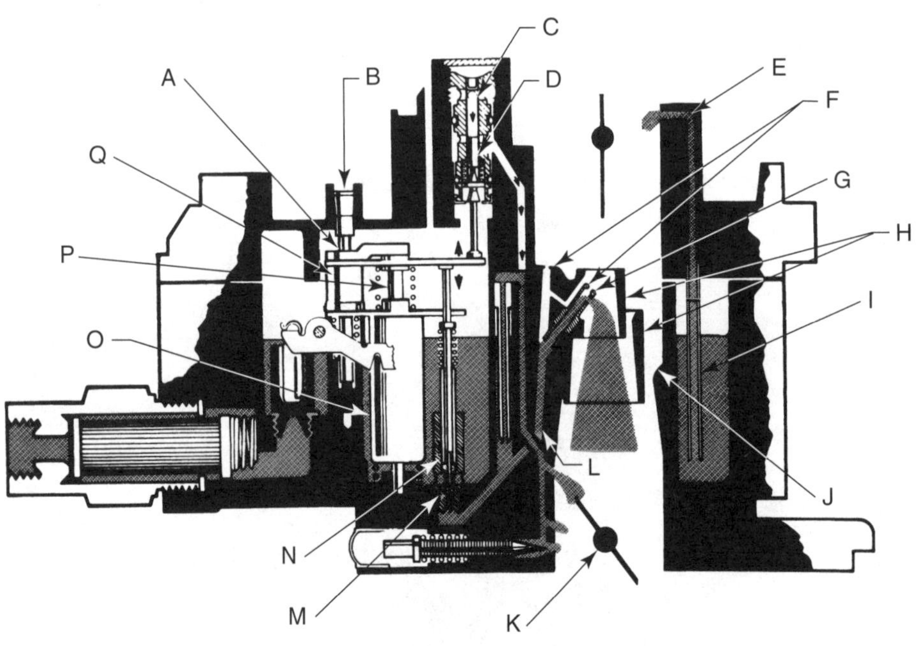

Name ______________________________

Identify the parts indicated on the power circuit below.

47. Venturi. 47. ______________________
48. Main system air bleed. 48. ______________________
49. Metering rods (2). 49. ______________________
50. Step-up piston. 50. ______________________
51. Main metering jets (2). 51. ______________________
52. Spring. 52. ______________________

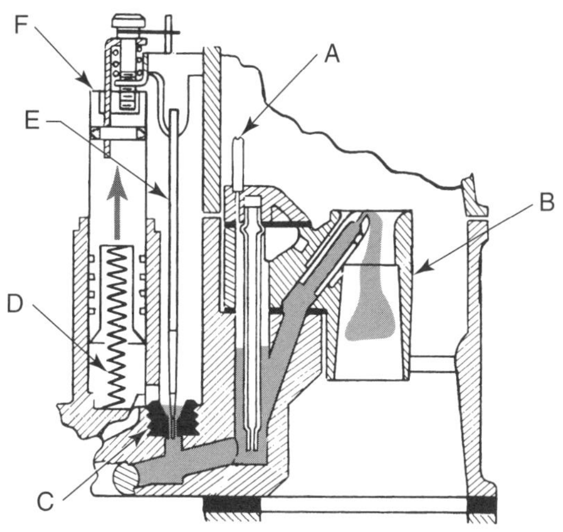

Identify the parts indicated on the accelerator pump below.

53. Intake check ball. 53. ______________________
54. Accelerator pump shaft. 54. ______________________
55. Discharge check ball. 55. ______________________
56. Jump drive spring. 56. ______________________
57. Pump arm. 57. ______________________
58. Accelerator pump plunger. 58. ______________________
59. "S" link. 59. ______________________
60. Discharge jet. 60. ______________________
61. Float bowl. 61. ______________________
62. Accelerator pump well. 62. ______________________

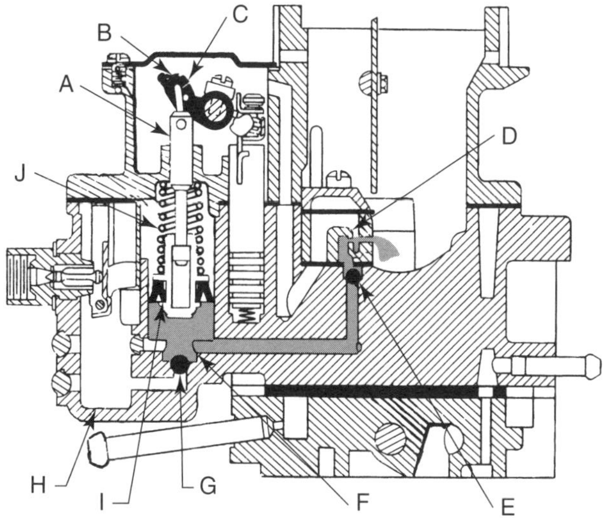

Name ______________________________

Completion

63. Choke _____-_____ assists in opening the choke plate a fraction of an inch. The "U"-shaped bend in the link determines how far the choke is opened. 63. ______________________

64. The crossover-type automatic choke is _____ controlled. 64. ______________________

65. The difference between the ______ (high, low) pressure within the cylinder and atmospheric pressure outside of the carburetor causes air and fuel to flow into the cylinder from the carburetor. 65. ______________________

66. The metering _____ varies the amount of fuel flowing through the jet. As speed increases, it is lifted out of the jet, allowing more fuel to flow. 66. ______________________

67. In a typical four-barrel carburetor, the primary side bores are _____ (smaller, larger) than the secondary bores. 67. ______________________

68. The only practical method for monitoring all engine variables at once is with the use on an on-board _____. 68. ______________________

69. The _____-______ carburetor is controlled by the computer. 69. ______________________

70. When an engine equipped with a computer-controlled carburetor is _____ (cold, hot), the computer operates from predetermined values and the fuel mixture is fixed at full rich. 70. ______________________

71. With manual shift cars in _____, and automatic transmission cars in _____, the idle speed can be checked and adjusted. 71. ______________________

72. Carburetor floats are either mounted in the _____ _____ or attached to the air horn assembly. 72. ______________________

Short Answer

73. What is occurring in the diagram at the top of the next page?

____

____

Name ______________________________

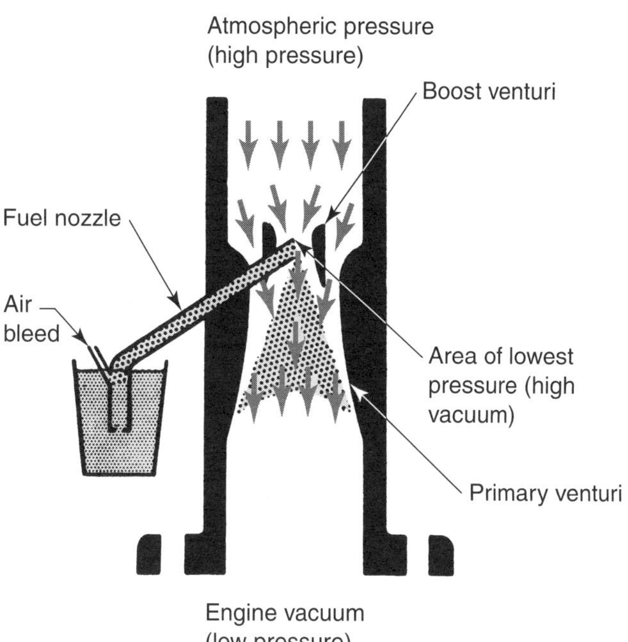

74. On 1980 and newer car models, the air-fuel mixture adjustment screws are sealed. Why has this been done?

____

____

75. What is being done in the diagram below?

____

____

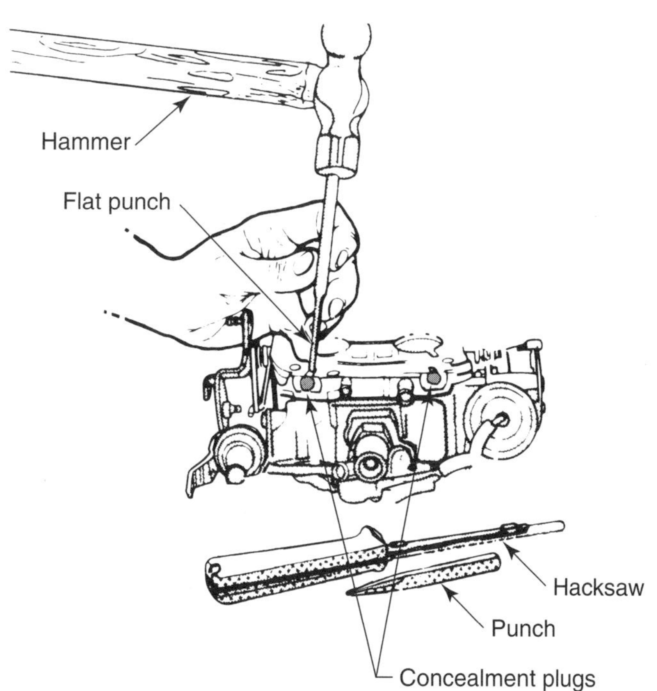

Chapter 22

Ignition System Fundamentals and Service

Name ______________________________

Date ________________ Instructor ________________

Score_______ Textbook pages 301–324

After studying the chapter in the text and completing this section of the workbook, you will be able to:

- ❑ Distinguish between the primary and secondary sides of the ignition system.
- ❑ Describe how a coil transforms battery voltage into the high voltage needed to ignite the air/fuel mixture.
- ❑ Explain how the different types of ignition systems operate.
- ❑ Diagnose common ignition system problems.
- ❑ Test and service individual ignition system components.

Multiple Choice

1. The ignition coil is constructed of primary and secondary windings that are wound around a soft _____ core.
   (A) copper
   (B) iron
   (C) steel
   (D) aluminum

   1. ______________________

2. Engine designers select spark plugs that give good performance for _____ driving conditions.
   (A) average
   (B) full-load
   (C) low-load
   (D) Both B and C.

   2. ______________________

3. What is the most common type of pickup assembly?
   (A) Optical.
   (B) Hall effect.
   (C) Magnetic.
   (D) None of the above.

   3. ______________________

Name ______________________________

4. A bad ignition coil may cause the engine to _____. 4. ______________________
   (A) miss
   (B) stall
   (C) not start at all
   (D) All of the above.

5. Under good conditions, most spark plugs last from _____ miles. 5. ______________________
   (A) 5,000 to 10,000
   (B) 15,000 to 50,000
   (C) 40,000 to 60,000
   (D) 70,000 to 100,000

Identification

Identify the parts of the ignition coil below.

6. Secondary winding. 6. ______________________
7. Low tension terminal. 7. ______________________
8. Iron core. 8. ______________________
9. Resistance unit. 9. ______________________
10. Connector strap. 10. ______________________
11. Low tension terminal. 11. ______________________
12. High tension terminal. 12. ______________________
13. Primary winding. 13. ______________________

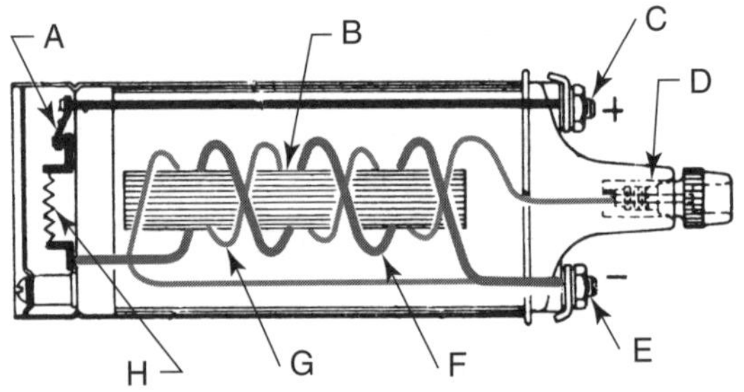

Identify the parts indicated on the diagram shown at the top of the next page.

14. High-voltage spark plug cable. 14. ______________________
15. Spark. 15. ______________________
16. High-voltage coil cable. 16. ______________________
17. Rotor. 17. ______________________
18. Shaft turns rotor. 18. ______________________
19. Spark plugs. 19. ______________________

Name ____________________

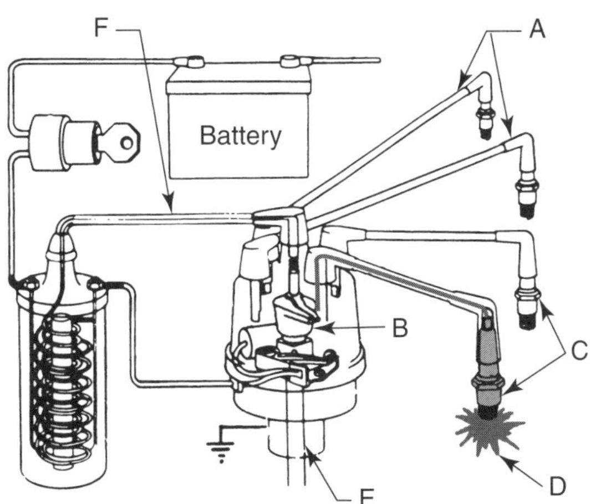

Identify the parts indicated on the spark plug shown below.

20. Copper-cored center electrode. 20. ____________________
21. Resistor. 21. ____________________
22. Inside gasket. 22. ____________________
23. Thread diameter. 23. ____________________
24. Terminal. 24. ____________________
25. Ground electrode. 25. ____________________
26. Siliment seals. 26. ____________________
27. Attached gasket. 27. ____________________
28. Five-rib insulator. 28. ____________________
29. Spark gap. 29. ____________________
30. Reach. 30. ____________________

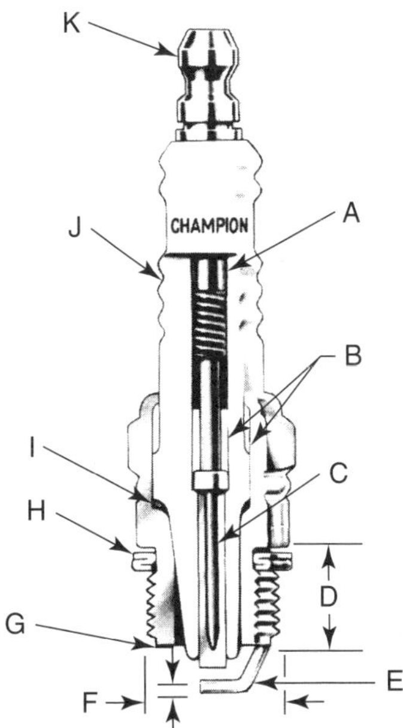

Name ______________________________

Completion

31. The _____ _____ ignites the air/fuel mixture in the cylinders at the correct moment to produce efficient combustion. 31. ______________________
32. The _____ _____ is a transformer designed to increase the primary voltage (battery voltage) to at least 30,000 V. 32. ______________________
33. The _____ _____ works in conjunction with the distributor and rotor to route the high voltage produced by the coil to the spark plugs. 33. ______________________
34. A distributor _____ is designed to rotate and distribute the high voltage from the center tower of the distributor cap to the outer towers. 34. ______________________
35. The _____ _____ in a spark ignition engine provides the gap across which the high tension voltage jumps. 35. ______________________
36. The _____ ignition system operates in the same manner as the distributorless ignition, but it uses one coil for each spark plug. 36. ______________________
37. In many cases, a _____ _____ (thin line of carbon-like substance) forms on the distributor cap when arcing is present. 37. ______________________
38. Ignition _____ must be adjusted whenever the distributor has been removed from and reinstalled in an engine. 38. ______________________
39. Before checking and adjusting the timing in a computerized ignition system, _____ timing must be activated. 39. ______________________
40. If the line on the _____ damper does not line up with the appropriate mark on the engine's front cover, the timing must be adjusted. 40. ______________________
41. A vacuum _____ can be used to check the vacuum advance diaphragm. 41. ______________________
42. Although dedicated testers are available to test ignition control module operation, the best way to identify a faulty module may be through the process of _____. 42. ______________________

Short Answer

43. What factors will affect the voltage needed to jump a certain gap?

____

____

____

____

Name ______________________________

44. How is the firing order of spark plugs determined?

45. List twelve variables that affect spark advance.

46. List six sensors commonly used in a computerized ignition system.

47. What is the advantage of a distributorless ignition system?

48. How can you check spark plug wire insulation?

49. What types of problems can a bad pickup coil produce?

50. Name two ways contact points can be adjusted.

Name ______________________________

Matching

51. Normal. 51. ______________________
52. Gap bridged. 52. ______________________
53. Oil fouled. 53. ______________________
54. Carbon fouled. 54. ______________________
55. Pre-ignition. 55. ______________________
56. Overheating. 56. ______________________
57. Fused spot deposit. 57. ______________________

D

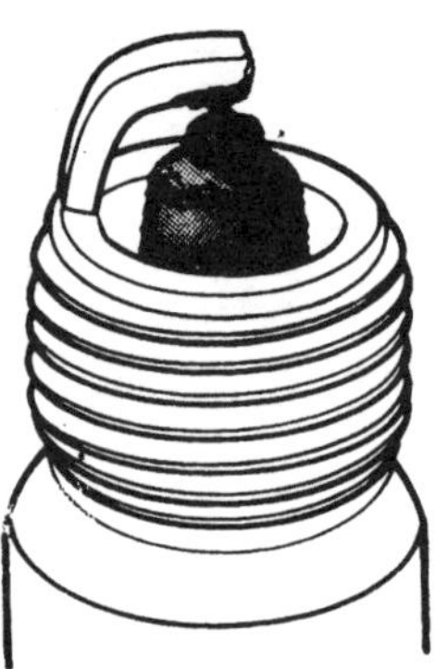

C

E

F

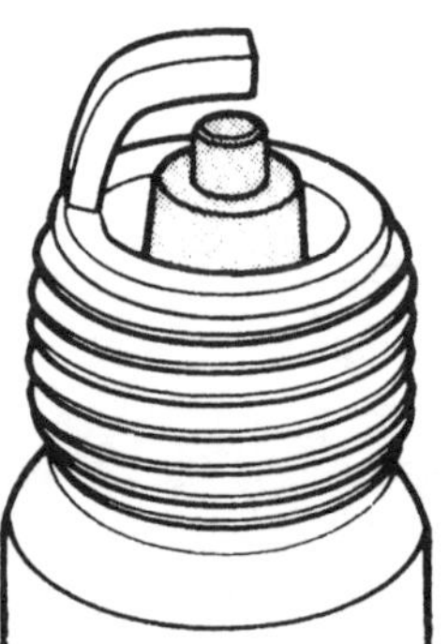

G

A

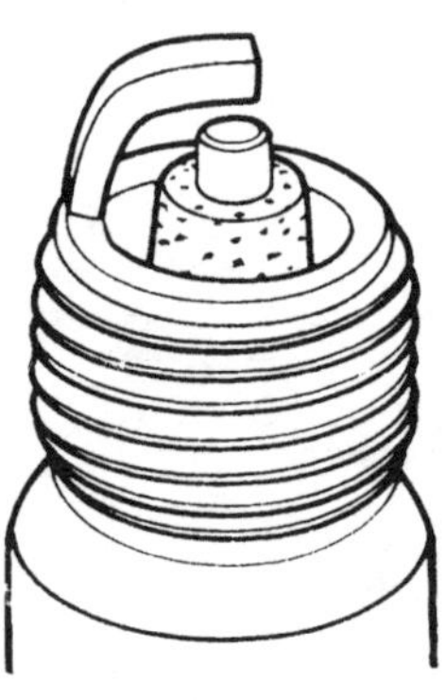

B

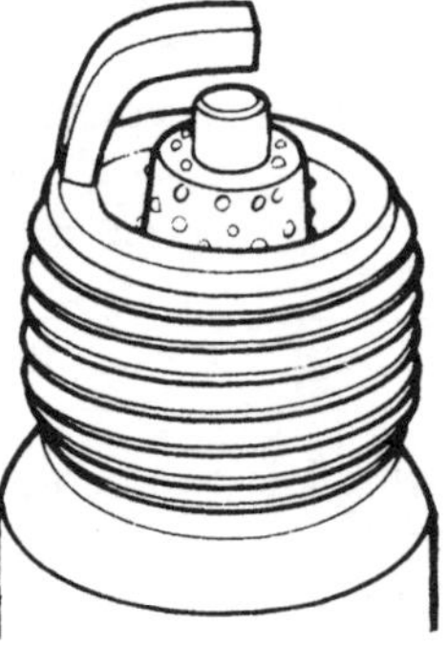

Chapter 23

Batteries and Battery Service

Name ____________________

Date __________ Instructor __________

Score______ Textbook pages 325–338

After studying the chapter in the text and completing this section of the workbook, you will be able to:

- ❑ State three functions of an automotive battery.
- ❑ List basic parts of a typical automotive battery.
- ❑ Give two methods of rating battery performance.
- ❑ Explain three methods of testing an automotive battery.
- ❑ List safe battery servicing practices.
- ❑ Identify four methods of charging a battery.
- ❑ State the sequence of steps for jump starting an engine.

Multiple Choice

1. The lead-acid storage battery used in automobiles and other vehicles is a(n) _____ device that converts chemical energy into electrical energy.
   (A) electrochemical
   (B) electrical
   (C) chemical
   (D) None of the above.

1. ELECTROCHEMICAL

2. Maintenance-free batteries have _____ than conventional batteries.
   (A) a greater electrolyte reserve above the plates
   (B) better overcharge resistance
   (C) less tendency toward terminal corrosion
   (D) All of the above.

2. D

3. Capacity of a battery depends on the _____.
   (A) number of plates in the cells
   (B) area of the plates in the cells
   (C) amount of electrolyte present
   (D) All of the above.

3. D

Name ______________________________

4. Capacity of cranking power _____.
   (A) stays constant with a drop in temperature
   (B) falls off sharply with a drop in temperature
   (C) increases sharply with a drop in temperature
   (D) None of the above.

4. B

5. A battery is considered "charged" if the state of charge is _____.
   (A) 25 percent or less
   (B) 50 percent or less
   (C) 75 percent or more
   (D) None of the above.

5. C

Identification

Identify the parts indicated on the maintenance-free battery shown below.

6. Polypropylene case. 6. D
7. Wrought lead-calcium grid. 7. G
8. Built-in hydrometer. 8. L
9. Molded symbols. 9. M
10. Cold forged terminals. 10. A
11. Built-in flame arrester. 11. B
12. Centered plate strap thru-the-cell partition cell connectors. 12. I
13. Electrolyte reservoir. 13. J
14. Liquid gas separator area. 14. K
15. High-density paste. 15. H
16. Separator envelopes. 16. F
17. Heat sealed covers. 17. C
18. Hold-down clamp. 18. E

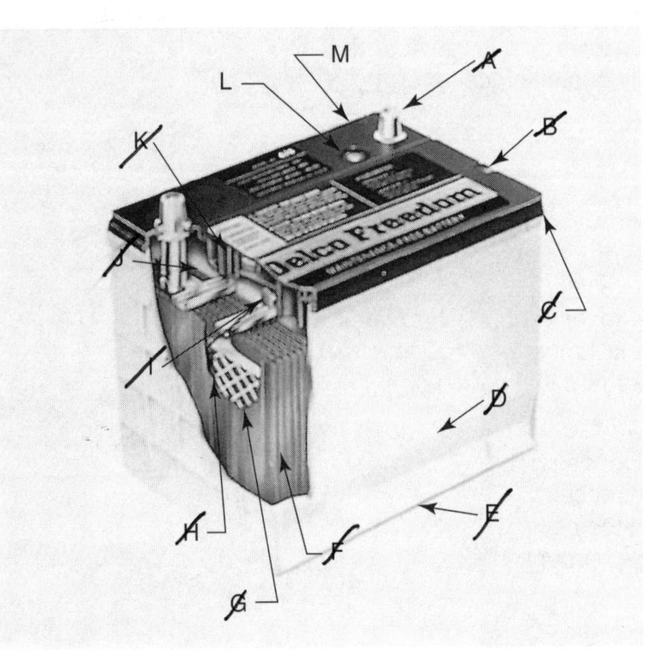

Name ______________________________

19. On the diagram below, indicate the proper jumper cable hookup order by placing numbers in the circles.

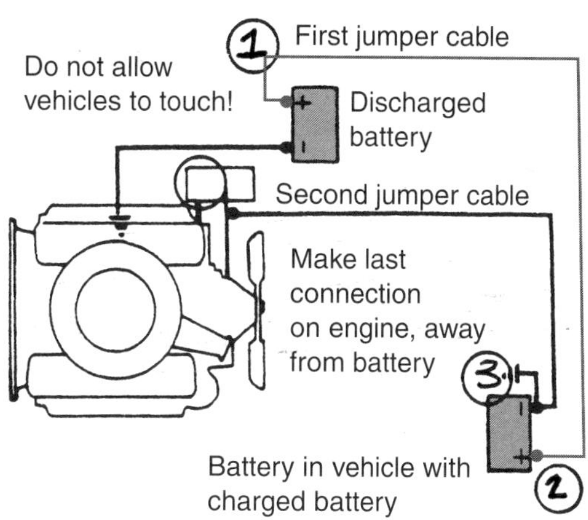

Completion

20. A typical 12-volt, lead-acid battery is made up of six _____ connected in series and filled with electrolyte. — 20. CELLS

21. A plate group is made by welding a number of plates of _____ (the same polarity, different polarities) to a post strap. — 21. THE SAME POLARITY

22. To ensure that adjacent plates do not touch each other, _____ are placed between them. — 22. SEPARATORS

23. The assembly of positive and negative plates and separators is called a(n) _____. — 23. ELEMENT

24. With the elements in place in the battery case, _____ connectors are inserted either through holes in the case partitions or over the partitions. — 24. INTERCELL

25. The _____ cycle occurs when an electric load is connected to the battery and current flows. — 25. DISCHARGE

26. The open circuit voltage (no load voltage) of a fully charged automotive battery is _____ volts or more for electrolyte of approximately _____ specific gravity. — 26. 12.6 / 1.265

27. The _____ of a battery is the amount of current it will deliver. — 27. CAPACITY

28. The _____ is an instrument used to determine the state of charge of battery by testing the specific gravity of the electrolyte. — 28. HYDROMETER

29. The _____ test is a good test of the battery's ability to perform under load. In this test, a good battery will produce current equal to 50 percent of its cold cranking rating (or equal to three times its ampere/hour rating) for 15 seconds and still provide minimum voltage to start the engine. — 29. LOAD

Name ______________________

30. An open circuit voltage test is made by connecting _____ leads across battery terminals.

30. TEST

31. When working on a battery, always disconnect the _____ (negative, positive) cable first and reconnect it last.

31. NEGATIVE

32. _____ _____ an engine involves using jumper cables to transfer power from a good (booster) battery to a discharged battery.

32. BOOST CHARGE

Short Answer

33. List the three main functions of a lead-acid automotive battery.

- STARTING AND IGNITION WHEN CRANKING
- ACTS AS A STABILIZER
- IT HELPS WITH ELECTRICAL WHEN ALTERNATOR CANT

34. How is a battery activated by the addition of electrolyte?

CHEMICAL ACTION TAKES PLACE AND THE ELECTROLYTE HELPS MOVE ELECTRIC CURRENT BETWEEN POLES

35. How can a discharged battery be restored to a charged condition?

ADD MORE ELECTROLYTE AND SLOW CHARGE IT

36. List the two methods of rating the performance of lead-acid batteries established by the Battery Council International. Describe what they mean.

HYDROMETER TEST - TEST THE ELECTROLYTE
~~LOAD~~ LOAD TEST - SEE IF IT WILL HOLD ITS CHARGE

37. Explain why you should strictly observe directions for jumper cable hookup sequence.

SO NO ONE GETS SHOCKED OR THE BATTERS DONT FRY

38. List four battery-charging methods.

HIGH-RATE FAST CHARGING
CONSTANT - POTENTIAL CHARGING
CONSTANT - CURRENT SLOW CHARGING
TRICKLE CHARGING

39. Explain why it is important to wear safety goggles or a face shield and observe all recommended safety practices when working on or near batteries.

THE AICD MIGHT EXPLODE OUT AND GET IN YOUR EYES

Chapter 24

Starting System Fundamentals and Service

Name ______________________________

Date ______________ Instructor ______________

Score________ Textbook pages 339–352

After studying the chapter in the text and completing this section of the workbook, you will be able to:

- ❑ Describe how the starting system works.
- ❑ Explain the principles of electric motor operation.
- ❑ Cite the function of an overrunning clutch.
- ❑ Give examples of possible causes of starting system problems.
- ❑ List the various steps of starter maintenance.
- ❑ Describe ways of testing a starting motor to determine its operating condition.

Multiple Choice

1. The voltage that forces current through the armature is the _____.
   (A) difference between the applied voltage and the CEMF
   (B) sum of the applied voltage and the CEMF
   (C) CEMF
   (D) applied voltage

1. B

2. Increased load on a series motor will cause its _____.
   (A) speed, current, and torque to rise
   (B) speed to rise, while current and torque will drop
   (C) speed to drop, while current and torque will rise
   (D) speed to remain the same, while current and torque will drop

2. A

3. If the lights become dim when the starter motor is cranking, the _____.
   (A) starter may be shorted out
   (B) battery may be weak
   (C) engine may be dragging due to mechanical problems
   (D) Any of the above.

3. D

Name ______________________

4. To prevent the starting motor from overheating, do not operate the starter for more than _____ seconds at a time.
   (A) 5
   (B) 15
   (C) 45
   (D) 60

4. C

5. To test a starting motor to determine its operating condition, begin by making _____.
   (A) on-car tests
   (B) a no-load test
   (C) bench tests
   (D) None of the above.

5. A

Identification

Identify the parts on the cross-sectional views revealing the internal parts of a typical positive engagement starting motor shown at the top of the next page.

6. Grounded brush holder. 6. B
7. Riser bars. 7. O
8. Switch terminal. 8. A
9. Grommet. 9. R
10. Brush. 10. C
11. Shift lever. 11. H
12. Insulated brush holder. 12. D
13. Plunger. 13. F
14. Armature. 14. M
15. Conductors from riser bars to armature. 15. N
16. Commutator. 16. Q
17. Solenoid. 17. E
18. Bushing. 18. I
19. Overrunning clutch. 19. K
20. Bushing. 20. P
21. Field coil. 21. L
22. Pinion stop. 22. J
23. Return spring. 23. G

Name ______________________

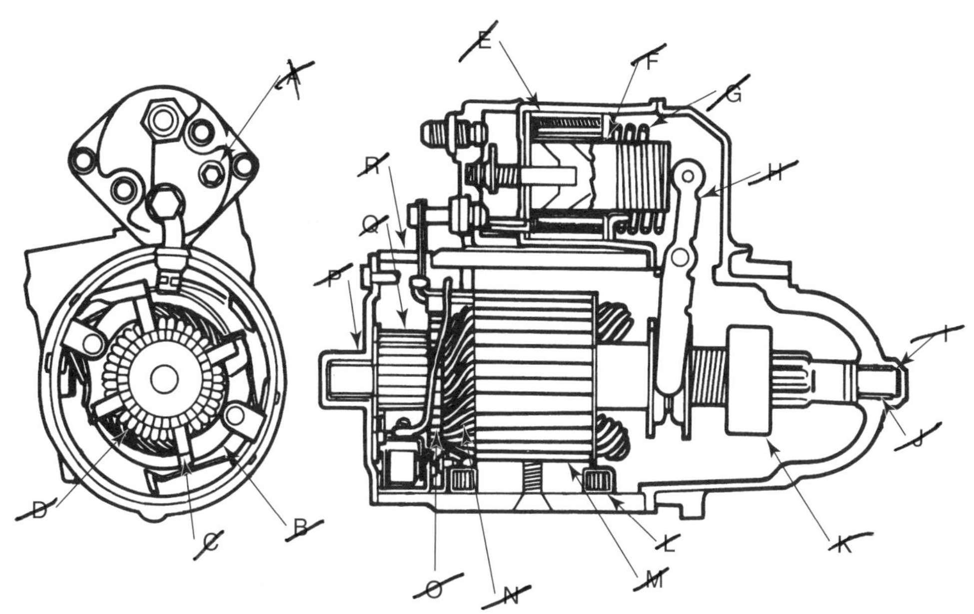

Identify the parts indicated on the sectional view of the positive engagement starting motor shown below.

24. Solenoid terminal. 24. G
25. Shift fork. 25. A
26. Solenoid. 26. H
27. Pinion. 27. B
28. Brush. 28. D
29. Battery terminal. 29. F
30. Overrunning clutch. 30. C
31. Bushing. 31. E

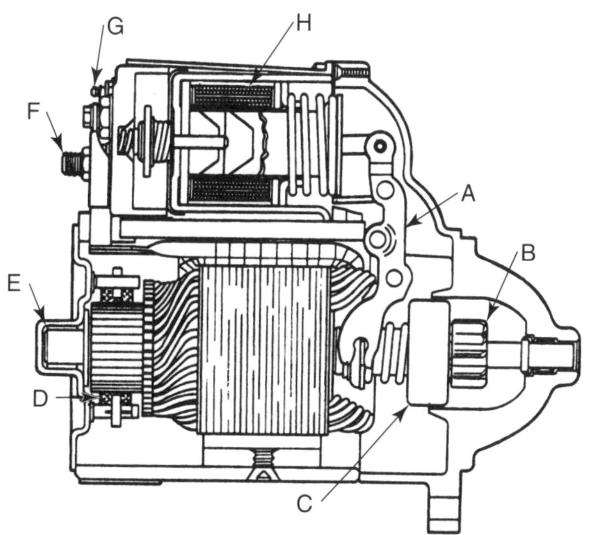

Name ______________________________

Identify the parts indicated on the permanent magnet starting motor shown below.

32. Output shaft. 32. E
33. Ring gear. 33. D
34. Brush holder. 34. A
35. Armature with winding. 35. G
36. Commutator. 36. B
37. Armature shaft. 37. C
38. Planet gears. 38. F

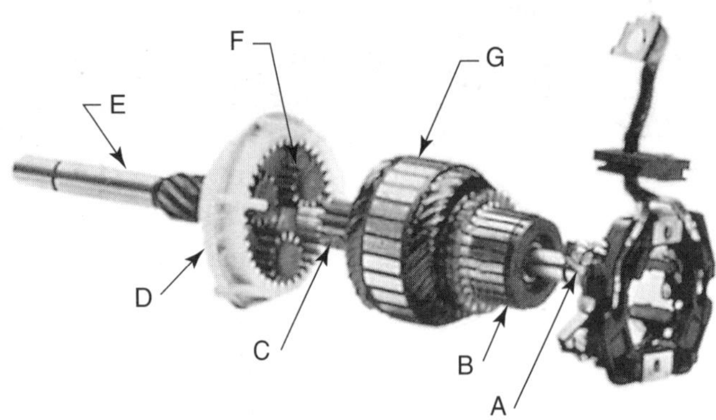

Identify the parts indicated on the sectional view of the overrunning clutch shown below.

39. Pinion and collar assembly. 39. C
40. Collar. 40. A
41. Spring. 41. H
42. Lock wire. 42. F
43. Clutch spring. 43. B
44. Shell and sleeve assembly. 44. E
45. Roller. 45. G
46. Bushings. 46. D

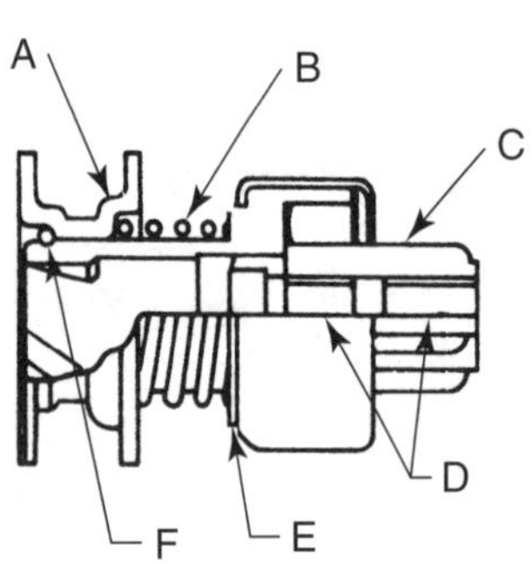

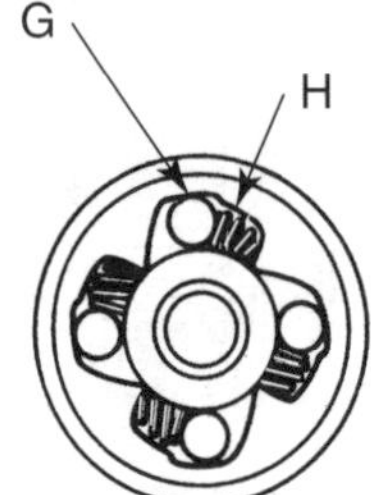

Name ______________________________

Identify the parts indicated on the diagram of the simplified starting system circuitry below.

47. Solenoid. 47. D
48. Start switch. 48. A
49. Cranking motor. 49. C
50. Battery. 50. E
51. Neutral safety switch. 51. B

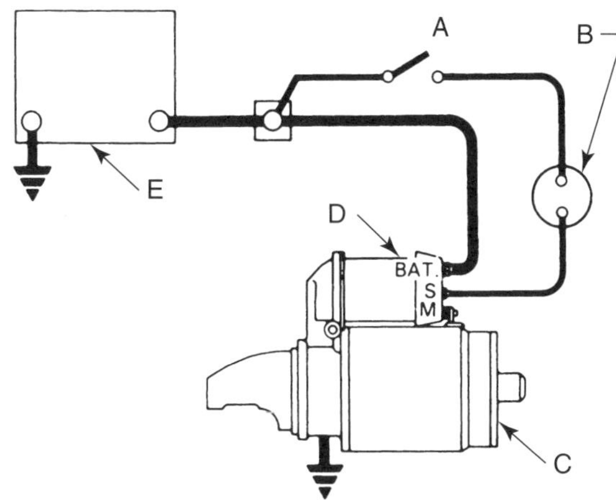

Completion

52. The automotive _____ _____ is an electromagnetic device that converts electrical energy into mechanical energy. It is designed specifically for cranking internal combustion engines at speeds that will permit starting. 52. ______________

53. Electric motors of the type used in "starters" operate on the principle that a current-carrying conductor will tend to move from a _____ (weak, strong) magnetic field to a _____ (weak, strong) magnetic field. 53. WEAK/STRONG

54. As the lines of force tend to straighten out, they exert a downward thrust on the conductor, which is converted into _____ motion. 54. ______________

55. Starting motors basically operate on the same principle: first using a light _____ to energize the relay and/or solenoid, then using a heavy current to power the starting motor. 55. ______________

56. Positive engagement starters use a(n) _____ _____ to provide positive meshing and demeshing of the starter drive pinion gear and flywheel ring gear. 56. ______________

57. All cars equipped with an automatic transmission are provided with a(n) _____ _____ switch, which eliminates the possibility of starting the engine when the transmission selector lever is in gear to drive the car. 57. ______________

58. Before disassembly of a starting motor, scratch _____ _____ on the field frame and end frame to ease reassembly. 58. ______________

Name ______________________________

Short Answer

59. Describe what is happening in the diagram below.

____

____

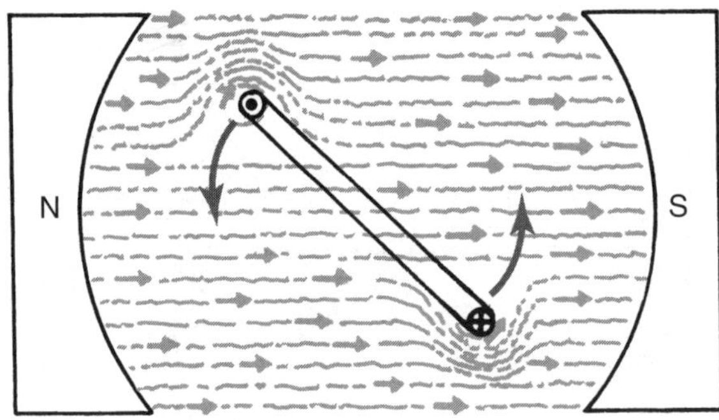

End view

60. List five possible causes of an inoperative starter and dim headlights.

____

____

____

61. List four possible causes of a starter turning, but the drive not engaging.

____

____

____

Chapter 25

Charging System Fundamentals

Name ______________________________

Date ______________ Instructor ______________

Score________ Textbook pages 353–366

After studying the chapter in the text and completing this section of the workbook, you will be able to:

- ❑ Explain the principle of electromagnetic induction.
- ❑ Describe how alternators differ from dc generators.
- ❑ Name the major components of an alternator.
- ❑ Tell how an alternator produces alternating current and then converts it to direct current at the output terminal.
- ❑ Give some examples of alternator design and construction differences.
- ❑ Tell why voltage regulation is necessary in a charging system.
- ❑ Discuss the three basic phases of voltage regulator development.
- ❑ Describe the operating principles of an electromagnetic voltage regulator.
- ❑ Describe the operating principles of an electronic voltage regulator.
- ❑ Explain how an electronic control unit can control alternator voltage output.

Multiple Choice

1. Each phase of the three-phase output of the alternator ranges from _____.
   (A) negative to positive and back to negative again
   (B) positive to negative and back to positive again
   (C) positive to negative
   (D) negative to positive

   1. ______________________________

2. Passenger car alternators range in rated output from _____ amps.
   (A) 10 to 15
   (B) 25 to 35
   (C) 40 to 85
   (D) None of the above.

   2. ______________________________

Name ______________________________

3. The task of the voltage regulator is to _____. 3. ______________
   (A) sense the amount of voltage present
   (B) determine when the battery needs to be charged
   (C) control the alternator output
   (D) All of the above.

4. Electronic voltage regulators _____. 4. ______________
   (A) use wire-wound coils
   (B) often contain contact points and bimetallic hinges
   (C) generally contain sealed-in transistors, diodes, resistors, and capacitors
   (D) All of the above.

5. In many late-model vehicles, the _____ controls the alternator output, eliminating the need for a conventional voltage regulator. 5. ______________
   (A) battery
   (B) engine computer
   (C) rotor
   (D) stator

Identification

Identify the parts indicated on the alternator below.

6. Protected terminals. 6. ______________
7. Internal fan. 7. ______________
8. Multi-function integrated circuit regulator. 8. ______________
9. High temperature insulation. 9. ______________
10. Rectifier bridge. 10. ______________
11. Double sealed ball bearing. 11. ______________
12. Double sealed ball bearing. 12. ______________

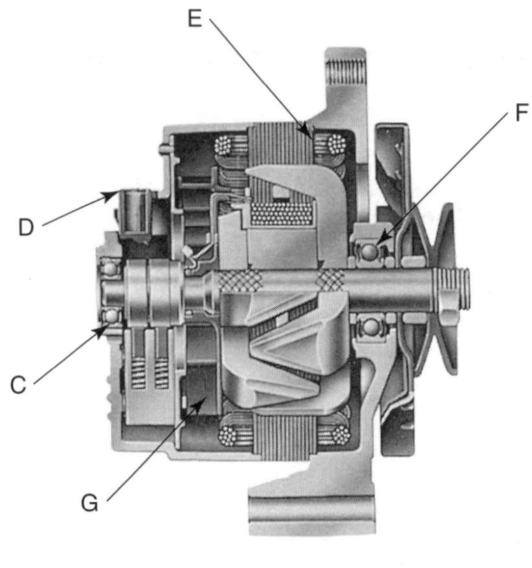

Name ______________________________

Identify the parts indicated on the diagram of the alternator below.

13. Drive end frame. 13. ____________________
14. Diode trio. 14. ____________________
15. Regulator. 15. ____________________
16. "Bat" terminal. 16. ____________________
17. No. 2 terminal (sensing). 17. ____________________
18. Rotor. 18. ____________________
19. Seal. 19. ____________________
20. Stator assembly. 20. ____________________
21. No. 1 terminal (field). 21. ____________________
22. Slip ring end frame. 22. ____________________
23. Brushes. 23. ____________________
24. Rectifier bridge. 24. ____________________
25. Slip rings. 25. ____________________
26. Bearing. 26. ____________________
27. Bearing. 27. ____________________

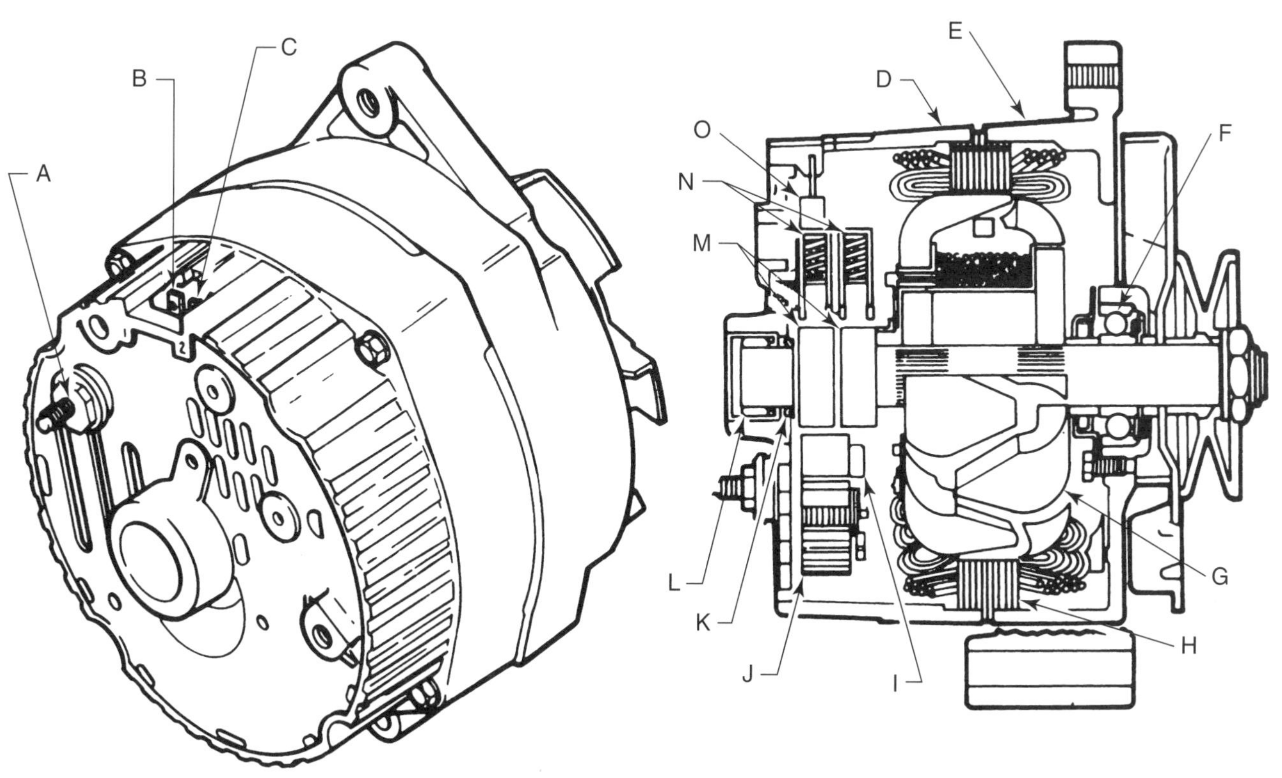

Name ______________________________

Identify the parts indicated on the diagram below.

28. Grounded heat sink. 28. ______________________
29. Regulator. 29. ______________________
30. Brush holder. 30. ______________________
31. Insulating washer. 31. ______________________
32. Insulated heat sink. 32. ______________________

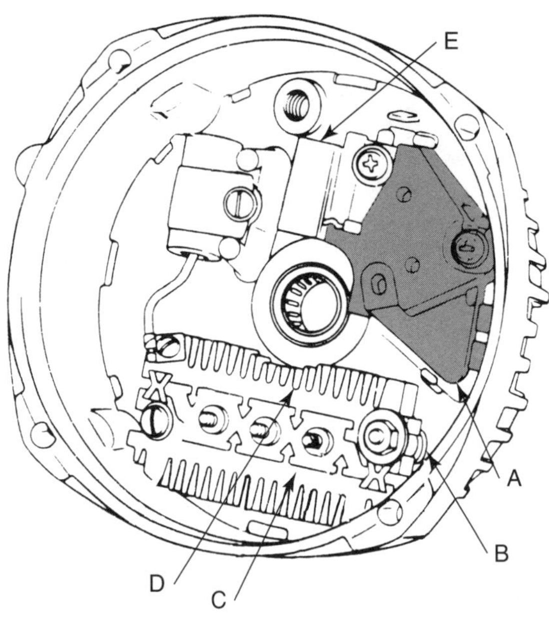

Completion

33. An automotive generator is an electromagnetic device that converts the mechanical energy supplied by the engine into _____ energy. 33. ______________________

34. Automotive alternators produce _____ (direct, alternating) current which, in turn, must be rectified to _____ (direct, alternating) current to satisfy the needs of the battery and the various electrical systems and accessories. 34. ______________________

35. In an ac generator, or alternator, the _____ field is rotated and voltage is generated in the stationary coils. Rectifiers, or diodes, are built into the alternator to limit current flow to one direction only to produce current at the _____ terminal. 35. ______________________

36. The _____ has three sets of windings assembled around the inside circumference of a laminated core. This core forms part of the exterior frame in most alternators, and it provides a path for the flow of _____ flux between two adjacent poles of the rotor. 36. ______________________

37. The rotor must be _____ (internally, externally) excited before it will deliver voltage and current. 37. ______________________

Name ______________________________

38. A(n) _____ diode acts as an automatic switch between the battery and alternator to block current flow back to the alternator and regulator when the alternator is not operating. 38. ______________________

39. Basically, the alternator voltage _____ is an automatic switch that controls charging system outputs so that voltage and current will not exceed predetermined values, causing damage to the battery, alternator, or other elements of the charging system. 39. ______________________

40. Voltage regulator units in some applications have been replaced by functions within engine _____ modules. 40. ______________________

41. _____ regulators are built into the alternator. 41. ______________________

42. Electronic regulators are factory calibrated, sealed, and _____ (adjustable, nonadjustable). 42. ______________________

Short Answer

43. List the three major units in an alternator and describe the purpose of each.

____

____

____

44. Name three types of regulators most commonly used with alternators.

____

____

____

Chapter 26

Charging System Service

Name ______________________________

Date ________________ Instructor ________________

Score_______ Textbook pages 367–374

After studying the chapter in the text and completing this section of the workbook, you will be able to:

- ❑ State precautions concerning charging system testing and servicing.
- ❑ Give quick checks for solving charging system problems.
- ❑ Explain the need for follow-up current output and circuit resistance tests.
- ❑ Recognize the importance of service manual information.
- ❑ Describe bench testing of charging system components.
- ❑ Interpret charging system test results.

Multiple Choice

1 Which of the following tends to increase wear on alternator components?
   (A) High-speed operation.
   (B) High temperatures.
   (C) Dust and dirt.
   (D) All of the above.

1. ______________________________

2. The charging system fuse (fusible) link _____.
   (A) is designed to "blow" if heavy current flows in the circuit
   (B) should be replaced with a "matching" link if the link is blackened or "open"
   (C) should be bypassed or replaced with any piece of wire
   (D) Both A and B.

2. ______________________________

3. To test for a(n) _____ circuit, connect one test lamp lead to the rotor shaft and the other lead to one slip ring.
   (A) short
   (B) open
   (C) grounded
   (D) None of the above.

3. ______________________________

Name ______________________________

4. Which of the following could cause the charge indicator light to stay on? 4. ______________________
   (A) Defective voltage indicator.
   (B) Corroded or loose battery cable clamps or terminals.
   (C) Loose, worn, or broken alternator belt.
   (D) All of the above.

5. Which of the following could result in excessive charging? 5. ______________________
   (A) Faulty alternator.
   (B) Defective voltage regulator.
   (C) Bent pulley flanges.
   (D) All of the above.

Identification

Identify the parts indicated on the illustration below.

6. Adjusting bolts. 6. ______________________
7. A/C mounting bracket. 7. ______________________
8. Washers. 8. ______________________
9. Adjusting bracket. 9. ______________________
10. Bolt. 10. ______________________
11. Nut. 11. ______________________
12. Alternator. 12. ______________________
13. Nut. 13. ______________________
14. Mounting bolt. 14. ______________________
15. Adjusting bolt nut. 15. ______________________
16. Bracket to engine mounting bolt. 16. ______________________
17. Bolt. 17. ______________________
18. Spacer. 18. ______________________

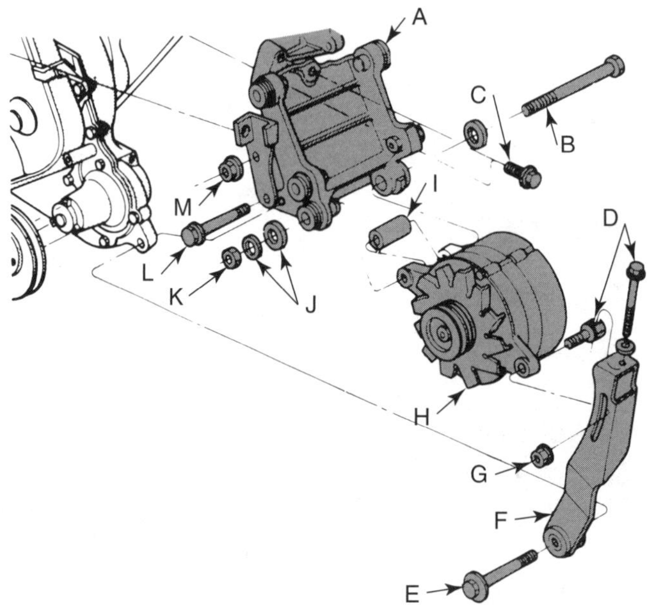

Name ______________________________

Completion

19. If "undercharging" is a problem, a good way to begin electrical tests of the charging system is to bypass the voltage regulator, which is called _____ _____ because the alternator field winding is receiving full current input. 19. ______________________

20. When making tests or performing service operations, consult the car manufacturer's _____ _____ for step-by-step instructions, test equipment and tools needed, test procedures, and acceptable values or ranges for a comparison with test results. 20. ______________________

21. With all major parts _____ (assembled, disassembled), parts may be tested for condition by making various "bench tests." 21. ______________________

Short Answer

22. List four precautions that should be taken when testing or servicing an alternator.

____

____

____

____

23. What is being done in the illustration below?

____

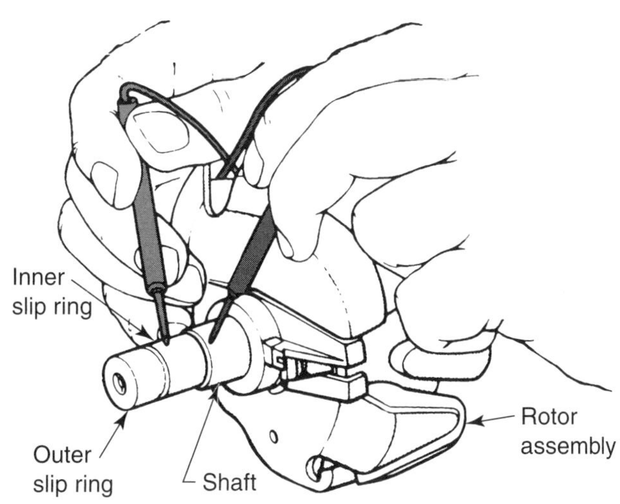

Name ____

24. What is being done in the illustration below?

____

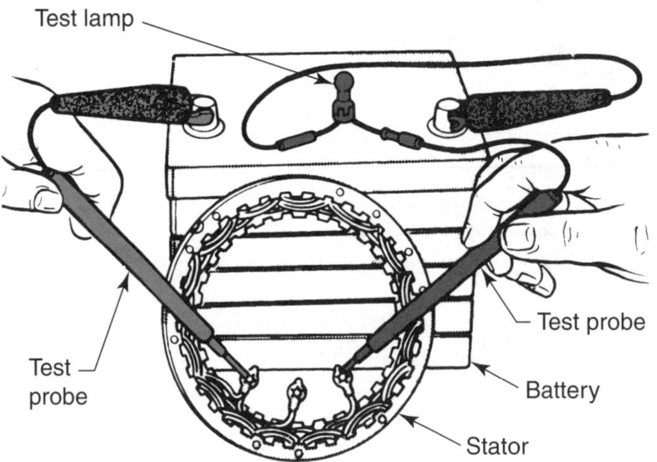

Chapter 27

Computer System Fundamentals and Service

Name ____________________

Date ____________ Instructor ____________

Score________ Textbook pages 375–396

After studying the chapter in the text and completing this section of the workbook, you will be able to:

- ❑ Explain the stages of computer control system operation.
- ❑ Explain the function and operation of various sensors and actuators.
- ❑ Troubleshoot and service sensors, actuators, and electronic control modules.

Multiple Choice

1. The most important tool for troubleshooting and servicing computer control systems is _____.
   (A) mechanical aptitude
   (B) a thorough understanding of how they operate
   (C) a computer
   (D) None of the above.

1. ____________________

2. The three stages of computer control system operation—the input stage, the processing stage, and the output stage—are _____ during control system operation.
   (A) repeated continuously
   (B) repeated intermittently
   (C) seldom repeated
   (D) None of the above.

2. ____________________

3. Multiplexing _____ wiring that is needed in a vehicle.
   (A) increases the amount of
   (B) reduces the amount of
   (C) eliminates the
   (D) None of the above.

3. ____________________

Name ____________________

4. Most computer system problems are caused by _____.
   (A) loose connections
   (B) leaking vacuum hoses
   (C) physical damage
   (D) Any of the above.

4. ____________________

5. When installing a PROM chip, _____.
   (A) use your fingers
   (B) use a special tool
   (C) it can be installed either forward or backward
   (D) None of the above.

5. ____________________

6. Tampering with the flash memory _____.
   (A) may have a negative effect on exhaust emission levels and fuel efficiency
   (B) is a good way to "customize" the memory
   (C) may void the manufacturer's warranty
   (D) Both A and C.

6. ____________________

Identification

Identify the various computer control system components indicated on the diagram shown on the next page.

7. IAC valve. 7. CC
8. EGR valve. 8. D
9. Crankshaft position sensor. 9. V
10. Ignition coil. 10. U
11. Knock sensor 1. 11. T
12. Camshaft position sensor 1. 12. X
13. Mass airflow sensor. 13. BB
14. Malfunction indicator lamp. 14. G
15. Throttle position sensor. 15. A
16. Ignition sensor. 16. AA
17. Knock sensor 2. 17. W
18. EFI main relay. 18. Q
19. EGR gas temperature sensor. 19. N
20. Fuel pump resistor. 20. S
21. Circuit opening relay. 21. P
22. Diagnostic link connector. 22. I
23. Ignition switch. 23. E
24. Heated oxygen sensor (bank 2, sensor 1). 24. R
25. Fuel pump relay. 25. O

Name ____________________

26. Heated oxygen sensor (bank 2, sensor 2). 26. L
27. Engine coolant temperature sensor. 27. Y
28. Heated oxygen sensor (bank 1, sensor 1). 28. M
29. Park/neutral position switch. 29. J
30. Injector. 30. C
31. Fuel pump. 31. F
32. Camshaft position sensor 2. 32. Z
33. Electronic control module. 33. B
34. Heated oxygen sensor (bank 1, sensor 2). 34. K
35. Vehicle speed sensor. 35. H
36. Igniters. 36. DD

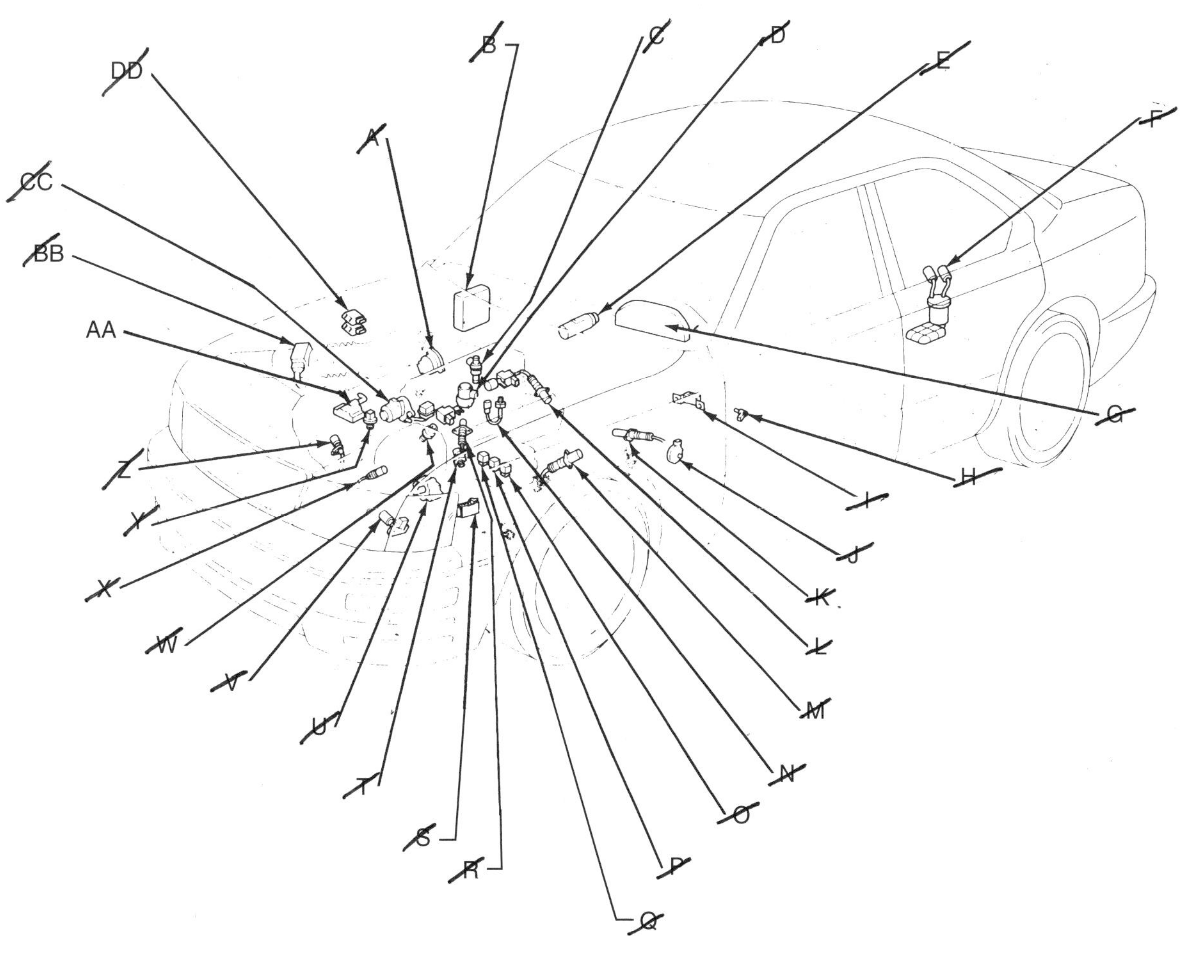

Name ______________________________

Identify the parts indicated on the engine speed sensor shown below.

37. Non-magnetic feeler gauge. 37. C
38. Pickup coil adjustment. 38. A
39. Reluctor. 39. E
40. Run pickup. 40. B
41. Run pickup connector. 41. D

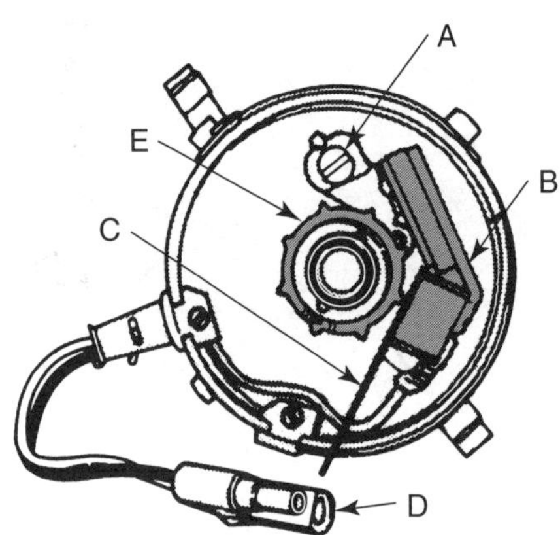

Identify the parts indicated on the typical coolant temperature sensor below.

42. Case. 42. B
43. Electrical connector. 43. A
44. Thermistor. 44. C

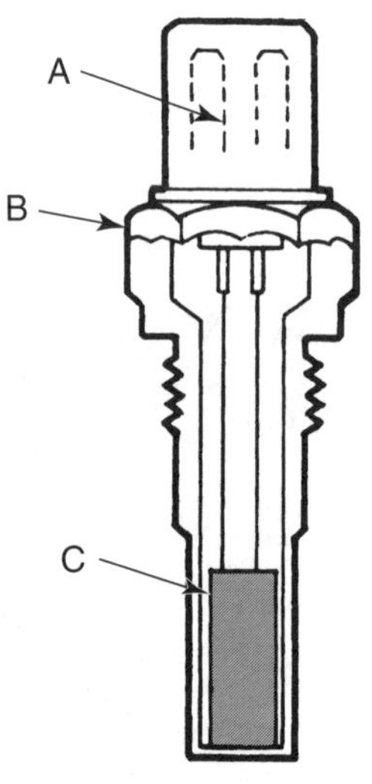

Name ______________________

Identify the sections indicated on the diagram of the functions of the electronic control module shown below.

45. Input signal. 45. A
46. Control section. 46. D
47. Memory. 47. B
48. Output. 48. C

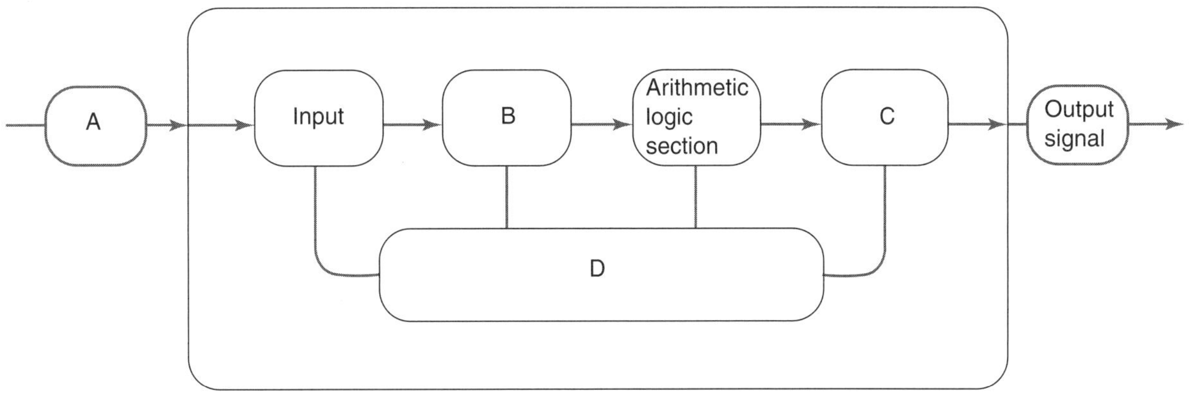

Completion

49. _____ convert physical conditions to electrical input signals. 49. ACTIVE SENSOR

50. The electronic _____ _____ processes input signals and supplies output data based on these inputs. 50. CONTROL MODULE

51. _____ convert output signals from the computer into physical actions. 51. ______

52. During the _____ stage of computer control system operation, data is collected by sensors. 52. ______

53. During the _____ stage of computer control system operation, the ECM interprets data and calculates appropriate output. 53. ______

54. During the _____ stage of computer control system operation, the actuator converts output data to physical movement. 54. ______

55. The _____ sensor is usually located in the exhaust manifold or near the catalytic converter and monitors the amount of oxygen in the exhaust gases. 55. ______

56. The ECM uses information from the _____ speed sensor to calculate fuel injection timing and ignition timing. 56. ______

57. The _____ speed sensor tells the computer how fast the car is traveling. 57. ______

58. A(n) _____ sensor converts abnormal engine vibrations into electrical signals so the ECM can retard the ignition timing to correct the condition. 58. ______

59. The manifold air temperature sensor monitors the temperature of the air entering the _____ manifold. 59. ______

Name ______________________________

60. The _____ _____ _____ sensor monitors the temperature of the engine coolant. 60. ______________

61. The _____ sensors monitor the amount of air entering a vehicle's throttle body or carburetor. 61. ______________

62. The manifold _____ pressure sensor monitors the engine's intake manifold pressure. 62. ______________

63. The _____ pressure sensor measures atmospheric pressure. 63. ______________

64. The _____ _____ sensor is one of the only computer control system components that is mechanical in nature. 64. ______________

65. A(n) _____ sensor is used to monitor oil pressure on many vehicles. 65. ______________

66. Modern _____ _____ can be used to troubleshoot computer control systems. 66. ______________

Short Answer

67. Name three active sensors.

OXYGEN SENSOR

SPEED SENSOR

DETONATION

68. Name seven passive sensors.

MANIFOLD AIR TEMP SENSORS

COOLANT TEMP SENSORS

AIRFLOW SENSORS

MANIFOLD ABSOLUTE PRESSURE SENSORS

BAROMETRIC PRESSURE SENSORS

THROTTLE POSITION SENSORS

SWITCHING SENSORS

69. Name the three types of memory commonly used in automotive ECMs.

ROM (READ ONLY MEMORY)

RAM (RANDOM ACCESS MEMORY)

PROM (PERMANENT READ ONLY MEMORY)

70. List five commonly used actuators.

FUEL INJECTORS

IDLE SPEED MOTORS

MIXTURE CONTROL SOLENOIDS

ELECTRIC FAN RELAYS

EGR VALVES

Name ___________________________

71. What have manufacturers done to simplify the troubleshooting and diagnosis of computer control systems?
THEY PUT IN AN ON-BOARD DIAGNOSTIC SYSTEMS

72. Name the six most common methods of retrieving trouble codes from a computer's memory.
SWITCHING A CONTROL MODE SELECTOR ON THE SIDE OF THE ECM
TURING THE IGNITION SWITCH ON AND OFF SEVERAL TIMES
CONNECTING A VOLTMETER
GROUNDING ONE OF THE TERMINALS ON THE DISGNOSTIC TEST LINK
USE A SCAN TOOL TO RETRIEVE CODES

73. List four pieces of traditional testing equipment used to check computer control system components.
HIGH IMPEDANCE MULTIMETER
TECHOMETER
VACUUM PUMP AND GAUGE
TIMING LIGHT

Matching

Match the term in the left column with its description in the right column. Place the corresponding letter in the blank.

74. Input section.	(A) Analyzes input information and calculates output data.	74. C
75. Memory section.	(B) Governs all the other sections in the computer.	75. D
76. Arithmetic logic section.	(C) Converts sensor signals to a form the computer can use.	76. A
77. Control section.	(D) Stores data until it is needed for processing operations.	77. E
78. Output section.	(E) Converts the computer's output signal to a form an output device can use to produce an appropriate control function.	78. B

Chapter 28
Exhaust Systems

Name ______________________

Date ____________ Instructor ______________

Score_______ Textbook pages 397–404

After studying the chapter in the text and completing this section of the workbook, you will be able to:
- ❑ List the components of the exhaust system.
- ❑ Explain the purpose of each component of the exhaust system.
- ❑ Describe what backpressure is and how it affects the operation of the engine.

Multiple Choice

1. Catalytic converters have been used in the exhaust systems of most cars since _____.
   (A) 1965
   (B) 1975
   (C) 1985
   (D) 1995

   1. ______________________

2. On an inline engine, ______.
   (A) the manifold is bolted to the side of the engine
   (B) separate manifolds are used for each side
   (C) a crossover pipe is used
   (D) None of the above.

   2. ______________________

3. A catalytic converter is installed to reduce _____.
   (A) hydrocarbons (HC)
   (B) carbon monoxide (CO)
   (C) nitrous oxide (NO_x)
   (D) All of the above.

   3. ______________________

4. Which of the following can reduce power and fuel economy?
   (A) A clogged catalytic converter.
   (B) A collapsed muffler.
   (C) Kinks in exhaust pipes.
   (D) All of the above.

   4. ______________________

Name ____________________

5. As backpressure increases, fuel consumption _____. 5. ____________
   (A) increases
   (B) decreases
   (C) remains the same
   (D) None of the above.

Identification

Identify the parts indicated on the diagram below.

6. Intermediate pipe. 6. ____________
7. Resonator. 7. ____________
8. Kick-up pipe. 8. ____________
9. Catalytic converter. 9. ____________
10. Muffler. 10. ____________
11. Crossover pipe. 11. ____________
12. Tail spout. 12. ____________

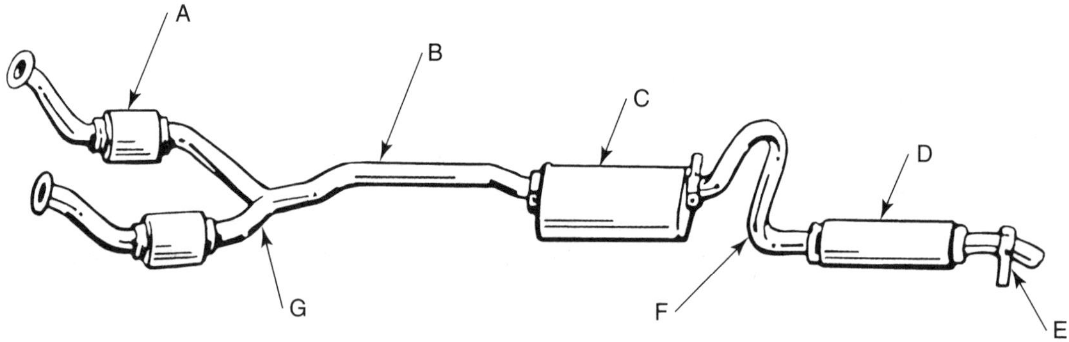

Identify the parts indicated on the reverse flow muffler below.

13. Reversing crossover passages. 13. ____________
14. Helmholtz tuning chambers. 14. ____________
15. High frequency tuning chamber. 15. ____________

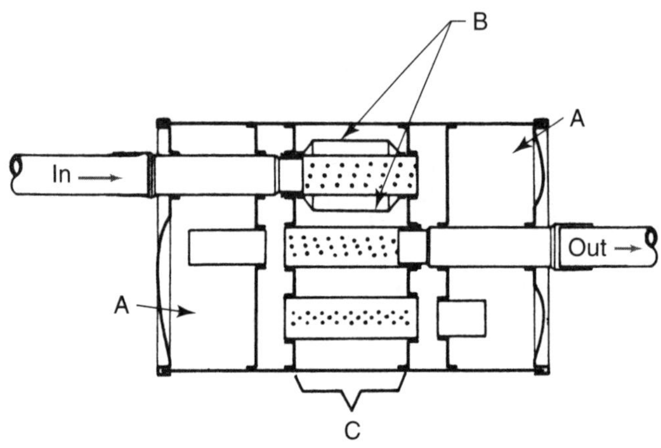

Name ______________________________

Completion

16. The exhaust system of an engine is designed to conduct _____ _____ to the rear of the car and into the air. 16. ______________________

17. On V-type engines, separate _____ are used for each side of the "V." 17. ______________________

18. _____ shields prevent heat created by the catalytic converter from being transferred into the passenger compartment. 18. ______________________

19. In order to reduce the noise of the combustion of an engine, exhaust gases from the engine are passed through a _____. 19. ______________________

20. Undercoating material should _____ (always, never) be applied to heat shields. 20. ______________________

Short Answer

21. Identify the items shown below.

____

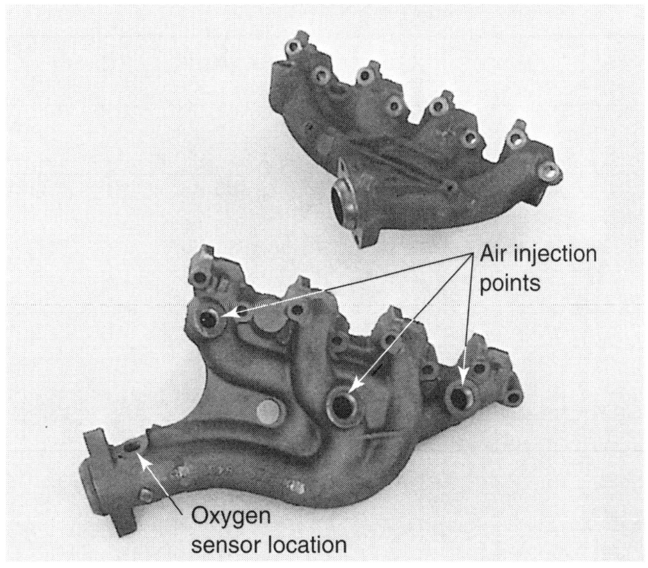

22. Explain how a catalytic converter works.

____

____

____

23. Why does the greatest amount of corrosion occur inside the exhaust system?

____

____

____

Chapter 29

Emission Controls

Name ______________________________

Date ______________ Instructor ______________

Score_______ Textbook pages 405–420

After studying the chapter in the text and completing this section of the workbook, you will be able to:

- ❑ Name the noxious automotive emissions that created the need for car manufacturers to install emission controls.
- ❑ Explain the function of the positive crankcase ventilation system.
- ❑ Cite the various engine design modifications made to combat emissions.
- ❑ Classify precombustion and post-combustion emission control systems.
- ❑ Give examples of emission control failures and services required.

Multiple Choice

1. As a result of the Clean Air Act, _____.
   (A) automotive emission standards were set
   (B) car manufacturers refused to cooperate
   (C) motor vehicle emissions are on the increase
   (D) None of the above.

   1. ______________________

2. If the PCV valve is sticking or hoses are plugged, the engine will _____.
   (A) have a rough idle
   (B) idle too slow
   (C) stall
   (D) Any of the above.

   2. ______________________

3. Which of the following parts of an air injection system prevents hot exhaust gases from backing up into the hose and pump?
   (A) Diverter valve.
   (B) Check valve.
   (C) Pressure relief valve.
   (D) None of the above.

   3. ______________________

Name ______________________________

4. The air injection system requires _____. 4. ______________
   (A) frequent lubrication
   (B) a great deal of maintenance
   (C) little maintenance
   (D) Both A and B.

5. If a catalytic converter is damaged or contaminated, it should be _____. 5. ______________
   (A) reconditioned
   (B) repaired
   (C) replaced with an original equipment converter or the equivalent
   (D) None of the above.

Identification

Identify the parts in the illustration below and use arrows to indicate the direction of fresh air and blowby gases.

6. Blowby gases. 6. ______________

7. Air cleaner. 7. ______________

8. PCV valve. 8. ______________

9. Air intake. 9. ______________

10. Crankcase inlet air cleaner. 10. ______________

11. Combustion chamber. 11. ______________

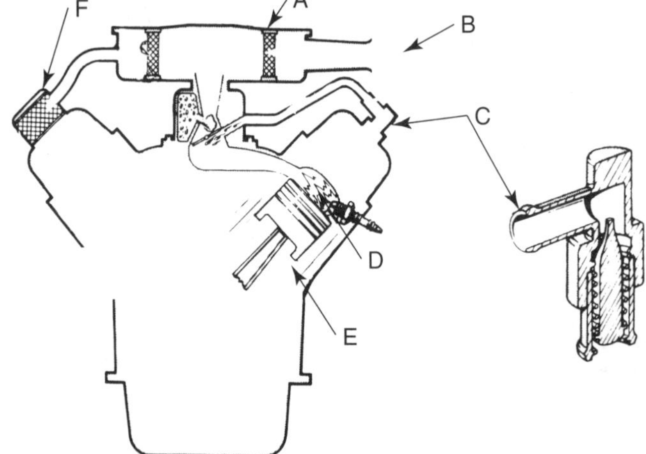

Identify the parts indicated on the evaporative emissions control system shown on the next page.

12. Throttle valve. 12. ______________

13. Non-vented fuel filler cap. 13. ______________

14. Rollover valve. 14. ______________

15. Vent line. 15. ______________

16. Purge valve. 16. ______________

17. Charcoal canister. 17. ______________

18. Purge line. 18. ______________

19. Fuel tank. 19. ______________

20. Vacuum line. 20. ______________

Name ______________________________

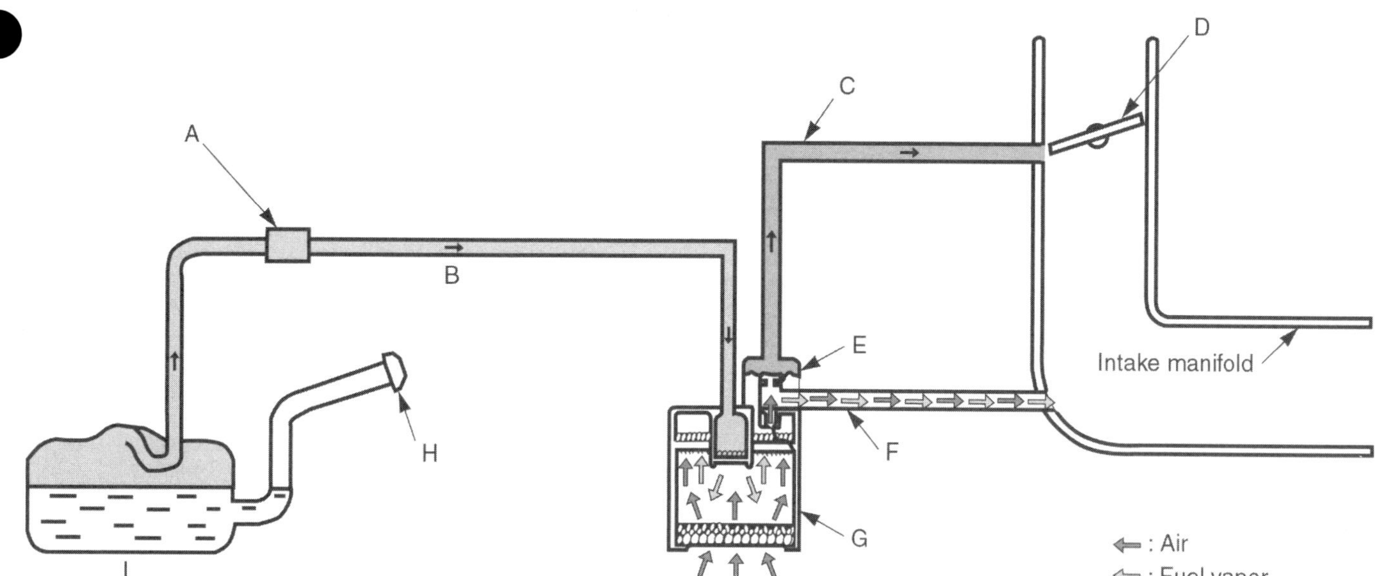

Identify the parts indicated on the illustration below and use arrows to indicate the direction of air intake and exhaust gas flow.

21. Calibrated carburetor port. 21. ______________________

22. EGR valve. 22. ______________________

23. Intake manifold. 23. ______________________

24. Exhaust gases. 24. ______________________

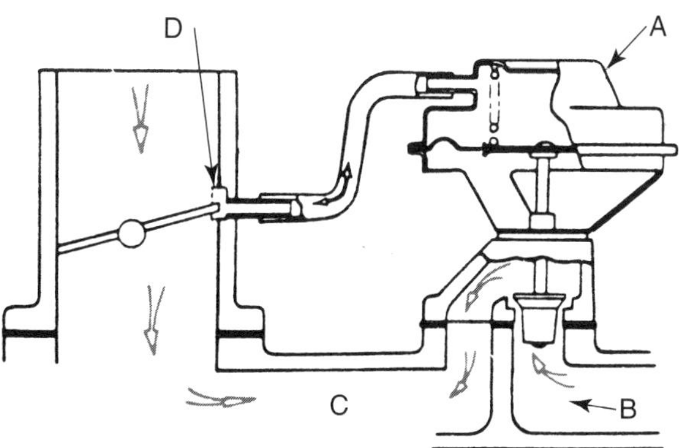

Name ______________________________

Identify the parts indicated on the air supply pump shown below.

25. Rear cover. 25. ______________________
26. Impeller air inlet. 26. ______________________
27. Housing. 27. ______________________
28. Rotor shaft. 28. ______________________
29. Centrifugal filter fan. 29. ______________________
30. Straight outlet. 30. ______________________
31. Air outlet. 31. ______________________
32. Drive hub. 32. ______________________

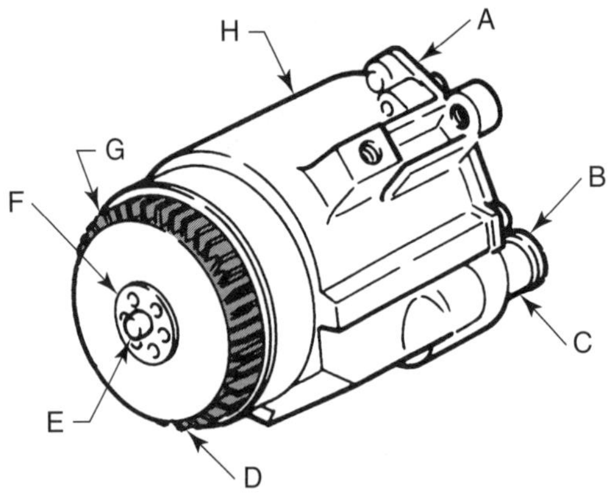

Completion

33. The function of the _____ valve is to restrict the flow of crankcase emissions when vacuum is high to preserve satisfactory engine idle. 33. ______________________

34. _____ controlled air cleaners control the temperature of the air entering the carburetor or fuel injection system, allowing leaner air/fuel mixtures and reducing hydrocarbon emissions. 34. ______________________

35. Evaporative emission controls prevent the escape of gasoline vapors from the fuel tank and throttle body or carburetor, whether or not the engine is running. Late-model engines use an activated _____ canister to trap the vapors when the engine is shut off. 35. ______________________

36. The exhaust gas _____ system is specially designed to lower NO_x (oxides of nitrogen) emission levels caused by high combustion temperatures by feeding exhaust gas back into the combustion chambers. 36. ______________________

37. The widely accepted _____ catalytic converter uses an upstream three-way catalyst to reduce HC, CO, and NO_x. The downstream catalyst and air provided by the air _____ system further reduce HC and CO emissions. 37. ______________________

38. A primary cause of catalyst damage or contamination is an overly _____ (rich, lean) air/fuel mixture. 38. ______________________

Name ______________________________

Short Answer

39. List and describe the two broad classes of emission controls.

____

____

____

____

40. As emission control standards became more stringent, how did car manufacturers' engineers solve the problem?

____

____

Chapter 30

Engine Troubleshooting

Name ______________________

Date ____________ Instructor ____________

Score______ Textbook pages 421–432

After studying the chapter in the text and completing this section of the workbook, you will be able to:

- ❑ Explain the process of engine troubleshooting.
- ❑ Tell why modern engine analyzers should be used to supplement visual inspection and manual checks.
- ❑ Explain strategy-based diagnostics.
- ❑ Describe self-diagnostic systems.
- ❑ List various engine troubles and identify possible causes.
- ❑ Elaborate on more common causes of engine overheating, excessive oil consumption, and engine noises.

Multiple Choice

1. Engine troubleshooting is supported throughout by _____.
   (A) analysis
   (B) deduction
   (C) elimination
   (D) All of the above.

1. ______________________

2. Strategy-based diagnostics involves _____.
   (A) doing unnecessary testing
   (B) taking logical, uniform steps to pinpoint a problem
   (C) guessing
   (D) None of the above.

2. ______________________

3. The compression pressure limit chart provided by the engine manufacturer is calculated so that the lowest reading on the compression tester is _____ percent of the highest reading.
   (A) 55
   (B) 65
   (C) 75
   (D) 85

3. ______________________

Name ______________________________

4. When performing a vacuum gauge test, if the vacuum gauge reading does not drop on sudden acceleration and then recover, _____. 4. ______________________
   (A) the piston rings may be worn
   (B) an engine valve is sticking
   (C) a spark plug is not firing
   (D) a burned valve is indicated

5. One of the most difficult of all troubleshooting jobs is to locate _____. 5. ______________________
   (A) the source of oil leakage
   (B) the reason for engine overheating
   (C) the source of noise or "knocks"
   (D) None of the above.

Completion

6. Engine _____ is a process of studying the symptoms of the existing trouble and reasoning possible causes and corrections. 6. ______________________

7. When a malfunction is detected and a diagnostic trouble code is stored, the _____-_____ system illuminates a malfunction indicator lamp on the vehicle's instrument panel. 7. ______________________

8. Trouble codes can be retrieved using a _____ tool. 8. ______________________

9. Troubleshooting _____ have been a traditional means of relating specific symptoms of trouble to possible causes. 9. ______________________

10. The vacuum gauge test is made with the engine running at normal operating temperature and the vacuum gauge attached to the _____ _____. 10. ______________________

Short Answer

11. What is the item below and what is its purpose?

____

____

Name ______________________________

12. What type of diagnostic procedure is shown below?

____

____

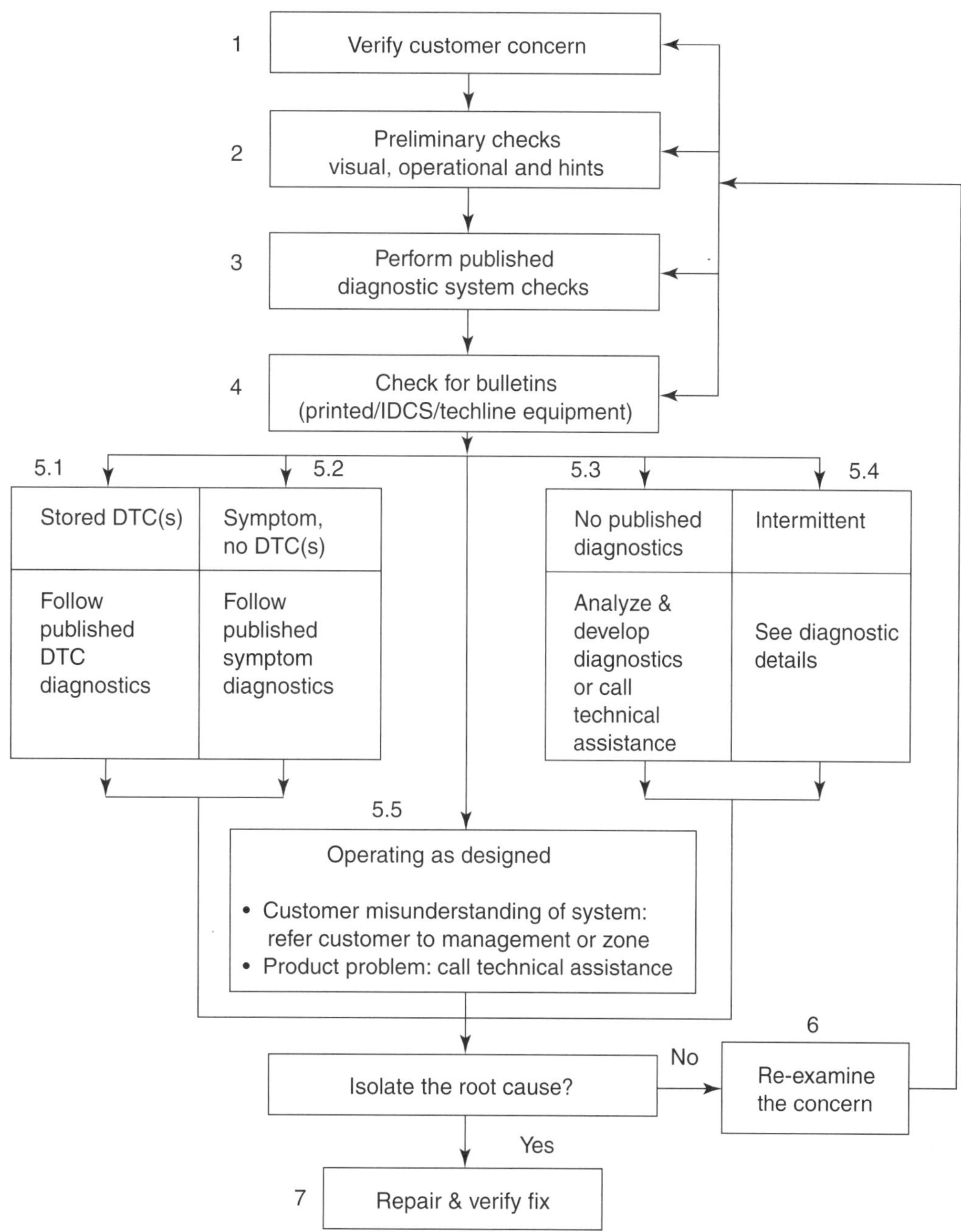

Name ____________________

13 to 48. Imagine that you are a professional automotive technician. Your customers have come to your shop with the following problems. After each problem, list one possible cause.

13. Engine will not start.

____

14. Engine starts, but will not run.

____

15. Hard starting.

____

16. Rough idle.

____

17. Engine stalls.

____

18. Engine stalls on quick stops.

____

19. Loss of power.

____

20. Engine hesitates on acceleration.

____

21. Engine misses on acceleration.

____

22. Engine misses under load.

____

23. Engine misses at high speed.

____

24. Engine backfires.

____

25. Engine speed surges.

____

26. Excessive fuel consumption.

____

27. Engine vibration.

____

28. Engine runs cold.

____

29. Engine overheats.

____

Name ____________________

30. Excessive oil consumption.

____

31. External oil leakage.

____

32. Low oil pressure.

____

33. Ping or spark knock.

____

34. Engine knocks.

____

35. Noisy connecting rods or bearings.

____

36. Noisy pistons, pins, or rings.

____

37. Noisy main bearings.

____

38. Noisy valves.

____

39. Burned valves and seats.

____

40. Dieseling.

____

41. Hard starting (diesel engine).

____

42. Engine surges while idling (diesel engine).

____

43. Loss of power (diesel engine).

____

44. Engine misses under load (diesel engine).

____

45. Excessive fuel consumption (diesel engine).

____

46. Engine cannot be shut off (diesel engine).

____

47. Black smoke and poor performance (diesel engine).

____

Name ______________________________

48. White or blue smoke (diesel engine).

____

49. What is a well-accepted method of checking the condition of the internal components of the engine?

____

____

50. What is the purpose of the stethoscope tool shown below?

____

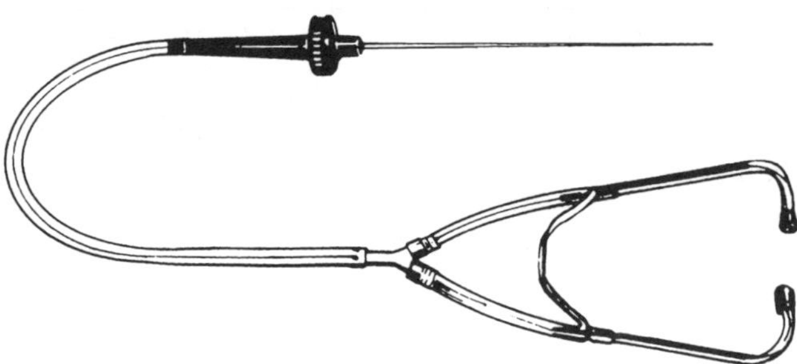

Chapter 31 Driveability and Tune-up

Name ______________________________

Date ______________ Instructor ______________

Score_______ Textbook pages 433–442

After studying the chapter in the text and completing this section of the workbook, you will be able to:

- ❑ Define engine tune-up.
- ❑ Explain the close relationship of engine tune-up and emission controls.
- ❑ Describe test equipment needed to tune up late-model engines.
- ❑ State necessary preliminary tests and inspections required to determine whether or not an engine is "tunable."
- ❑ List the steps of a logically sequenced engine tune-up test procedure.
- ❑ Assess the value of compression pressure tests and the use of a vacuum gauge to diagnose engine problems.

Multiple Choice

1. Engine tune-up specifications _____. 1. ______________
   (A) vary from car to car—even for the same make and model
   (B) are based on the type of fuel system and ignition system
   (C) are based on accessory equipment installed on the vehicle
   (D) All of the above.

2. According to the results of research conducted by a spark plug manufacturer, a tuned engine produces _____ carbon monoxide at idle and 48% fewer hydrocarbons than an untuned engine. 2. ______________
   (A) 25% more
   (B) 85% more
   (C) 57% less
   (D) 78% less

Name ______________________________

3. An engine tune-up can correct _____.	3. ______________
   (A) faulty valves
   (B) worn crankshaft lobes
   (C) an internal coolant leak
   (D) None of the above.

4. If one or more cylinders is "out-of-specification" during a compression test, _____.	4. ______________
   (A) proceed carefully with the tune-up
   (B) tune up the engine to correct the problem
   (C) there is no use tuning the engine until the cause has been determined and corrected
   (D) None of the above.

5. When interpreting vacuum gauge readings, which of the following would cause the needle to read in normal range when the engine is first started, sink to zero, and then rise slowly to below normal?	5. ______________
   (A) Restricted exhaust.
   (B) Spark plug gaps.
   (C) Late timing.
   (D) Defective valve action.

Identification

Identify the items indicated on the illustration below.

6. Spark plug gap.	6. ______________
7. Spark plug.	7. ______________
8. Wire feeler.	8. ______________
9. Insulator.	9. ______________

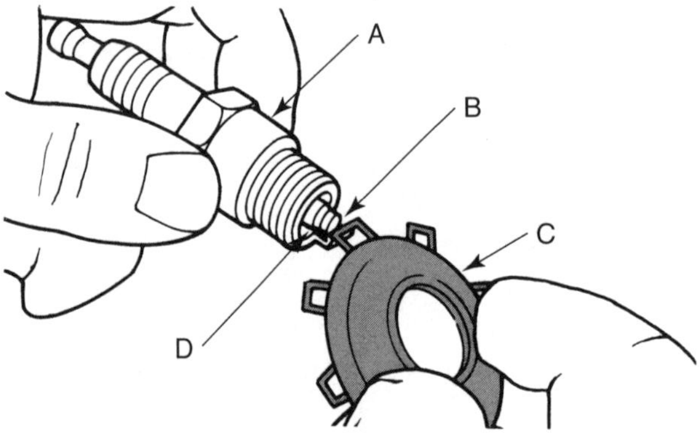

A
B
C
D

Completion

10. An engine tune-up is a service operation designed to restore the engine's best level of performance while maintaining good fuel economy and minimum exhaust _____.	10. ______________

Name ______________________________

11. With the engine warmed up to operating temperature and running slightly higher than at low idling speed, attach a vacuum gauge to the intake manifold. If an engine is in good internal condition and operating properly, the vacuum gauge needle will hold steady at a reading between _____ and _____ at idling speed. 11. ______________________

12. Government regulations _____ (allow, forbid) removing, disconnecting, disengaging, or otherwise rendering emission controls inoperative. 12. ______________________

Short Answer

13. Describe the ways that tune-ups have changed over the years.

____

____

____

____

14. What is the purpose of the label shown below?

____

____

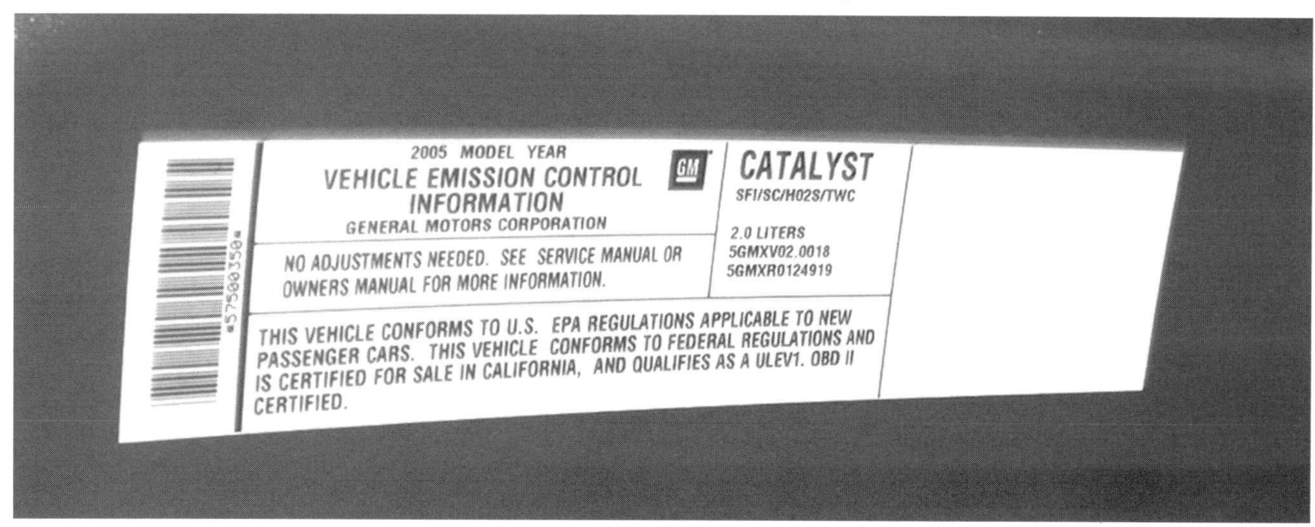

Name ______________________________

15. What is the purpose of the analyzer shown below?

____

____

Chapter 32
Clutches

Name ____________________

Date ____________ Instructor ____________

Score_______ Textbook pages 443–456

After studying the chapter in the text and completing this section of the workbook, you will be able to:

- ❑ Explain the purpose of an automotive clutch.
- ❑ Describe the operation of major components of a clutch assembly and its actuating parts.
- ❑ Give examples of various cable-operated clutch control mechanisms.
- ❑ List typical clutch service procedures and precautions.
- ❑ Recognize symptoms of pending clutch failure.

Multiple Choice

1. The transmission, pressure plate, flywheel housing, clutch disc, flywheel, and crankshaft must be properly aligned to prevent _____.
   (A) slippage
   (B) vibration
   (C) noise
   (D) All of the above.

   1. ____________________

2. You should punch mark the clutch cover and flywheel before removing the clutch cover _____.
   (A) to allow for air circulation
   (B) so you can reinstall the cover in the same relative position
   (C) to release moisture
   (D) None of the above.

   2. ____________________

3. Clutch pedal free play should be _____.
   (A) 0.5″
   (B) 1″
   (C) 1.5″
   (D) 2″

   3. ____________________

Name ______________________________

4. When clutch troubleshooting, which of the following could cause slipping? 4. ____________
   (A) Worn clutch disc facing.
   (B) Oil or grease on disc facing.
   (C) Warped or distorted disc.
   (D) Any of the above.

5. When clutch troubleshooting, which of the following could cause squeaks? 5. ____________
   (A) Dry clutch release bearing.
   (B) Oil or grease on clutch facing.
   (C) Insufficient clutch pedal free play.
   (D) Both B and C.

Identification

Identify the parts indicated on this exploded view of a mechanical clutch system used with a manual transmission.

6. Clutch fork ball stud. 6. D
7. Flywheel. 7. A
8. Clutch housing cover. 8. H
9. Clutch housing. 9. E
10. Driven plate assembly. 10. G
11. Pressure plate and cover assembly. 11. B
12. Clutch fork. 12. F
13. Clutch release bearing. 13. C

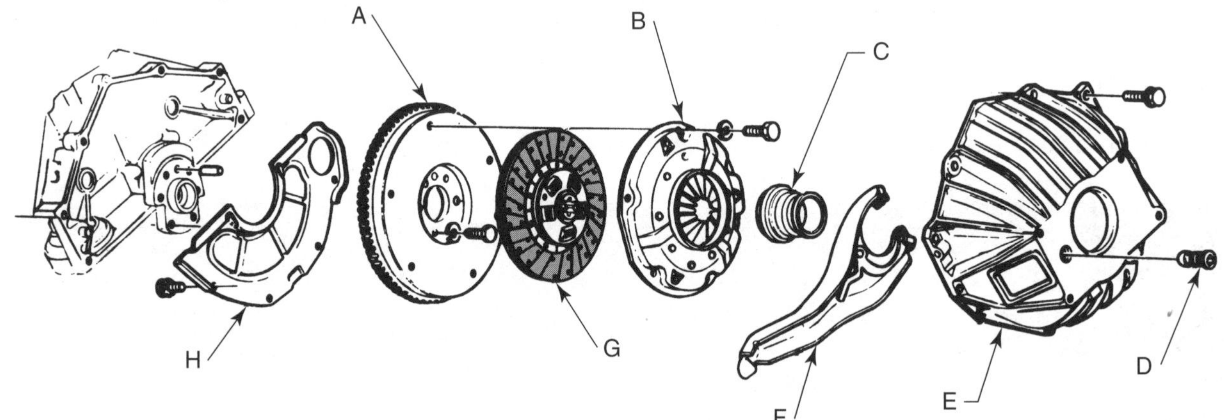

Identify the items indicated on the exploded view of the mechanical clutch system used with the manual transaxle shown at the top of the next page.

14. Clutch release bearing. 14. D
15. Transaxle. 15. C
16. Flywheel. 16. A
17. Driven plate assembly. 17. E
18. Pressure plate and cover assembly. 18. B

Name ______________________

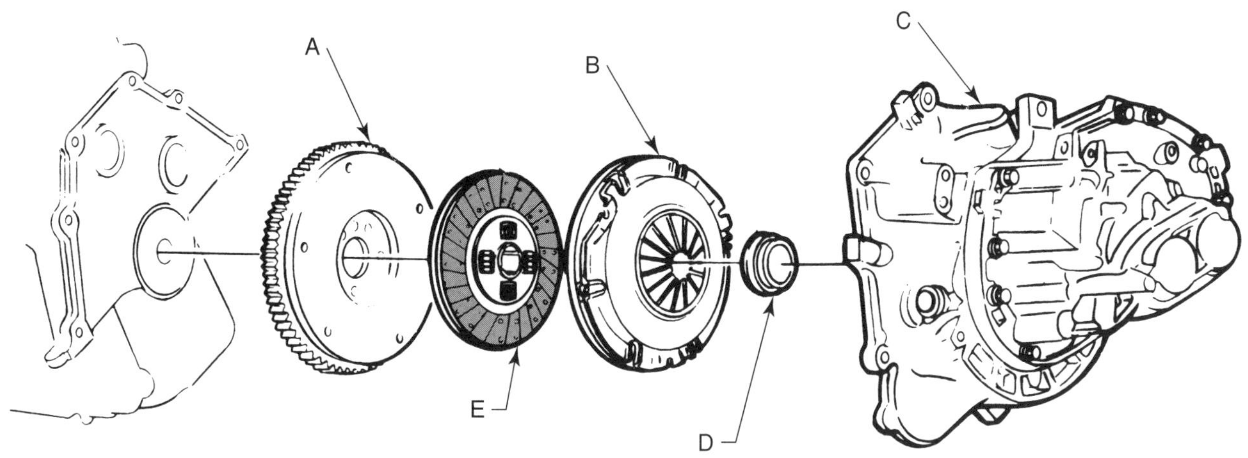

Identify the parts indicated on the cross section of the clutch assembly shown below.

19. Driven plate. 19. I
20. Flywheel. 20. F
21. Clutch release bearing. 21. C
22. Retracting spring. 22. E
23. Dowel hole. 23. G
24. Diaphragm spring. 24. A
25. Clutch fork. 25. D
26. Pilot bushing. 26. H
27. Pressure plate. 27. J
28. Clutch cover. 28. B

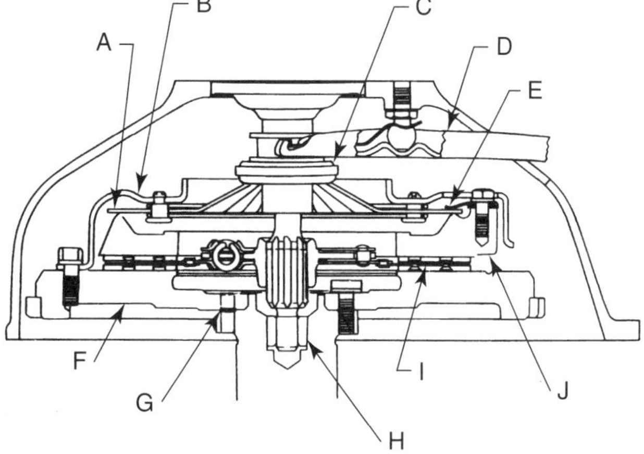

Identify the parts indicated on the diagram on the next page.

29. Clutch and brake pedal bracket. 29. A
30. Frame side rail. 30. G
31. Hook. 31. B
32. Pedal rod. 32. I
33. Release fork. 33. D

Name ______________________________

34. Torque shaft assembly. — 34. F

35. Clutch pedal. — 35. H

36. Over-center spring. — 36. C

37. Fork rod. — 37. E

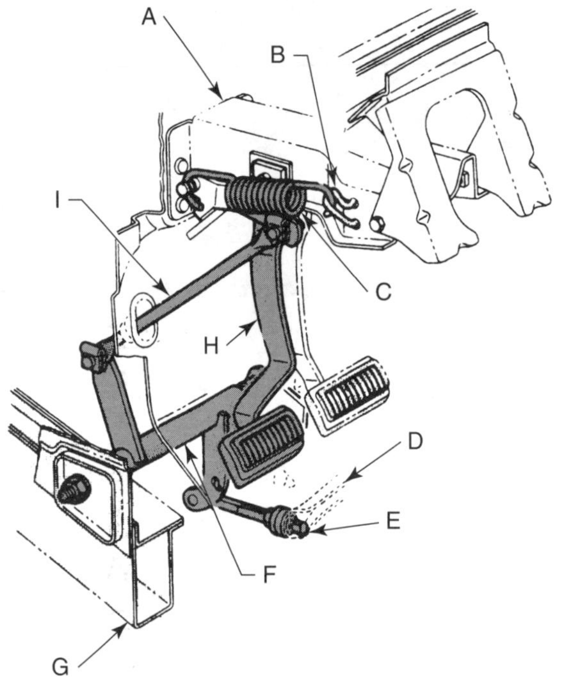

Completion

38. A clutch is a(n) _____ device used to connect and disconnect a driving force from a driven member. — 38. FRICTION

39. Dust created when servicing clutch assemblies may contain _____ fibers (a known carcinogen). When working on clutches, be sure to wear a mask with a government-approved filter and flush clutch parts with water or use a vacuum source. — 39. ASBESTOS

40. The clutch release bearing or _____ bearing, in most cases, is a ball bearing assembly with a machined face on one side that is designed to contact the pressure plate diaphragm release fingers during disengagement. — 40. THROWOUT

41. Transaxle clutch assemblies generally use a different arrangement of connecting the _____ to the clutch fork and the fork to the clutch release bearing. In transaxle applications, the release bearing is constantly _____ (engaged, disengaged) with the release fingers of the pressure plate diaphragm. — 41. LINKAGE, ENGAGED

Short Answer

42. What is the principal cause of damaged clutch release bearings in manual transmission applications?

THE BARING

Chapter 33
Manual Transmission Fundamentals

Name ______________________________

Date ______________ Instructor ______________

Score_______ Textbook pages 457–468

After studying the chapter in the text and completing this section of the workbook, you will be able to:

- ❑ Explain the function of a transmission in an automotive vehicle.
- ❑ Give examples of various gear combinations that provide different ratios to produce more power and less speed or more speed and less power at the output shaft of the transmission.
- ❑ Trace the power flow through each "gear" of three-speed and four-speed manual transmissions.
- ❑ Tell how the three basic elements of a planetary gearset work together to provide the gear reduction or direct drive.
- ❑ Trace the power flow through each "gear" of a five-speed manual transmission, including fifth-gear overdrive.

Multiple Choice

1. A modern transmission provides _____.
   (A) speed
   (B) friction
   (C) power
   (D) Both A and C.

   1. ______________________

2. Gear ratios in transmissions are _____.
   (A) not standardized
   (B) are engineered to fit changes in the engine, vehicle weight, etc., in order to achieve maximum performance
   (C) are standardized
   (D) Both A and B.

   2. ______________________

3. Overdrive is an arrangement of gearing that produces more revolutions of the driven shaft than the driving shaft. This means _____.
   (A) the engine rpm will be reduced about 30 percent while the vehicle maintains the same road speed
   (B) fuel consumption is reduced
   (C) engine life is prolonged
   (D) All of the above.

   3. ______________________

Name ______________________

4. If the ring gear is held and the pinion carrier is driven by the sun gear and the pinions in an overdrive planetary transmission, the speed of the drive shaft will _____.
   (A) increase
   (B) decrease
   (C) remain the same
   (D) None of the above.

4. ______________________

5. In a five-speed overdrive transmission, when the third- and fourth-speed clutch sleeve assembly is moved forward to mesh with the input shaft main drive gear, this engagement results in _____.
   (A) overdrive
   (B) direct drive
   (C) reverse
   (D) neutral

5. ______________________

Identification

Identify the parts indicated on the synchronizer assembly shown below.

6. Hub. 6. ______________________
7. Blocker ring. 7. ______________________
8. Keys. 8. ______________________
9. Spring. 9. ______________________
10. Sleeve. 10. ______________________
11. Blocker ring. 11. ______________________
12. Spring. 12. ______________________

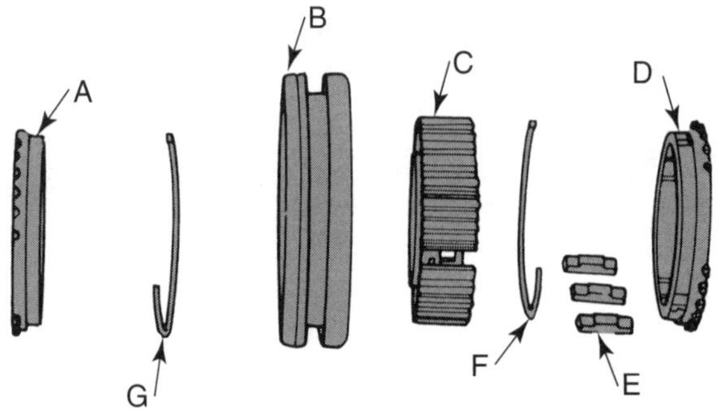

A
B
C
D
E
F
G

Completion

13. A transmission is a(n) _____ and _____ changing device installed at some point between the engine and driving wheels of a vehicle.

13. ______________________

14. Gears are simply a means of applying leverage to rotating parts. The _____ (smaller, larger) the number of teeth on the driving gear, the slower the driven gear rotates, but with multiplied power.

14. ______________________

Name ______________________________

15. The _____ clutch is a drum or sleeve that slides back and forth on the splined output shaft by means of the shifting fork. Generally, it has a bronze cone on each side that engages with a tapered mating cone on the second- and _____-speed gears. 15. ______________________

16. The diagram below is that of a _____-speed manual transmission. It is fully synchronized. 16. ______________________

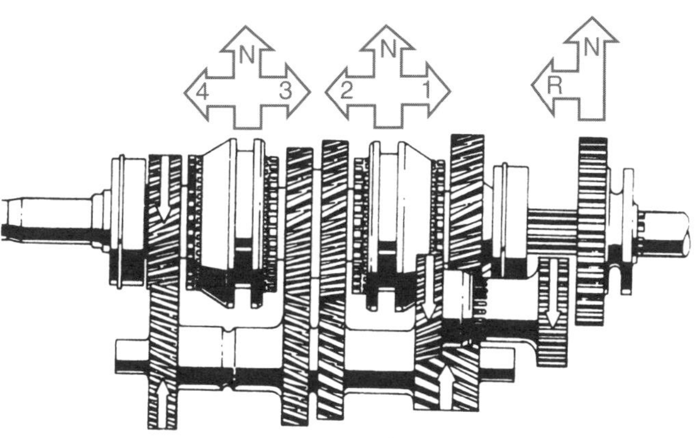

17. As shown in the end view of the planetary gearset below, the gears are in _____ at all times. As different elements are "held" from turning, different gear _____ are affected. 17.

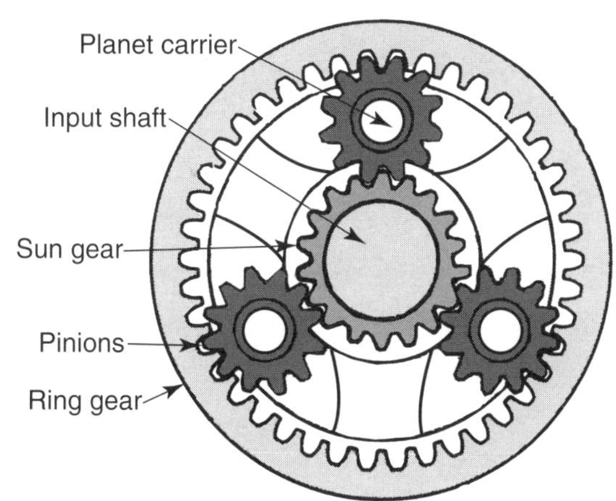

Short Answer

18. Explain the function of a transmission in an automotive vehicle.

____

____

____

____

____

____

Chapter 34

Manual Transmission Service

Name ______________________________

Date ______________ Instructor ______________

Score________ Textbook pages 469–486

After studying the chapter in the text and completing this section of the workbook, you will be able to:

- ❑ Name six manual transmission maintenance operations.
- ❑ List various manual transmission troubles and identify possible causes.
- ❑ Explain general procedure for manual transmission removal and reinstallation.
- ❑ Describe procedures for manual transmission disassembly and internal parts cleaning and inspection.
- ❑ Describe procedure for manual transmission reassembly.

Multiple Choice

1. A methodical run-through of gearshift operation in _____ should be part of any manual transmission maintenance routine.
   (A) all gear ranges
   (B) each forward position
   (C) the reverse position
   (D) None of the above.

   1. ______________________

2. The principal cause of a transmission slipping out of gear is _____.
   (A) a damaged output shaft pilot bearing
   (B) a badly worn or broken gear
   (C) misalignment between the transmission and engine
   (D) improper adjustment of the shift linkage

   2. ______________________

3. The need for major transmission service usually is signaled by _____.
   (A) noisy operation or gear clash
   (B) the transmission jumping out of gear
   (C) the transmission not shifting gears or being locked in one gear
   (D) Any of the above.

   3. ______________________

Name ______________________________

4. When removing the transmission from a vehicle, be very careful because _____.   4. ______________________
   (A) transmissions are very light and delicate
   (B) transmissions are extremely heavy
   (C) transmissions are likely to explode
   (D) None of the above.

5. If gears have worn, cracked, or chipped teeth, _____.   5. ______________________
   (A) ignore them
   (B) file them
   (C) replace them
   (D) replace both the teeth and the mating gears

Identification

Identify the items indicated on the countershaft assembly below.

6. Washer (bronze).   6. ______________________
7. Washer.   7. ______________________
8. Countershaft gear.   8. ______________________
9. Washer.   9. ______________________
10. Pin.   10. ______________________
11. Bearings.   11. ______________________
12. Bearings.   12. ______________________
13. Washer (plastic).   13. ______________________
14. Shaft.   14. ______________________

A
B
C
D
E
F
G
H
I

Completion

15. The manual check and refill point is generally located at the fill plug hole in the _____ (top, side) of the transmission case.   15. ______________________

16. After disassembly, use fresh _____ to clean the transmission case and all parts.   16. ______________________

17. Wash bearings in a fresh cleaning solution, rotating each bearing to flush away oil and dirt. Dry bearings with a clean, _____-_____ cloth.   17. ______________________

Name ______________________________

18. To reinstall a manual transmission in a car, place the transmission in gear. Lift the transmission and align it with the ______ ______ in the clutch disc. Slide the transmission forward while slowly rotating the output shaft to align splines in the transmission input shaft with splines in the clutch disc hub. When splines align, slide the transmission into place against the clutch housing.

18. ______________________________

Short Answer

19. List six routines involved in manual transmission maintenance.

____

____

____

____

____

____

20. When removing a manual transmission, the final step is to unscrew the transmission-to-clutch housing attaching bolts. Why is it important to pull the transmission straight back, holding it level?

____

____

21. What is occurring in the illustration below?

____

____

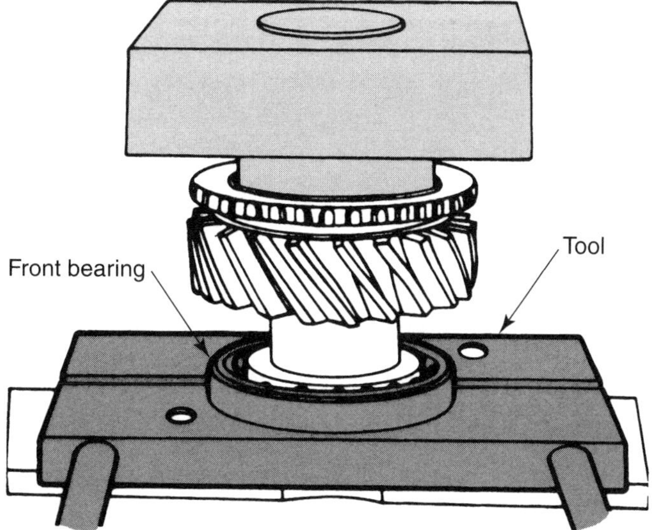

Chapter 35
Automatic Transmission Fundamentals

Name ____

Date ________________ Instructor ________________

Score_______ Textbook pages 487–506

After studying the chapter in the text and completing this section of the workbook, you will be able to:

- ❑ State the primary difference between a fluid coupling and a torque converter.
- ❑ Explain how a torque converter multiplies engine torque.
- ❑ Tell how a converter clutch locks the turbine to the impeller in direct drive.
- ❑ Discuss the function of clutches and bands in automatic transmission operation.
- ❑ Detail the principles of planetary gearset operation.
- ❑ Trace power flow in the various modes of operation in a three-speed automatic transmission.
- ❑ Point out the path of power flow in the overdrive mode of a four-speed automatic transmission.

Multiple Choice

1. Which of the following multiplies and transmits engine torque to the input shaft and planetary gearsets of the automatic transmission?
   (A) Pressure regulator valve.
   (B) Torque converter.
   (C) Throttle valve.
   (D) None of the above.

   1. ______________________

2. Which of the following is connected to the output shaft of the transmission and controls line pressure and shift speeds?
   (A) Governor valve assembly.
   (B) Vacuum modulator valve.
   (C) Servos.
   (D) None of the above.

   2. ______________________

Name ______________________________

3. Which of the following automatically applies the converter clutch if the vehicle speed is above a predetermined speed (30–40 mph) in direct drive?
   (A) Fail-safe valve.
   (B) Multiple-disc clutches.
   (C) Lockup valve.
   (D) None of the above.

3. ______________________

4. In many late-model cars, the transmission is controlled _____.
   (A) mechanically
   (B) electronically
   (C) hydraulically
   (D) None of the above.

4. ______________________

5. Electronically controlled transmissions operate more efficiently than conventional transmissions by _____.
   (A) improving vehicle economy
   (B) smoothing shifts
   (C) increasing fuel economy
   (D) All of the above.

5. ______________________

6. The solenoids used in electronically controlled transmissions are used to control _____.
   (A) torque converter lockup
   (B) shift points
   (C) Both A and B.
   (D) Neither A nor B.

6. ______________________

7. CVTs are called ____ transmissions because they allow almost unlimited ratio changes between the engine and the final drive.
   (A) infinite
   (B) stepless
   (C) sliding
   (D) slush

7. ______________________

8. The CVT operates by varying the _____ two pulleys.
   (A) diameters of
   (B) relative speed of
   (C) distance between
   (D) None of the above.

8. ______________________

Name ______________________________

Identification

Identify the parts indicated on the cross-sectional view of the typical torque converter below.

9. Impeller. 9. ____________________
10. Stator. 10. ____________________
11. Stator overrunning clutch. 11. ____________________
12. Housing. 12. ____________________
13. Turbine. 13. ____________________

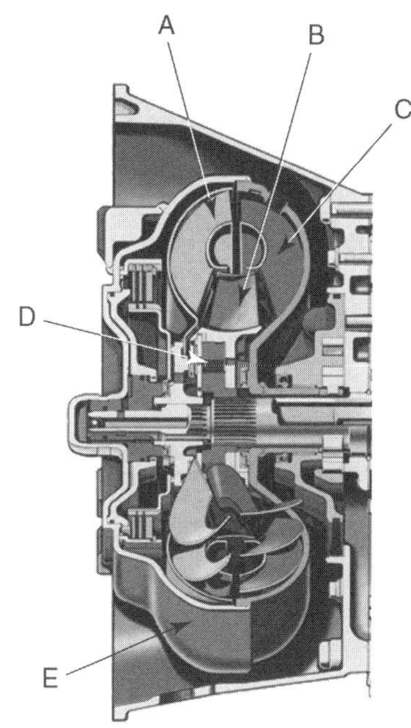

Identify the parts indicated on the cross-sectional view of a low-reverse band setup in an automatic transmission.

14. Piston stem. 14. ____________________
15. Low-reverse band. 15. ____________________
16. Cover. 16. ____________________
17. Apply pressure. 17. ____________________
18. Case. 18. ____________________
19. Servo piston. 19. ____________________

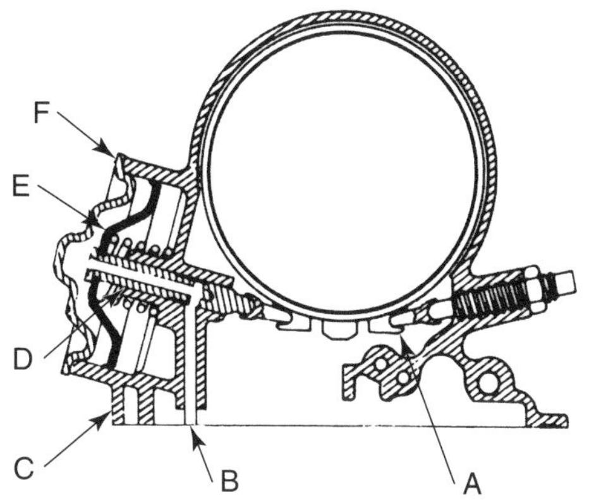

Name ______________________________

Identify the parts of the single planetary gearset shown below.

20. Drive shaft from planet pinion carrier. 20. ____________
21. Ring gear. 21. ____________
22. Sun gear. 22. ____________
23. Drive shaft sun gear. 23. ____________
24. Planet pinion. 24. ____________
25. Planet pinion carrier. 25. ____________

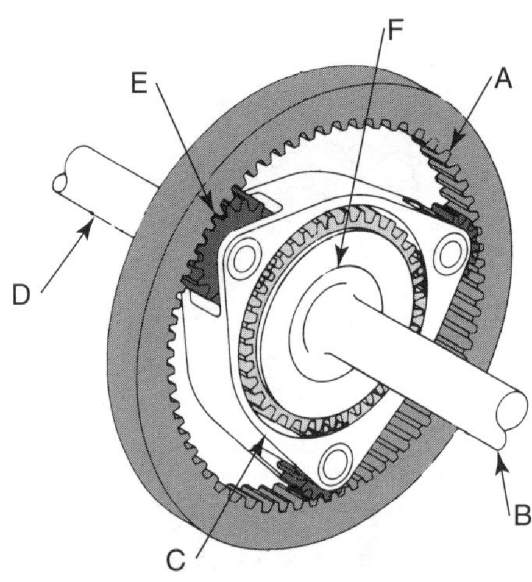

Identify the assemblies and components indicated on the three-speed automatic transmission shown on the next page.

26. Front clutch. 26. ____________
27. Lockup clutch. 27. ____________
28. Stator. 28. ____________
29. Rear planetary gear set. 29. ____________
30. Overrunning clutch. 30. ____________
31. Adapter housing. 31. ____________
32. Sun gear driving shell. 32. ____________
33. Turbine. 33. ____________
34. Front planetary gear set. 34. ____________
35. Output shaft. 35. ____________
36. Bearing. 36. ____________
37. Parking lock assembly. 37. ____________
38. Valve body. 38. ____________
39. Flexible drive plate. 39. ____________
40. Impeller. 40. ____________
41. Low and reverse (rear) band. 41. ____________
42. Seal. 42. ____________

Name ______________________________

43. Rear clutch. 43. ____________________
44. Governor. 44. ____________________
45. Oil filter. 45. ____________________
46. Engine crankshaft. 46. ____________________
47. Kickdown (front) band. 47. ____________________
48. Input shaft. 48. ____________________
49. Oil pump. 49. ____________________

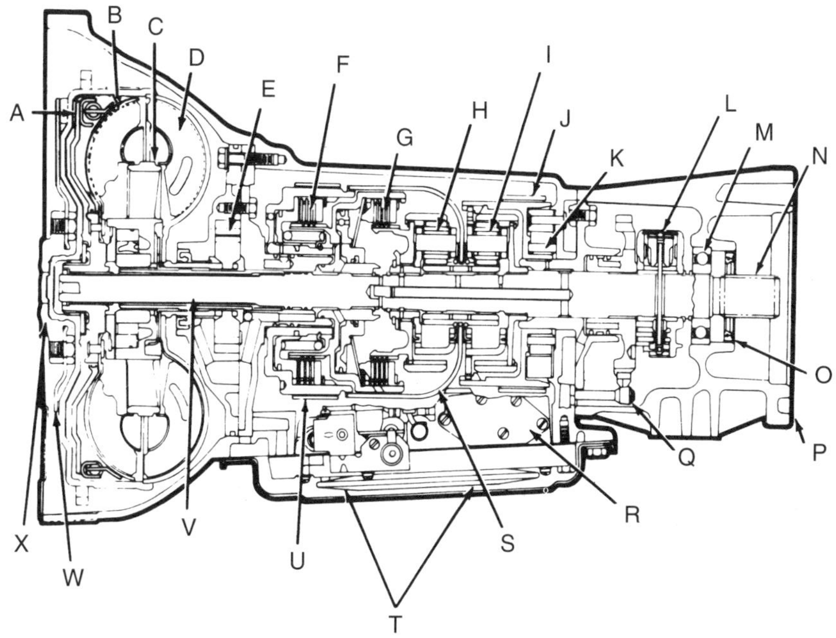

Identify the parts indicated on the automatic overdrive transmission shown on the following page.

50. 4th speed planetary gearset. 50. ____________________
51. 3rd speed clutch disc assembly. 51. ____________________
52. 1st and 2nd speed planetary gearset. 52. ____________________
53. Vane type variable capacity pump. 53. ____________________
54. Governor. 54. ____________________
55. Converter clutch assembly. 55. ____________________
56. Clutch friction surface. 56. ____________________
57. Intermediate speed band (2nd speed range). 57. ____________________
58. Forward clutch disc (1st speed range). 58. ____________________
59. Reactionary planetary gearset (manual 1st and reverse). 59. ____________________
60. Reverse clutch disc assembly. 60. ____________________
61. 4th speed clutch discs. 61. ____________________

Name ______________________________

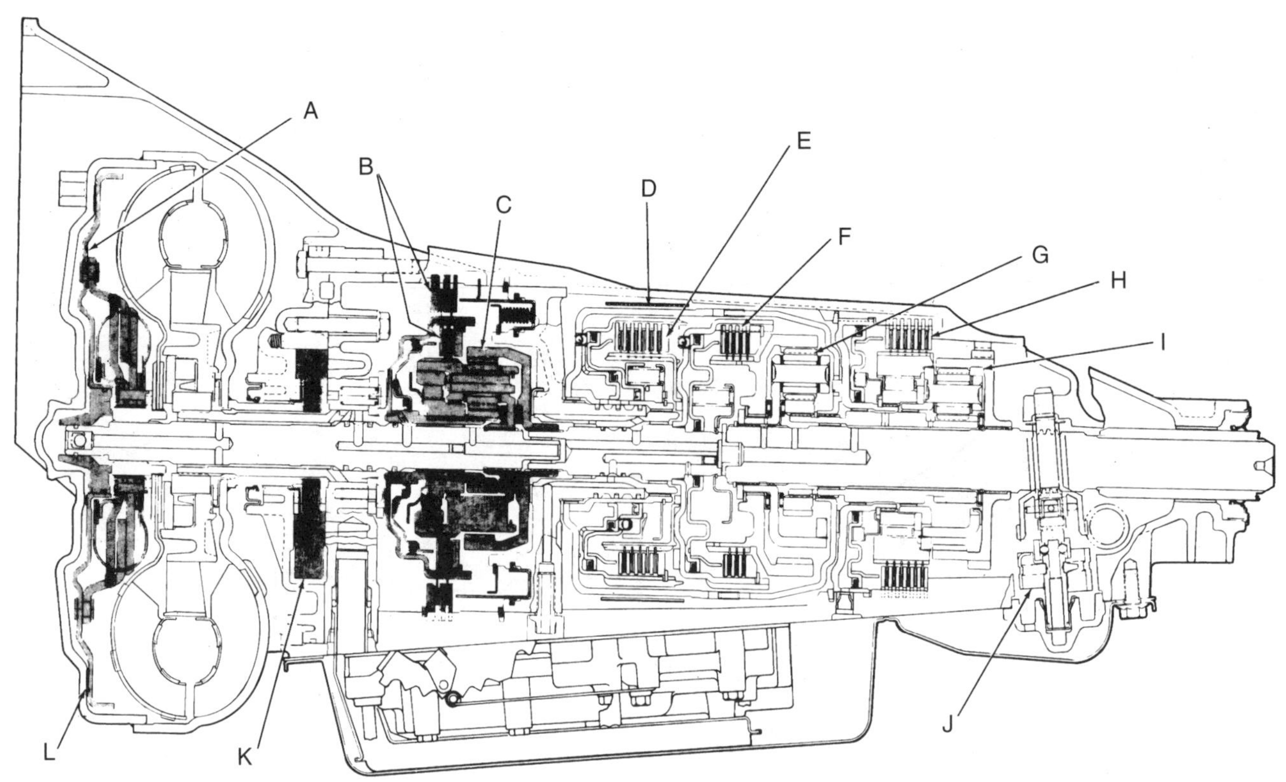

Completion

62. The engine _____ turns the converter housing and pump (impeller). The stator is mounted on the overrunning clutch.

62. ______________________________

63. To overcome slippage, lockup _____ converters are equipped with an internal locking mechanism called a "converter clutch" that locks the turbine to the impeller in direct drive.

63. ______________________________

64. The _____ _____ usually is located immediately behind the torque converter. It is driven by the converter and serves as the pressure supply system for the automatic transmission.

64. ______________________________

65. _____ apply and release bands that control the operation of drive shells and planetary gearsets.

65. ______________________________

66. _____ _____ clutches are the "drive" members of the automatic transmission.

66. ______________________________

67. When used in conjunction with multiple-disc clutches, bands, valve controls, and valves, _____ gearsets automatically provide all the forward and reverse gear ratios needed for efficient operation under normal driving conditions.

67. ______________________________

68. _____ _____ transmissions operate by varying the working diameters of two pulleys. The pulleys have V-shaped grooves in which the steel belt rides. The spacing of the pulley sheaves and working diameters of the pulleys determine output ratio and speed.

68. ______________________________

Name ______________________________

Short Answer

69. What are the two types of oil circulation within the unit when the torque converter is in operation?

____

____

70. List three advantages that the lockup converter has over the conventional converter.

____

____

____

____

Chapter 36 Automatic Transmission Service

Name ______________________________

Date ______________ Instructor ______________

Score________ Textbook pages 507–520

After studying the chapter in the text and completing this section of the workbook, you will be able to:

- ❑ Name the maintenance checks, adjustments, and services that will keep automatic transmissions in satisfactory operating condition.
- ❑ Demonstrate how to check level and condition of the automatic transmission fluid (ATF).
- ❑ Determine by inspection where an automatic transmission is leaking ATF.
- ❑ Change ATF and replace the filter.
- ❑ Explain how to adjust automatic transmission bands.
- ❑ Describe throttle linkage and gearshift linkage adjustments.
- ❑ Explain road testing, hydraulic pressure and air pressure testing, and stall testing procedures.

Multiple Choice

1. When making an automatic transmission fluid level check, the color of the fluid should be _____.
   (A) bright cherry red or dark red
   (B) dark brown or black
   (C) milky pink
   (D) None of the above.

   1. ______________________

2. Overfilling with automatic transmission fluid can result in _____.
   (A) not having to check the level for a long time
   (B) fluid loss, foaming, or erratic shifting
   (C) good transmission performance
   (D) None of the above.

   2. ______________________

3. The general rule for adjusting throttle linkage is to _____ the linkage.
   (A) remove some slack from
   (B) remove all slack from
   (C) add slack to
   (D) None of the above.

   3. ______________________

Name ______________________

4. The correct gearshift linkage adjustment properly positions the transmission manual valve in the valve body. Incorrect adjustment will cause _____.
   (A) creeping in Neutral
   (B) excessive clutch wear
   (C) delayed shifts or failure to start in Neutral or Park
   (D) All of the above.

4. ______________________

5. When performing a road test, operate the transmission in each gear range and check for _____.
   (A) slippage and shift points
   (B) harsh or spongy shifts
   (C) speeds at which upshifts and downshifts occur
   (D) All of the above.

5. ______________________

Identification

Identify the pressure port plugs that should be checked for automatic transmission fluid leakage.

6. Front servo release port. 6. ______________________
7. Line pressure port. 7. ______________________
8. Rear servo apply port. 8. ______________________

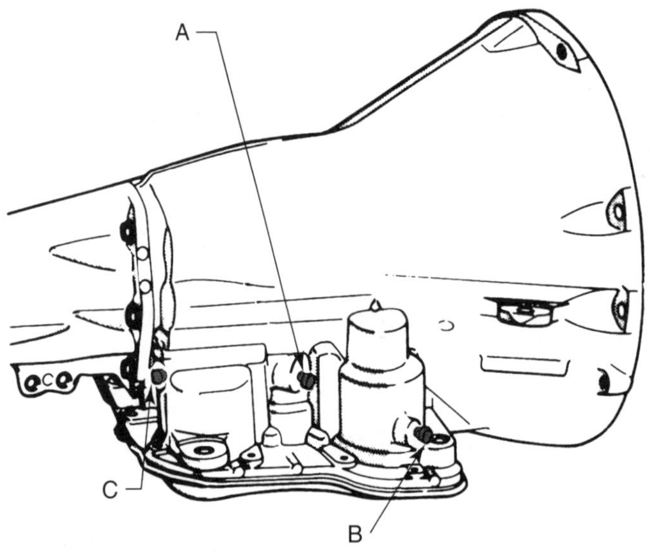

Identify the parts indicated on the diagram shown on the next page.

9. Line pressure adjusting screw. 9. ______________________
10. Spring retainer and line pressure adjusting screw bracket. 10. ______________________
11. Valve body. 11. ______________________
12. Manual lever assembly. 12. ______________________
13. Repair stand. 13. ______________________
14. Manual valve. 14. ______________________
15. Screw. 15. ______________________
16. Kickdown valve. 16. ______________________

Name ______________________________

17. Throttle lever and shaft. 17. ______________________________
18. Transfer plate. 18. ______________________________
19. Fluid filter. 19. ______________________________

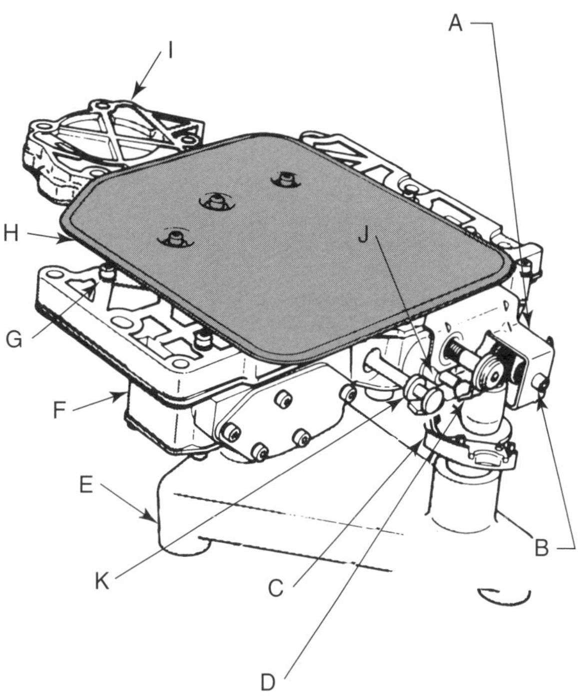

Completion

20. If the automatic transmission fluid appears to be in good condition but the level is low, add the manufacturer's specified ATF or the equivalent through the filler tube to bring the level to the _____ mark on the dipstick. 20. ______________________________

21. Make a careful, closeup inspection of the lower end of the dipstick for signs of _____ buildup or gum deposits. 21. ______________________________

22. If the throttle linkage setting is too _____ (short, long) early shifts and slippage between shifts may occur. If the throttle linkage setting is too _____ (short, long), shifts may be late and the part throttle downshifts may be overly sensitive. 22. ______________________________

23. _____ testing provides a means of checking the holding ability of the converter-stator overrunning clutch and front and rear clutches of the transmission. It basically determines the maximum engine rpm available at full throttle with the rear wheels locked and the transmission in _____. 23. ______________________________

Name ______________________________

Short Answer

24. What is the general procedure for automatic transmission band adjustment?

____

____

____

25. What does the air pressure testing procedure involve?

____

____

____

26. List seven causes of automatic transmission problems.

____

____

____

____

____

____

____

Chapter 37

Transaxles

Name ______________________________

Date ______________ Instructor ______________

Score_______ Textbook pages 521–536

After studying the chapter in the text and completing this section of the workbook, you will be able to:

- ❑ Define transaxle and state its function.
- ❑ Explain how transaxle gear ratios are determined.
- ❑ Describe the makeup and operation of a typical manual transaxle.
- ❑ Describe the makeup and operation of a typical automatic transaxle.
- ❑ Tell how to perform common maintenance checks and adjustments.
- ❑ Discuss the many ways in which manufacturers' service manuals provide technicians with helpful automotive service information.

Multiple Choice

1. Transaxles are used mainly in _____. 1. ______________
   (A) front-wheel drive applications
   (B) all-wheel drive cars
   (C) cars with rear-wheel drive
   (D) None of the above.

2. Automatic transaxles are _____-speed. 2. ______________
   (A) three
   (B) four
   (C) five
   (D) Either A or B.

3. With a four-speed automatic transaxle, in which gear does the input sun gear drive the pinion carrier and internal gear of the input gearset? 3. ______________
   (A) First gear.
   (B) Second gear.
   (C) Third gear.
   (D) Fourth gear.

Name ______________________________

4. Many manufacturers are installing _____ controlled automatic transaxles in their vehicles. 4. ______________
   (A) mechanically
   (B) electronically
   (C) hydraulically
   (D) None of the above.

5. Good automatic transaxle maintenance requires regular checks of _____, with corrective steps taken if necessary to help avoid problems. 5. ______________
   (A) fluid level and condition
   (B) gearshift control linkage
   (C) cable adjustment
   (D) All of the above.

Identification

Identify the parts on the diagram of the differential assembly shown below.

6. Speedometer drive gear. 6. ______________
7. Pinion gear thrust washer. 7. ______________
8. Side bearing shim. 8. ______________
9. Ring gear. 9. ______________
10. Differential case. 10. ______________
11. Side gear thrust washer. 11. ______________
12. Ring gear bolt. 12. ______________
13. Side bearing. 13. ______________
14. Cross pin. 14. ______________
15. Differential pinion gear. 15. ______________
16. Lock pin. 16. ______________
17. Differential side gear. 17. ______________

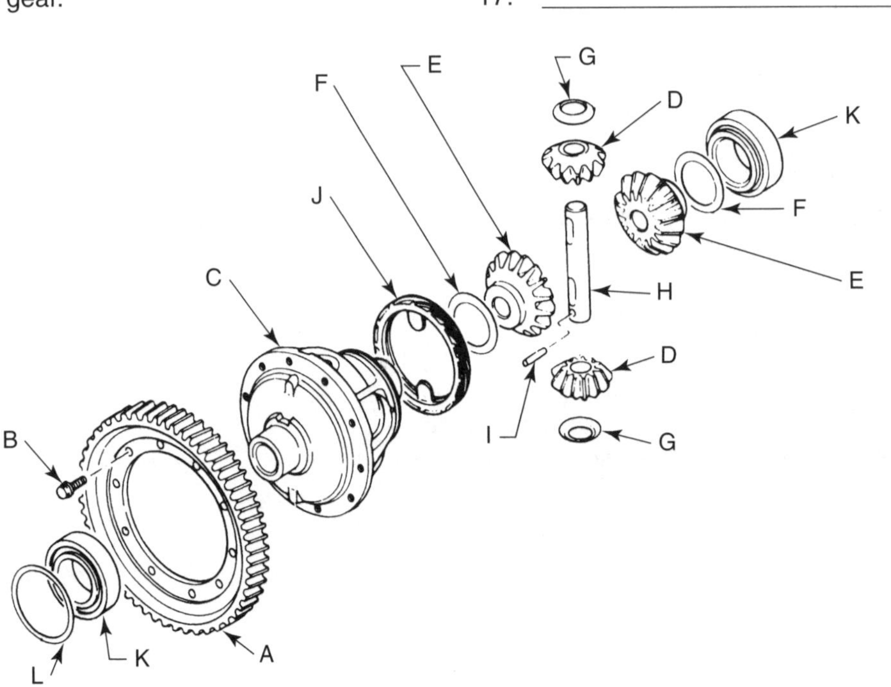

Name ____________________

Identify the parts indicated on the transaxle below.

18. End cover. 18. ____________________
19. Selector shaft. 19. ____________________
20. Lock pin. 20. ____________________
21. Fill plug. 21. ____________________
22. Vent. 22. ____________________

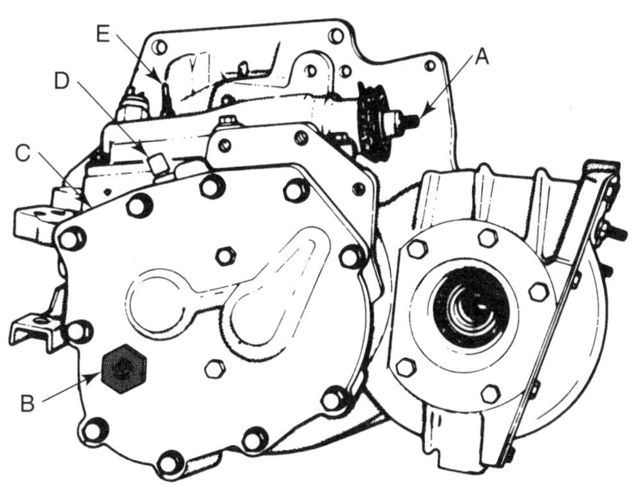

Completion

23. As with manual transmissions, transaxle gear _____ are determined by the number of teeth on the input cluster gear and the number of teeth on the matching gear on the main shaft. 23. ____________________

24. In a typical manual transaxle, power flow from the _____ is from the input cluster gear to the matching gear on the main shaft, from the main shaft and pinion gear to the _____ ring gear, and through the differential assembly to the half shafts and the driving wheels. 24. ____________________

25. Some automotive transaxles are equipped with a converter clutch that locks the converter turbine to the _____ in direct drive. In effect, the converter clutch provides a direct, mechanical drive to eliminate hydraulic converter slippage for greater efficiency and economy. 25. ____________________

Short Answer

26. What is a transaxle?

____

____

Name ____

27. List five steps involved in checking the condition of the transaxle mount.

____

____

____

____

____

Chapter 38

Driveline, Universal Joints, Differentials, and Driving Axles

Name ________________________________

Date ________________ Instructor ________________

Score________ Textbook pages 537–552

After studying the chapter in the text and completing this section of the workbook, you will be able to:

- ❑ Trace the transfer of power in the drive train of a rear-wheel drive vehicle.
- ❑ Discuss the need for universal joints in the driveline.
- ❑ State the principles of operation of the differential.
- ❑ Distinguish between Hotchkiss drive, torque tube drive, and control arm drive.
- ❑ Explain the types and functions of various constant velocity joints.
- ❑ Give examples of several different front-wheel drive driving axle systems.

Multiple Choice

1. The drive train includes the _____.
   (A) engine and transmission
   (B) driveline and differential assembly
   (C) driving axles
   (D) All of the above.

1. ________________________

2. On turns, the pinion gears turn on their axes and roll around the side gears to permit the driving wheels to rotate at _____ speeds.
   (A) equal
   (B) unequal
   (C) high
   (D) low

2. ________________________

3. The differential housing will tilt _____ when engine torque is relayed from the drive shaft to the drive pinion and rear axle housing.
   (A) upward
   (B) downward
   (C) sideways
   (D) None of the above.

3. ________________________

Name ______________________________

4. Each time the drive pinion shaft is taken apart or reassembled, _____.
   (A) the spacer must be repaired
   (B) the old spacer must be lubricated
   (C) a new spacer must be installed
   (D) None of the above.

4. ______________________________

5. The key element in the driveline of a _____ drive vehicle is a power transfer mechanism called a transaxle.
   (A) front-wheel
   (B) rear-wheel
   (C) four-wheel
   (D) None of the above.

5. ______________________________

Identification

Identify the types of drive setups below.

6. Control arm drive.

6. ______________________________

7. Hotchkiss drive.

7. ______________________________

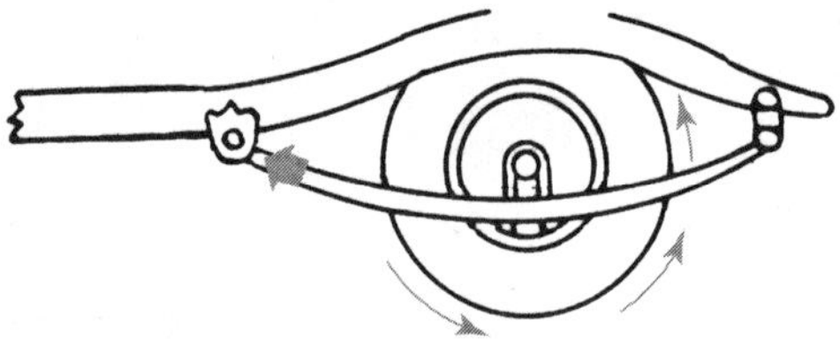

A

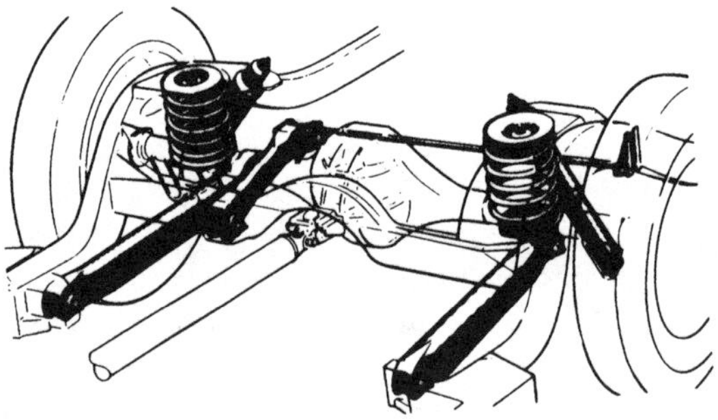

B

Identify the parts indicated on the typical differential case assembly shown at the top of the next page.

8. Pinion gear thrust washer. 8. ______________________________

9. Case. 9. ______________________________

10. Shaft. 10. ______________________________

11. Side gear thrust washer. 11. ______________________________

12. Differential pinion gear. 12. ______________________________

13. Screw. 13. ______________________________

14. Side gear. 14. ______________________________

Name ______________________________

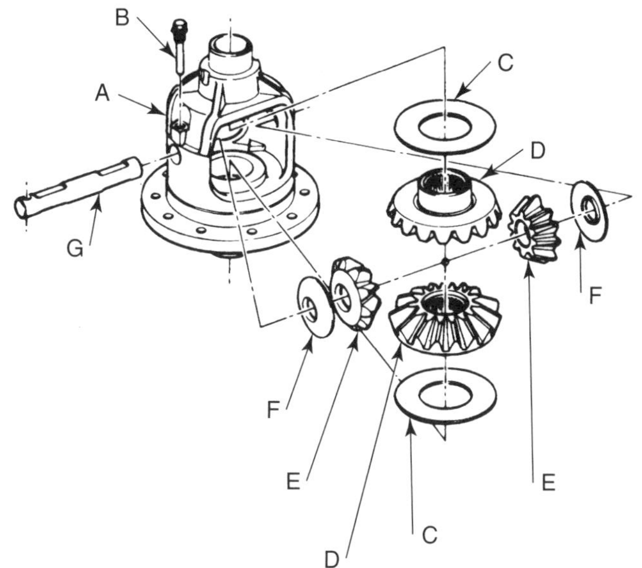

Completion

15. In basic passenger car design, the _____ connects the transmission with the driving axles. 15. ______________________

16. _____ _____ at both ends of the drive shaft compensate for changes in the angularity of the driveline. 16. ______________________

17. The _____ is a gear system that transfers power from the drive shaft to the driving axles. 17. ______________________

18. The _____ _____ of a rear-wheel drive passenger car are used to hold, align, and drive the rear wheels and support the weight of the vehicle. 18. ______________________

19. The _____ type of drive features a leaf spring rear suspension and an open drive shaft with two universal joints. 19. ______________________

20. In _____ _____ drive, driving and braking forces are transferred to the front end of heavy-duty control arms. 20. ______________________

21. Generally, differential bearing preload and ring gear _____ are adjusted by shims located between the differential bearing cup/races and the carrier housing. 21. ______________________

22. In front-wheel drive vehicles, the _____ _____ is compacted into an engine/transaxle/driving axles (halfshafts) "package" that provides torque force to the front wheels. 22. ______________________

23. The term *driving axles* is used when referring to front-wheel drive _____-_____-_____ assemblies that extend from inboard constant velocity joints to outboard constant velocity joints. 23. ______________________

Name ______________________________

Short Answer

24. As part of the driving axle assembly, what are the constant velocity joints (CV joints) designed to do?

____

____

____

Chapter 39

Driveline Service

Name ______________________________

Date ________________ Instructor ________________

Score________ Textbook pages 553–568

After studying the chapter in the text and completing this section of the workbook, you will be able to:

- ❑ Identify elements of rear-wheel drive and front-wheel drivelines.
- ❑ Describe differential pinion gear/ring gear adjusting procedures for obtaining correct tooth contact.
- ❑ Tell how to check angularity of drive shaft on rear-wheel drive vehicles.
- ❑ Cite driveline lubrication requirements.
- ❑ Explain driving axle services, both on rear-wheel drive and front-wheel drive systems.

Multiple Choice

1. Service problems with differentials are usually limited to _____.
   (A) lubricant leakage at the drive pinion oil seal
   (B) noisy operation of the differential
   (C) Both A and B.
   (D) None of the above.

1. ______________________________

2. When removing a drive shaft, place scribe marks on the drive shaft and the companion flange to aid in _____.
   (A) reinstallation
   (B) lubrication
   (C) maintaining balance
   (D) Both A and C.

2. ______________________________

3. CV joint components _____.
   (A) are matched
   (B) can be used with components from other CV joints
   (C) cannot be interchanged with components from another CV joint
   (D) Both A and C.

3. ______________________________

Name ______________________

4. Front-wheel driving axles must be handled with care to avoid damage to the _____.
   (A) boots
   (B) CV joints
   (C) shafts
   (D) All of the above.

4. ______________________

5. When servicing drivelines, you must ensure freedom of operation of moving parts to help _____.
   (A) eliminate friction
   (B) eliminate wear
   (C) furnish maximum power transfer to the driving wheels
   (D) All of the above.

5. ______________________

Identification

Identify the parts indicated on the illustration below.

6. Bearing retaining ring. 6. ______________________
7. Cross. 7. ______________________
8. Needle roller. 8. ______________________
9. Bearing retainer. 9. ______________________
10. Slip yoke. 10. ______________________
11. Tube yoke. 11. ______________________
12. Assembly held by injection molded plastic. 12. ______________________
13. Bearing seal. 13. ______________________
14. Injection hole. 14. ______________________
15. Round bearing cup. 15. ______________________

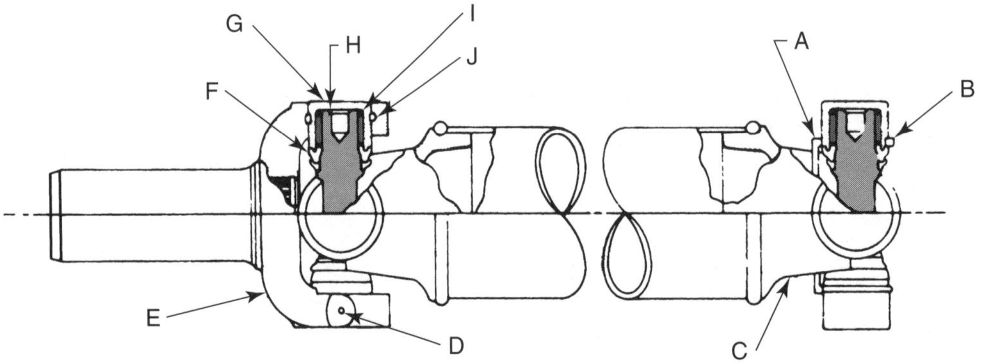

Identify the parts indicated on the CV joint shown at the top of the next page.

16. Outer bearing race. 16. ______________________
17. Inner bearing race. 17. ______________________
18. Dust seal. 18. ______________________
19. 26-tooth spline. 19. ______________________
20. Ball bearing. 20. ______________________

Name ______________________________

21. Stub shaft. 21. ______________________

22. Bearing cage. 22. ______________________

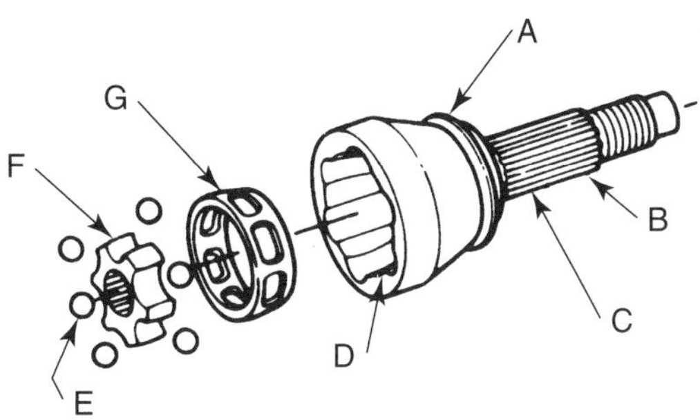

Completion

23. The _____ of a rear-wheel drive vehicle consists of one or more universal joints, the drive shaft, and the differential drive pinion gear. 23. ______________________

24. Noisy operation of a differential unit is usually caused by worn or damaged _____ or bearings. 24. ______________________

25. _____ between mating teeth is adjusted using bearing adjusting shims. Shims of varied thicknesses are used to move the entire case and ring gear assembly closer to or farther from the drive pinion gear. 25. ______________________

26. During removal and installation of front-wheel drive driving axles, always support the free end, or ends, of the driving axle assemblies at the CV joint _____. 26. ______________________

Short Answer

27. What is the drive shaft?

____

____

28. What is being done in the illustration below?

____

____

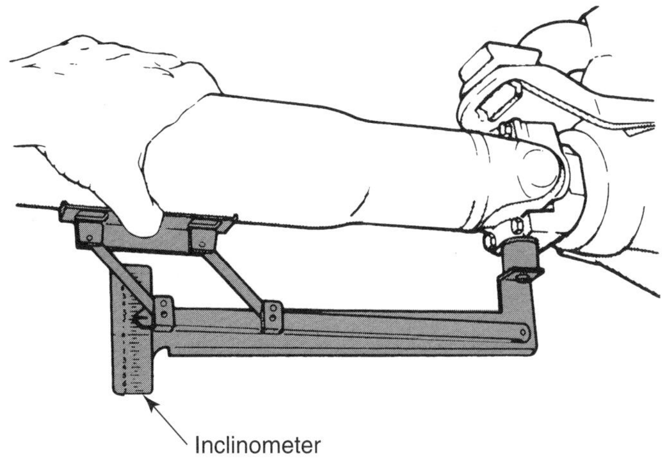

Chapter 40

Four-wheel Drive Systems

Name ______________________________

Date ______________ Instructor ______________

Score_______ Textbook pages 569–578

After studying the chapter in the text and completing this section of the workbook, you will be able to:

- ❑ Define four-wheel drive.
- ❑ Explain how four-wheel drive and all-wheel drive differ.
- ❑ Tell how a viscous coupling in a four-wheel drive system builds internal resistance and provides "limited-slip" action.
- ❑ State why differential "locks" are used in four-wheel drive systems.
- ❑ Identify some typical four-wheel drive troubles and give possible causes.

Multiple Choice

1. In all-wheel drive applications, the shifting is _____.
   (A) manual
   (B) automatic
   (C) Either A or B.
   (D) None of the above.

   1. ______________________

2. All four-wheel drive systems affect or are affected by _____.
   (A) at least two drivelines
   (B) all four driving axles
   (C) Either A or B.
   (D) None of the above.

   2. ______________________

3. To prevent vehicles from wandering, tire pressure should be within _____ psi from wheel to wheel.
   (A) 1/2 to 1
   (B) 1 to 1 1/2
   (C) 1 1/2 to 2
   (D) 2 to 2 1/2

   3. ______________________

Name ______________________________

4. Which of the following might cause lubricant leaks? 4. ______________
   (A) Yoke seals worn or damaged.
   (B) Vent closed or restricted.
   (C) Overfill condition in transfer case.
   (D) Any of the above.

5. Vibration or shudder can result from _____. 5. ______________
   (A) defective or loose steering linkage
   (B) defective steering damper
   (C) faulty universal joints
   (D) Any of the above.

Identification

Identify the parts indicated on the Eagle Select Drive system shown below.

6. Full-time transfer case. 6. ______________

7. Logic switch. 7. ______________

8. Front axle disconnect. 8. ______________

9. Viscous biasing unit. 9. ______________

10. Selector 2WD–4WD. 10. ______________

11. Transmission. 11. ______________

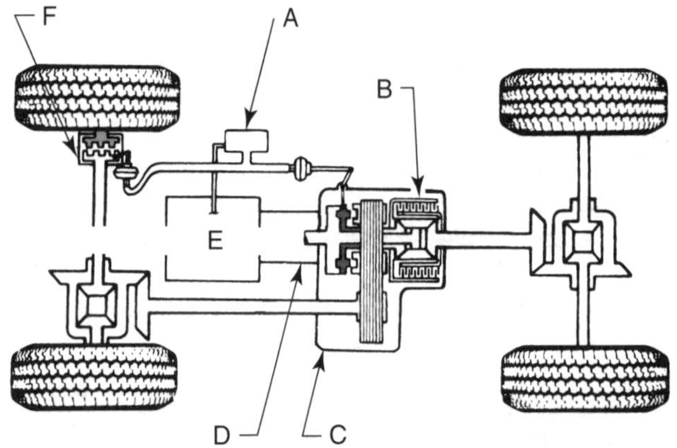

Identify the parts indicated on the four-wheel drive control system shown at the top of the next page.

12. Differential gears. 12. ______________

13. Speed sensor. 13. ______________

14. Drive shaft. 14. ______________

15. Automatic hub lock. 15. ______________

16. Automatic hub lock. 16. ______________

17. Neutral sensing switch. 17. ______________

18. Shaft motor and worm drive. 18. ______________

19. Electromagnetic clutch. 19. ______________

20. Chain. 20. ______________

21. Rear output shaft. 21. ______________

22. Transfer case. 22. ______________

Name ______________________________

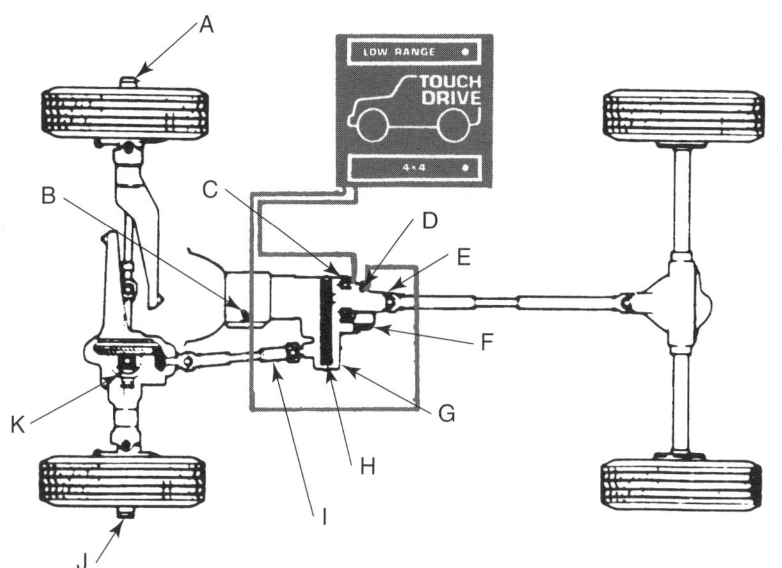

Identify the parts indicated on the diagram below.

23. AWD On-Off switch. 23. ____________________

24. Limited slip differential. 24. ____________________

25. Transfer case. 25. ____________________

26. Vacuum reservoir. 26. ____________________

27. Drive shaft. 27. ____________________

28. Vacuum shift motor. 28. ____________________

29. Exhaust. 29. ____________________

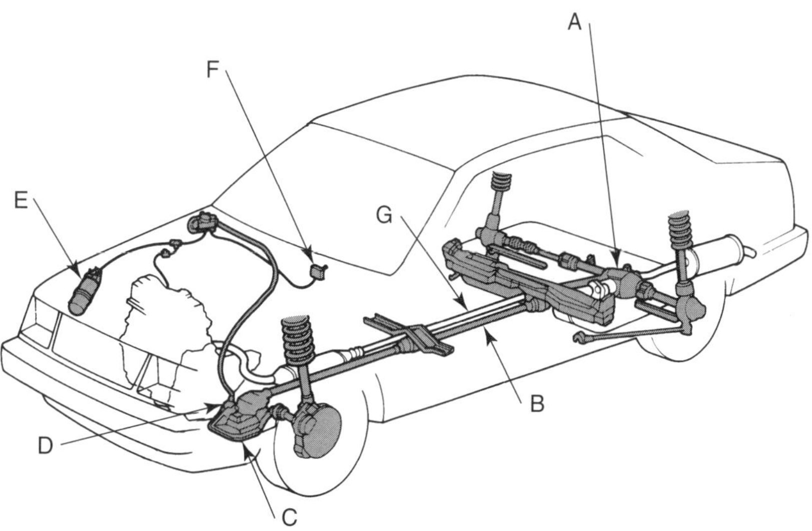

Completion

30. Most four-wheel drive vehicles have a(n) _____ device so the front-wheel drive or rear-wheel drive can be disengaged, if desired, and the vehicle becomes two-wheel drive. 30. ____________________

Name ______________________________

31. The Select Drive system used on some Eagle models has a dash-mounted switch that controls _____ _____ to provide either 2WD or 4WD capacity.

31. ______________________________

32. With Ford's "Touch Drive" electrical shift selector system, shifts between 2WD and _____-range 4WD can be made at any speed or with the vehicle stopped. Shifts into or out of _____-range 4WD require that the vehicle is stopped with the transmission in neutral.

32. ______________________________

33. Volkswagen has an automatically engaging, permanent all-wheel drive system based on the use of a _____ _____.

33. ______________________________

Short Answer

34. Identify the item shown below and describe how it works.

____

____

Chapter 41

Suspension and Steering Systems

Name ______________________________

Date ________________ Instructor ________________

Score_______ Textbook pages 579–600

After studying the chapter in the text and completing this section of the workbook, you will be able to:

- ❑ Explain the function of the various front and rear suspension components and assemblies.
- ❑ Name the three basic types of front and rear suspension systems.
- ❑ Tell how a typical "automatic level control system" works.
- ❑ Describe the makeup of manual rack-and-pinion and recirculating ball types of steering systems.
- ❑ State the operating principles of a power rack-and-pinion steering gear assembly and the integral power steering gear assembly.
- ❑ Identify some typical suspension and steering system troubles and give possible causes.

Multiple Choice

1. The sprung weight of a vehicle includes the _____. 1. ______________________
   (A) wheels
   (B) engine
   (C) tires
   (D) brake assemblies

2. Which of the following twists to exert resistance against up-and-down movement? 2. ______________________
   (A) Leaf spring.
   (B) Torsion bar.
   (C) Coil spring.
   (D) All of the above.

3. Which of the following front suspension systems is most often used on subcompact and compact cars with front-wheel drive? 3. ______________________
   (A) Independent front suspension.
   (B) Solid-axle suspension.
   (C) MacPherson strut suspension.
   (D) None of the above.

Name ______________________________

4. Which of the following is installed on over 90% of new domestic automobiles?
   (A) Power steering systems.
   (B) Manual steering systems.
   (C) Worm and roller steering.
   (D) None of the above.

4. ______________________________

5. Most modern power steering pumps contain a flow control valve that limits fluid flow to the power cylinder to about _____ gallon(s) per minute.
   (A) 1
   (B) 2
   (C) 5
   (D) 8

5. ______________________________

Identification

Identify the parts indicated on the independent front suspension shown below.

6. Steering spindle.	6. ______________
7. Upper control arm.	7. ______________
8. Steering arm.	8. ______________
9. Anchor plate.	9. ______________
10. Front crossmember.	10. ______________
11. Adapter.	11. ______________
12. Steering knuckle.	12. ______________
13. Shock absorber.	13. ______________
14. Coil spring.	14. ______________
15. Lower control arm.	15. ______________

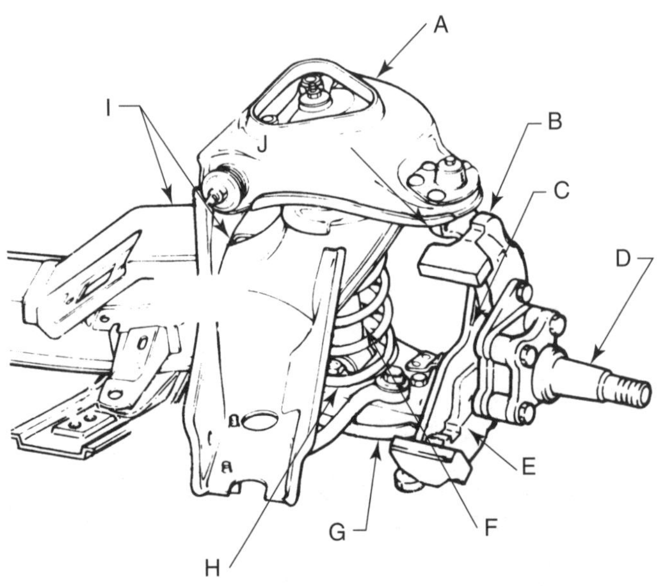

Name ____________________

Identify the parts indicated on the following diagram of a MacPherson strut arrangement.

16. Stabilizer bar. 16. ____________________

17. MacPherson strut assembly. 17. ____________________

18. Frame rail. 18. ____________________

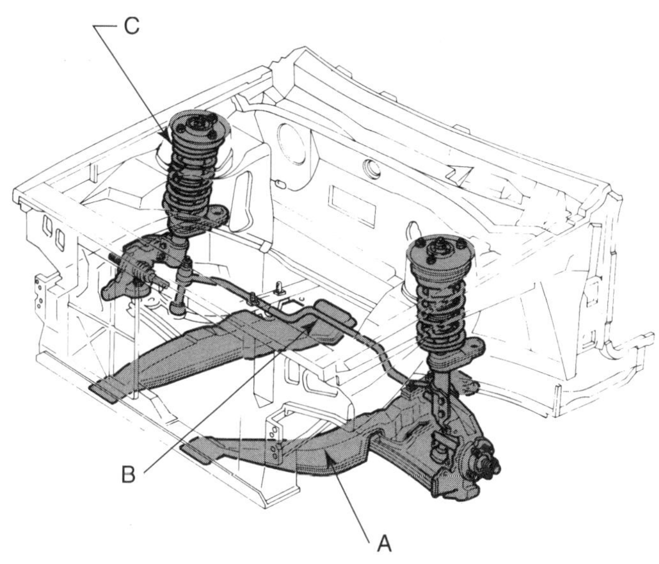

Identify the parts indicated on the diagram below.

19. Spindle and knuckle. 19. ____________________

20. Stabilizer bar. 20. ____________________

21. Coil spring. 21. ____________________

22. Control arm and bushing. 22. ____________________

23. Tie rod. 23. ____________________

24. Link. 24. ____________________

25. MacPherson strut. 25. ____________________

Name ______________________________

Identify the parts indicated on the diagram below.

26. Worm bearing race (upper). 26. ______________________
27. Locknut. 27. ______________________
28. Ball guides. 28. ______________________
29. Adjuster. 29. ______________________
30. Pitman shaft (sector). 30. ______________________
31. Wormshaft seal. 31. ______________________
32. Worm bearing race (lower). 32. ______________________
33. Worm bearing (upper). 33. ______________________
34. Wormshaft. 34. ______________________
35. Ball nut. 35. ______________________
36. Worm bearing (lower). 36. ______________________

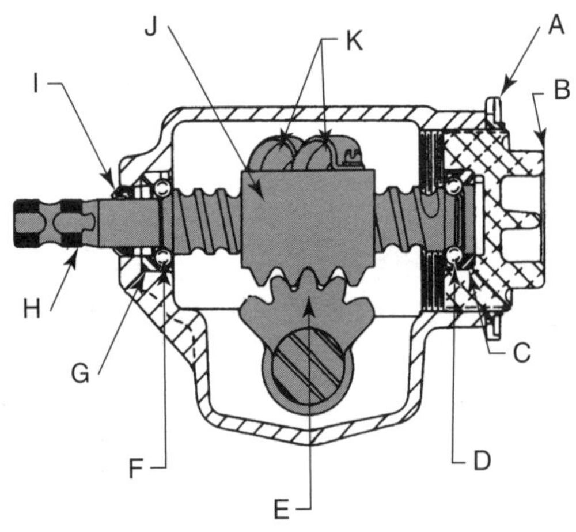

Identify the items indicated on the power steering pump shown below.

37. Rotor. 37. ______________________
38. Slipper. 38. ______________________
39. Shaft. 39. ______________________
40. Spring. 40. ______________________
41. Pump housing. 41. ______________________

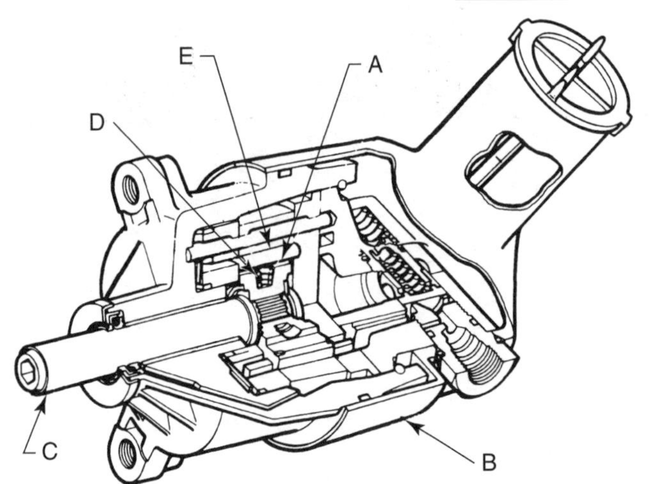

Name ______

Completion

42. When ______ ______ are used in both front and rear suspensions, three or four control arms are placed between the rear axle housing and the frame to carry driving and braking torque.

42. ______

43. ______ ______ suspension systems usually operate through coil springs or torsion bars, upper and lower control arms, and direct double-acting shock absorbers.

43. ______

44. Generally, the rack-and-pinion steering system is installed on ______-wheel drive cars. The integral power steering gear is used on many ______ -wheel drive cars.

44. ______

45. A typical power rack-and-pinion steering gear assembly is a hydraulic-mechanical unit with an integral piston and rack assembly. An internal ______ valve directs power steering fluid and controls pressure to reduce steering effort.

45. ______

Short Answer

46. What is the operating principle of direct-acting hydraulic shock absorbers?

______

______

47. List three types of rear suspension arrangements used on front-wheel drive vehicles.

______

______

______

48. List three types of rear suspension setups for rear-wheel drive vehicles.

______

______

______

49. List the three types of power steering pumps.

______

______

______

Chapter 42

Tires and Tire Service

Name ______________________________

Date ______________ Instructor ______________

Score________ Textbook pages 601–614

After studying the chapter in the text and completing this section of the workbook, you will be able to:

- ❑ Compare basic tire types and tire structures.
- ❑ Interpret the meaning of tire sidewall markings.
- ❑ Describe excessive and uneven treadwear patterns and possible causes.
- ❑ Outline steps for checking wheel and tire radial and lateral runout.
- ❑ Demonstrate proper techniques for using a power operated tire changer to demount and mount tires on wheels.
- ❑ State several methods for making satisfactory permanent tire repairs.

Multiple Choice

1. Which of the following causes wear in the center of the tire tread? 1. ______________
   (A) Underinflation.
   (B) Overinflation.
   (C) Incorrect camber.
   (D) Excessive toe-out.

2. Puncture holes in radial tires are repairable only in the _____. 2. ______________
   (A) sidewall portion
   (B) shoulder area
   (C) tread area
   (D) Both A and B.

3. Which of the following is not an acceptable method of repairing a tire? 3. ______________
   (A) Repairing a tire from the outside.
   (B) Chemical or heat repair units.
   (C) One-piece patch/plug units.
   (D) Combination plug/patch repairs.

Name ______________________________

4. Faulty tires should be replaced with new ones that are equivalent to original equipment wheels for _____.
   (A) load capacity
   (B) diameter and rim width
   (C) offset and mounting configuration
   (D) All of the above.

4. ______________________________

5. A tire's speed rating designation is located _____.
   (A) after the load index number
   (B) between the aspect ratio and the tire construction designation
   (C) Both A and B.
   (D) Neither A nor B.

5. ______________________________

Identification

Identify the parts indicated on the cross section of the tubeless tire shown below.

6. Carcass plies. 6. ______________________________
7. Tread. 7. ______________________________
8. Rim. 8. ______________________________
9. Beads. 9. ______________________________

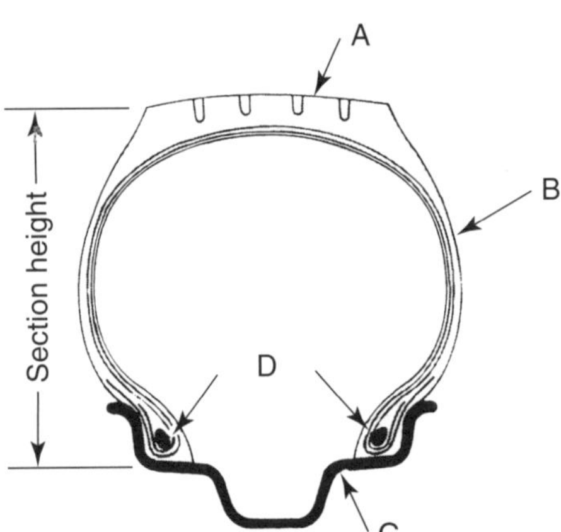

Identify the three basic types of tire construction shown below.

10. Belted radial. 10. ______________________________
11. Belted bias. 11. ______________________________
12. Bias. 12. ______________________________

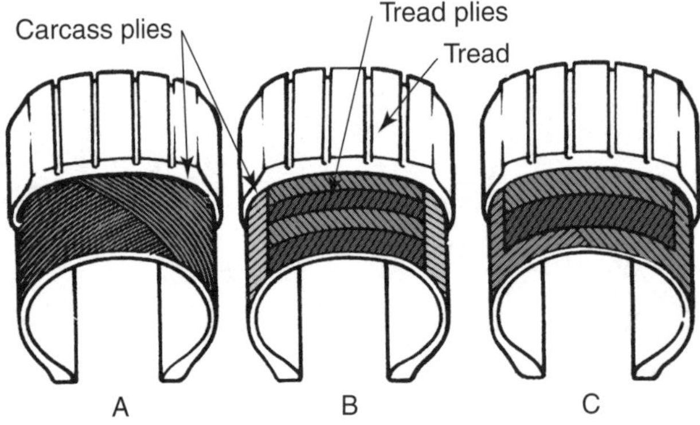

Name ______________________________

Identify the items indicated on the diagram below.

13. Snap-on rubber valve stem. 13. ____________

14. Valve core. 14. ____________

15. Cap. 15. ____________

16. Wheel rim. 16. ____________

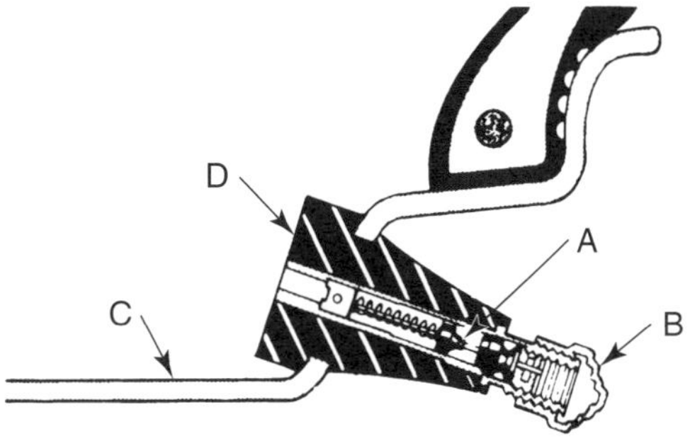

D
A
B
C

Completion

17. The _____ of a tire is made up of layers of cord materials such as rayon, nylon, polyester, fiberglass, or steel wire strands. The cords are laid parallel in layers and impregnated with rubber to form plies arranged at various angles and in different combinations of layers and belts. 17. ____________

18. A tire's load _____ is an indication of its load-carrying capacity. 18. ____________

19. Excessive or uneven _____ _____ results from underinflation, rapid stops, fast acceleration, misalignment, unbalanced conditions, gravel roads, and/or rough finished concrete. 19. ____________

20. _____ means adding a top strip of synthetic or reclaimed rubber to the buffed and roughened surface of a worn tire. 20. ____________

Short Answer

21. The U.S. Department of Transportation (DOT) has established the Uniform Tire Quality Grading for passenger car tires. On what areas are tires graded in accordance with DOT test procedures?

____

____

____

22. When should wheels be replaced?

____

____

Chapter 43

Wheel Alignment

Name ______________________________

Date ______________ Instructor ______________

Score_______ Textbook pages 615–624

After studying the chapter in the text and completing this section of the workbook, you will be able to:

- ❑ Explain why four-wheel alignment is necessary.
- ❑ Explain how various elements have an influence on tire-to-road contact.
- ❑ List preliminary steps required before wheel alignment angles are set.
- ❑ Identify and describe the angles involved in front wheel alignment.

Multiple Choice

1. For satisfactory wheel alignment, both front tires should _____.
   (A) be the same brand, size, and type
   (B) have varying degrees of tread wear and air pressure
   (C) carry different weights
   (D) All of the above.

   1. ______________________________

2. Which of the following is the equal distribution of weight on each side of the vertical centerline of the wheel and tire assembly?
   (A) Dynamic balance.
   (B) Static balance.
   (C) Unbalance.
   (D) None of the above.

   2. ______________________________

3. Before making alignment checks, make sure the vehicle's frame is _____.
   (A) straight
   (B) square
   (C) level
   (D) All of the above.

   3. ______________________________

Name ______________________________

4. Measurements for suspension height should be made with _____.
   (A) the car parked on a level floor and the tires equally inflated
   (B) the fuel tank full
   (C) no passenger load
   (D) All of the above.

4. ______________________________

5. Which of the following is the backward or forward tilt of the steering axis that tends to stabilize steering in a straight direction?
   (A) Camber.
   (B) Caster.
   (C) Toe-in.
   (D) Steering axis inclination.

5. ______________________________

Identification

Identify the parts indicated on the diagram below.

6. Centerline of tire. 6. ______________________________

7. Steering axis inclination. 7. ______________________________

8. True vertical. 8. ______________________________

9. Positive camber. 9. ______________________________

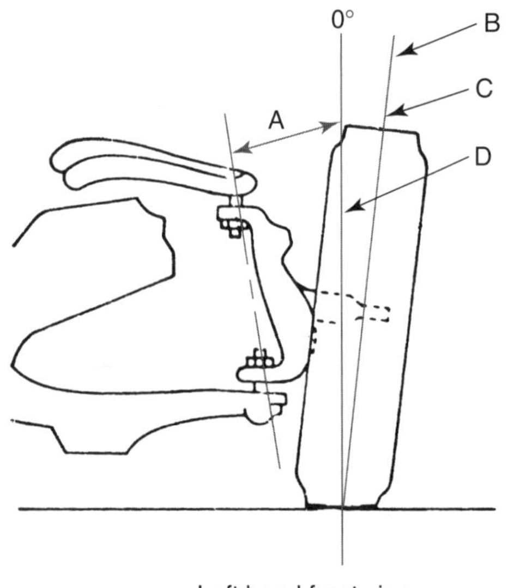

Left hand front view

Completion

10. Aligning a vehicle's front wheels involves balancing the _____ _____ with the physical forces being exerted.

10. ______________________________

11. The _____, which is the distance between the centers of the front and rear wheels, must measure as specified by the manufacturer and be exactly equal on each side of the vehicle.

11. ______________________________

Name ______________________________

12. Tread _____ is the distance between the center points of the left tire tread and the right tire tread as they come in contact with the road. 12. ______________________

13. The four wheel alignment procedure is required so that correct _____ (front, rear) wheel track is established. The _____ (front, rear) wheels steer the vehicle, but the _____ (front, rear) wheels direct it. 13. ______________________

14. If the front and rear wheels are realigned so the _____ _____ and the frame centerline agree, correct rear wheel track will be achieved. 14. ______________________

15. _____ is the backward or forward tilt of the steering axis that tends to stabilize steering in a straight direction. It places the weight of the vehicle either ahead or behind the area of tire-to-road contact. 15. ______________________

16. _____ is the inward or outward tilt of the wheel at the top. It is built into the wheel spindle by forming the spindle with a downward tilt to provide positive camber. 16. ______________________

17. Steering _____ _____ is the inward tilt of the steering knuckle. 17. ______________________

18. The combination of the camber and steering axis inclination forms the _____ _____. 18. ______________________

19. _____-_____ is the term used to specify the amount (in fractions of an inch) that the front wheels are closer together in the front than at the rear, when measured at hub height. 19. ______________________

Short Answer

20. In addition to aligning the front wheels, list seven items that must be considered and corrected if necessary when performing a four-wheel alignment.

____

____

____

____

____

____

____

Chapter 44

Wheel Alignment Correction

Name ______________________________

Date ________________ Instructor ________________

Score_______ Textbook pages 625–636

After studying the chapter in the text and completing this section of the workbook, you will be able to:

- ❑ Define the six front wheel alignment angles and list the order in which they should be checked.
- ❑ List preliminary steps that are necessary before making measurements of caster, camber, and toe-in.
- ❑ Give examples of typical front wheel caster and camber adjustment methods on both rear-wheel drive and front-wheel drive cars.
- ❑ Describe how various front wheel toe-in adjustments are made.
- ❑ Explain the importance of "rear wheel tracking."
- ❑ Give examples of typical rear wheel camber and toe-in checks and adjustments.

Multiple Choice

1. Most manufacturers recommend wheel alignment checks at least _____.
   (A) every six months
   (B) once a year
   (C) every two years
   (D) every five years

   1. ______________________

2. Ordinarily, cars should be checked for alignment at _____.
   (A) curb height or trim height
   (B) curb weight
   (C) Both A and B.
   (D) None of the above.

   2. ______________________

3. Which of the following can result from incorrect or unequal tire pressures?
   (A) Shimmy or wheel tramp.
   (B) Wander to either side.
   (C) Uneven tire tread wear.
   (D) All of the above.

   3. ______________________

Name ______________________________

4. If a car leads to one side, the cause could be _____. 4. ______________
   (A) loose shock absorber mountings
   (B) incorrect or uneven wheel alignment
   (C) excessive rotor or brake drum runout
   (D) None of the above.

Identification

Identify the parts indicated on the diagram below.

5. Upper control arm. 5. ______________
6. Cam. 6. ______________
7. Cam bolt. 7. ______________
8. Cam. 8. ______________
9. Cam bolt. 9. ______________
10. Cam. 10. ______________

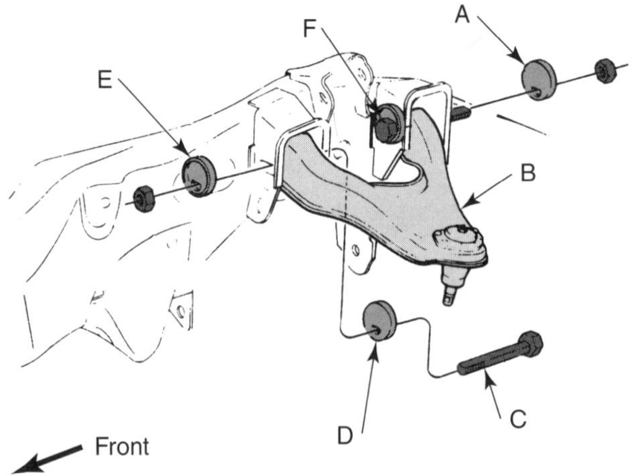

Identify the parts indicated on the diagram below.

11. Sleeve. 11. ______________
12. Tie rods. 12. ______________
13. Clamp. 13. ______________

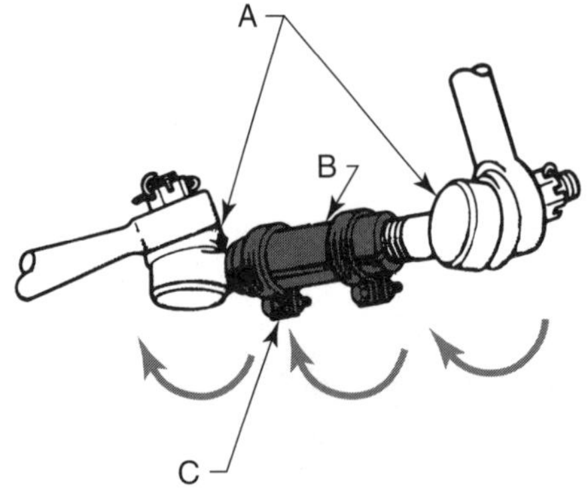

Name ______________________

Completion

14. ______ wheel track can be checked by running the car in and out of a wet area and examining the tread marks left by the front and rear tires. 14. ______________

15. To make caster adjustments on systems with adjustable strut rods, loosen the locknuts at the forward end of the struts and then shorten the rods to ______ caster or lengthen the rods to ______ caster. 15. ______________

16. ______ is the angle formed by the true vertical centerline and the vertical centerline of the tire. 16. ______________

17. Steering ______ ______ is created by the inward tilt of the steering knuckle and is not adjustable. 17. ______________

Short Answer

18. The method of wheel alignment inspection and detection varies with the type of equipment, but the angles should generally be checked in the following order:

Step 1: ______________

Step 2: ______________

Step 3: ______________

Step 4: ______________

Step 5: ______________

Step 6: ______________

19. Explain how to make a toe-in adjustment.

____

____

____

20. List the steps indicated on the rear camber and toe adjusting points below.

Step 1: ______________

Step 2: ______________

Step 3: ______________

Step 4: ______________

Step 5: ______________

5
3
4
Front
1
2

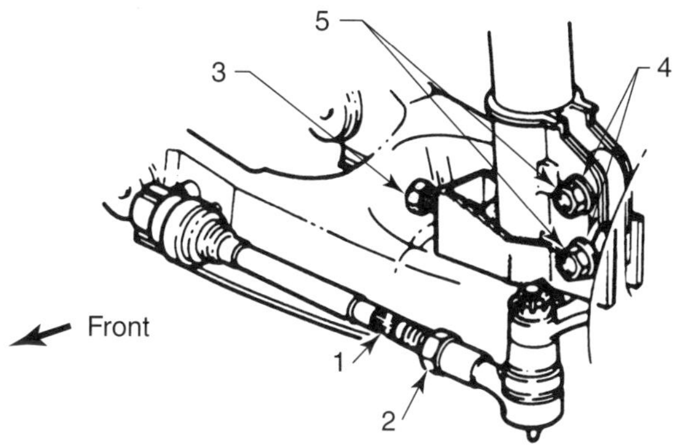

Chapter 45
Hydraulics and Pneumatics

Name ______________________________

Date ______________ Instructor ______________

Score________ Textbook pages 637–646

After studying the chapter in the text and completing this section of the workbook, you will be able to:

- ❑ Give examples of the principles of hydraulics.
- ❑ Cite the advantages of hydraulic systems.
- ❑ Define pressure and force.
- ❑ Describe various automotive applications of hydraulic principles.
- ❑ Define pneumatics.
- ❑ Name various automotive applications of pneumatic systems.
- ❑ State Boyle's Law.
- ❑ State Charles' Law.

Multiple Choice

1. The science of hydraulics includes the _____.
   (A) manner in which liquids act in tanks and pipes
   (B) laws of floating bodies and the behavior of liquids on submerged surfaces
   (C) flow of liquids under various conditions and methods of directing this flow to do useful work
   (D) All of the above.

   1. ______________________________

2. In automotive service work, specific gravity is used in _____.
   (A) testing antifreeze solutions to determine at what temperature the solution in the cooling system will freeze
   (B) measuring the state of charge in a starting battery
   (C) Both A and B.
   (D) None of the above.

   2. ______________________________

Name ______________________

3. If a force of 25 lb. is applied to a small piston, a pressure of 5 psi will be produced in the hydraulic fluid. This 5 psi will act over the entire area of a large piston with its 250 sq. in. surface. The resulting force will be _____ lb. 3. ______________
   (A) 250
   (B) 1250
   (C) 5000
   (D) 7500

4. In air brakes, which of the following factors is involved in the force developed? 4. ______________
   (A) The quantity of air action on the piston.
   (B) The air pressure.
   (C) The area of the piston on which the air pressure is acting.
   (D) Both B and C.

Identification

Look at the illustration below. Arrows illustrate the difference in the action of forces. Which is the liquid and which is the solid?

5. Liquid. 5. ______________

6. Solid. 6. ______________

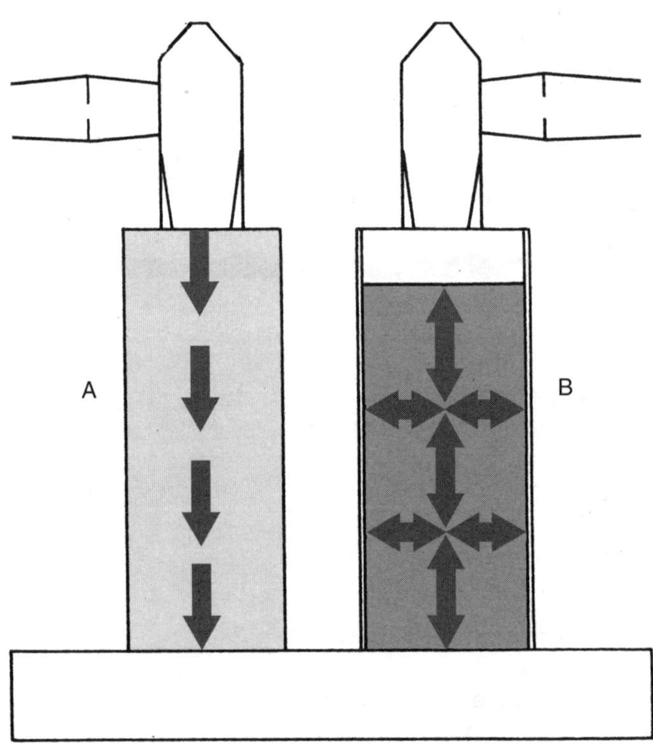

Name ____________________

Identify the parts indicated on the hydrometer shown below.

7. Float. 7. ____________________
8. Bulb. 8. ____________________
9. Thermometer. 9. ____________________
10. Barrel. 10. ____________________

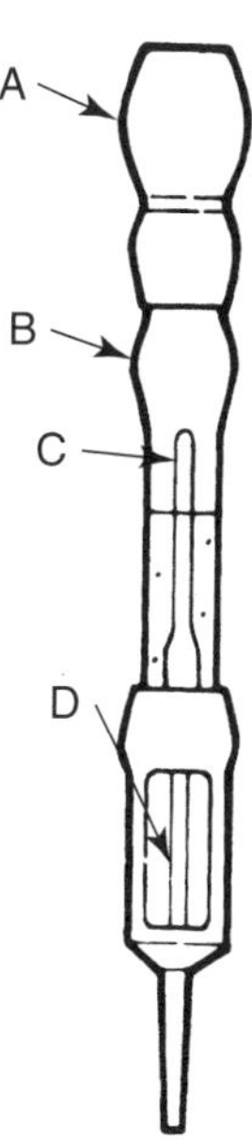

Identify the items indicated on the diagram below.

11. Push rod. 11. ____________________
12. Intake manifold vacuum. 12. ____________________
13. Vacuum control valve. 13. ____________________
14. Atmospheric pressure. 14. ____________________
15. Output force. 15. ____________________
16. Pedal input force. 16. ____________________
17. Atmospheric valve. 17. ____________________
18. Diaphragm. 18. ____________________

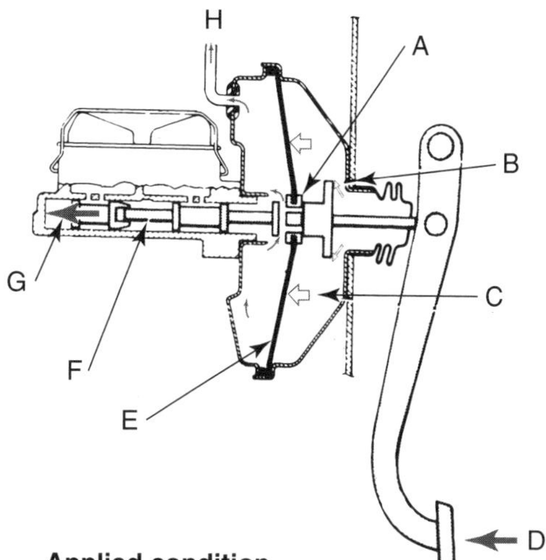

Applied condition

Name ______________________________

Completion

19. The study of _____ is concerned with liquids under pressure and in motion. 19. ____________________
20. To measure the specific gravity of a solution, an instrument known as a(n) _____ is used. 20. ____________________
21. _____ is the strength or power exerted on an object. _____ is defined as the force divided by the area over which it is distributed. 21. ____________________
22. Force applied to a fluid in a confined system is transmitted equally in all directions throughout the system regardless of its _____. 22. ____________________
23. If the output piston is larger than the input piston, the force will be _____ (increased, decreased) in the same proportion as the areas of the two pistons. 23. ____________________
24. Forces can be _____ (multiplied, divided) if the output piston is larger than the input piston. 24. ____________________
25. _____ is the study of the mechanical properties of air and other gases. 25. ____________________
26. Air and other gases are highly _____ and completely fill any containing vessel. 26. ____________________
27. The pressure of air at sea level under normal conditions is _____ psi. 27. ____________________
28. Vacuum is measured in inches of _____ and designated as inches Hg. 28. ____________________

Short Answer

29. List five advantages of hydraulic systems.

____
____
____
____
____

30. Describe Pascal's law.

____
____

31. Describe the principle of operation of the floating or sliding caliper disc brake.

____
____
____
____
____

Name ______________________________

32. Explain why the venturi tube is important.

33. What is Boyle's law?

34. What is Charles' law?

35. List five ways the principles of pneumatics are put to use in vehicles.

Chapter 46

Automotive Brakes

Name ______________________________

Date ______________ Instructor ______________

Score_______ Textbook pages 647–684

After studying the chapter in the text and completing this section of the workbook, you will be able to:

- ❑ Explain the forces and factors involved when braking a vehicle.
- ❑ Describe brake system materials, hydraulic components, and mechanical parts.
- ❑ State how disc brakes and drum brakes operate.
- ❑ Describe how various power brake systems and anti-lock brake systems operate.
- ❑ Tell how to service brake hydraulic systems.
- ❑ Give steps of performing disc brake overhaul and drum brake overhaul.
- ❑ Solve brake troubleshooting problems.
- ❑ Give examples of power brake system and anti-lock brake system service operations.

Multiple Choice

1. If a 75 lb. pull is required to slide a 100 lb. weight, then the coefficient of friction would be _____.
   (A) 0.75
   (B) 75
   (C) 750
   (D) 7500

   1. ______________________

2. If both the weight and speed of a vehicle are doubled, the stopping power must be increased _____ times.
   (A) 2
   (B) 4
   (C) 8
   (D) 16

   2. ______________________

3. Drum braking action involves _____.
   (A) self-energization of the primary shoe by the drum rotation
   (B) servo wedging action of the primary shoe against the drum
   (C) duo-servo action as the primary shoe pushes the secondary shoe against the drum with increased force
   (D) All of the above.

   3. ______________________

Name ______________________________

4. When cleaning the boots, cups, grommets, diaphragms, or any rubber parts, the proper cleaning fluid is _____.
   (A) alcohol
   (B) solvents
   (C) gasoline
   (D) All of the above.

4. ______________________________

5. Which of the following is a safe practice to follow when servicing anti-lock brake systems?
   (A) Loosen the brake lines before relieving system pressure.
   (B) Relieve system pressure before loosening the brake lines.
   (C) Refer to the manufacturer's manual for proper procedures.
   (D) Both B and C.

5. ______________________________

Identification

Identify the parts on the disc brake assembly shown below.

6. Piston seal. 6. ______________________________
7. Bleeder valve. 7. ______________________________
8. Bolt boot. 8. ______________________________
9. Caliper housing. 9. ______________________________
10. Boot. 10. ______________________________
11. Inboard shoe and lining. 11. ______________________________
12. Mounting bolt. 12. ______________________________
13. Piston. 13. ______________________________
14. Outboard shoe and lining. 14. ______________________________
15. Sleeve. 15. ______________________________

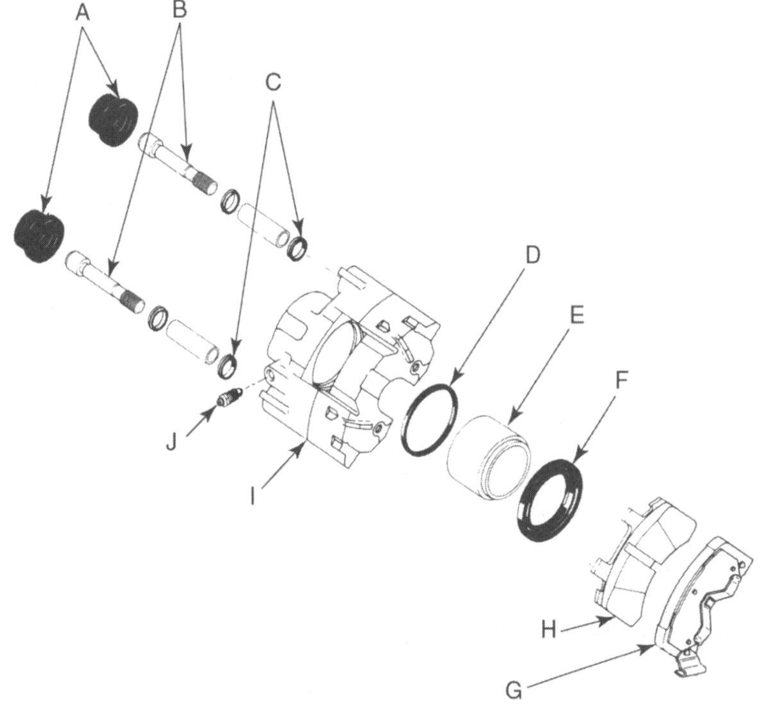

Name ______________________________

16. Using different colors (or double lines and single lines), indicate the primary (single) and secondary (double) systems of a typical dual diagonal braking system on the illustration below.

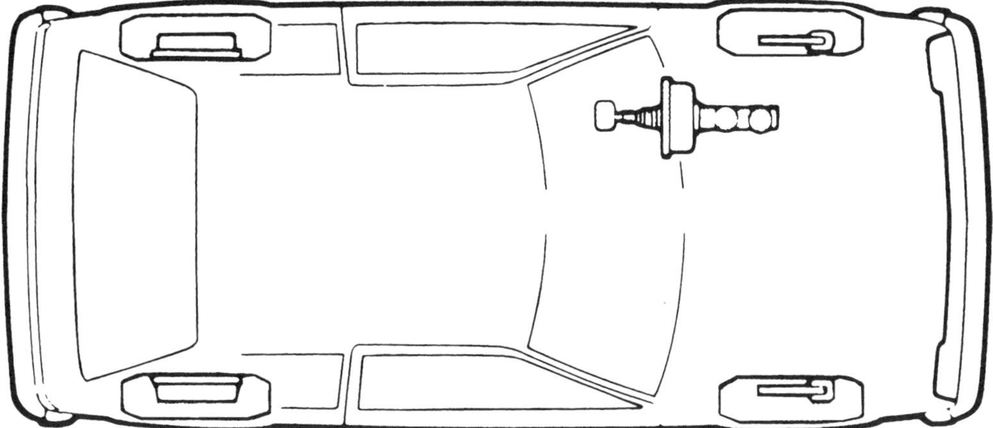

Identify the parts indicated on the master cylinder shown on the next page.

17. Cylinder body.	17.	______________
18. Lock ring.	18.	______________
19. Reservoir cover.	19.	______________
20. Reservoir.	20.	______________
21. Primary seal.	21.	______________
22. Primary piston assembly.	22.	______________
23. Reservoir diaphragm.	23.	______________
24. Secondary seal.	24.	______________
25. Spring retainer.	25.	______________
26. Grommets.	26.	______________
27. Secondary seal.	27.	______________
28. Secondary piston.	28.	______________

Name ____________________

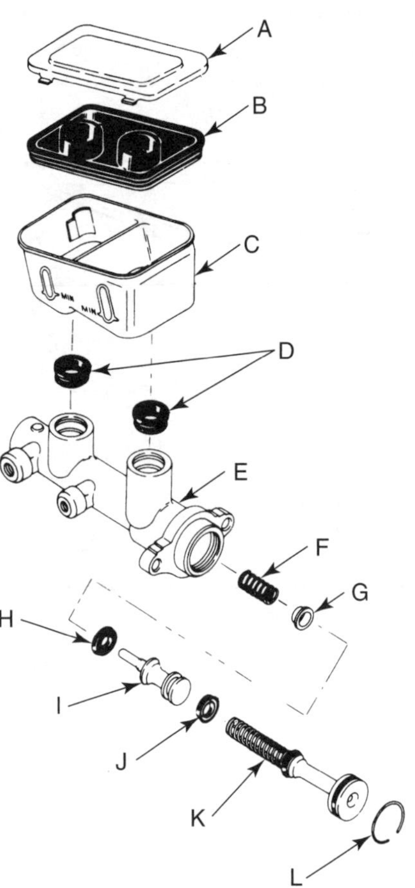

Completion

29. The brake system is a balanced set of mechanical and hydraulic devices used to retard the motion of the vehicle by means of _____, which is the resistance to relative motion between two bodies in contact. 29. ____________________

30. The amount of friction developed by any two bodies in contact with each other is their _____ of _____. 30. ____________________

31. Disc brake _____ surfaces are precisely machined for quality of finish, thickness, parallelism, and absence of lateral runout. 31. ____________________

32. With single piston disc brake calipers, the _____ slides or floats on mounting bolts, sleeves on the mounting bolts, or pins to apply friction pads to the _____ surfaces of a rotating disc. 32. ____________________

33. The _____-_____ brake principle involves actuating a lever to rotate an adjusting screw by driving the vehicle in reverse and making repeated "hard" stops with one forward brake application between each reverse stop. 33. ____________________

34. A basic brake _____ system usually consists of a dual reservoir master cylinder; a combination valve; front disc brake calipers; rear drum brake wheel cylinders; and the connecting brake lines, hoses, and fittings. 34. ____________________

Name ______________________________

35. Most brake hydraulic systems with disc brakes in _____ (front, rear) and drum brakes at the _____ (front, rear) utilize a combination valve that generally combines a pressure differential valve, metering valve, and proportioning valve. 35. ______________________

36. The diagram below illustrates the _____ (applied, unapplied) condition of a single diaphragm power brake unit. Both sides of the diaphragm are _____ (open, closed) to intake manifold vacuum. 36. ______________________

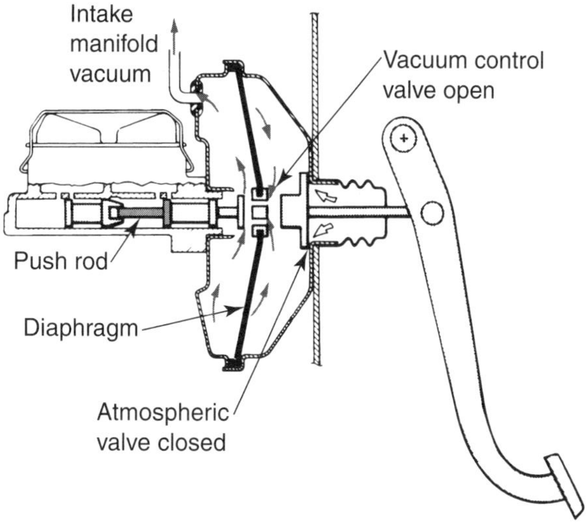

37. _____-_____ brake systems use electronic and hydraulic components to help prevent wheel lockup during periods of hard braking. 37. ______________________

38. Drum brakes utilize _____ (internal, external) expanding brake shoe assemblies to create the friction and heat required to slow and stop the rotating drums. 38. ______________________

Short Answer

39. List the three basic types of brake linings in current original equipment use.

____

____

____

40. Define *disc brake rotor.*

____

____

41. List six factors that contribute to the effectiveness of drum brakes.

____

____

____

____

____

____

Name ______________________________

42. The SAE J1703 specification requires that brake fluids pass certain tests. Name six.

____

____

____

____

____

____

43. List the four types of power brake units used on passenger cars.

____

____

____

____

44. Explain how to remove a caliper piston.

____

____

____

45. What is the purpose of the item shown below?

____

____

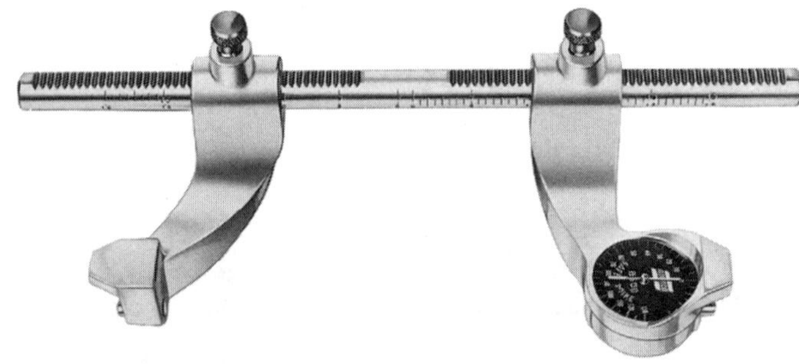

Chapter 47

Automobile Air Conditioning

Name ______________________________

Date ________________ Instructor ________________

Score_______ Textbook pages 685–708

After studying the chapter in the text and completing this section of the workbook, you will be able to:

- ❑ Describe the fundamentals of air conditioning.
- ❑ List the major parts of an air conditioning system and the purpose of each.
- ❑ Summarize the principles of air conditioning.
- ❑ Explain why R-134a is being used in the air conditioning systems of late-model vehicles.
- ❑ Explain how the heating system works.
- ❑ Tell how an air conditioning compressor and clutch operate.
- ❑ List the different types of air conditioning systems.
- ❑ Explain how to service an air conditioning system, including proper refrigerant recovery techniques.
- ❑ Troubleshoot an air conditioning system.

Multiple Choice

1. Changes from a liquid to a vapor are often accomplished by means of _____.
   (A) heat and evaporation
   (B) cooling and condensation
   (C) heat and condensation
   (D) cooling and evaporation

   1. ______________________________

2. Changes from vapor to a liquid are often accomplished by means of _____.
   (A) heat and condensation
   (B) heat and evaporation
   (C) cooling and condensation
   (D) cooling and evaporation

   2. ______________________________

Name ______________________________

3 Which of the following is the storage tank for liquid refrigerant and also contains a filter and a desiccant to remove foreign particles and moisture from the circulating refrigerant?
(A) Compressor.
(B) Condenser.
(C) Receiver-drier.
(D) Evaporator.

3. ______________________________

4. To protect the earth's ozone layer, _____.
(A) the production of chlorofluorocarbons was banned in 1996
(B) manufacturers are now using R-134a in their air conditioning systems
(C) manufacturers are using R-12 in their air conditioning systems
(D) Both A and B.

4. ______________________________

5. When handling refrigerants, _____.
(A) always wear goggles
(B) discharge refrigerant slowly into a recovery/recycling unit
(C) do not have sparks or open flames in work area
(D) All of the above.

5. ______________________________

Identification

Identify the parts of the compressor clutch assembly shown below.

6. Dust shield. 6. ______________________________
7. Clutch hub. 7. ______________________________
8. Clutch pulley. 8. ______________________________
9. Pulley bearing. 9. ______________________________
10. Compressor. 10. ______________________________
11. Field coil snap ring. 11. ______________________________
12. Pulley snap ring. 12. ______________________________
13. Clutch field coil. 13. ______________________________

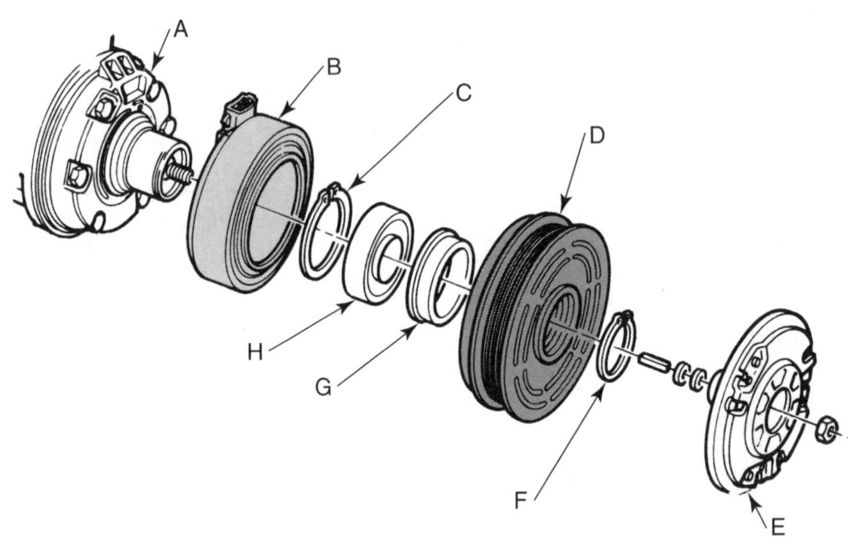

Name ______________________

Identify the parts indicated on the manifold gauge set shown below.

14. Low-pressure gauge. 14. ______________
15. High-pressure gauge. 15. ______________
16. Hose to shop exhaust system. 16. ______________
17. Manifold gauge set. 17. ______________
18. Pressure test fittings. 18. ______________

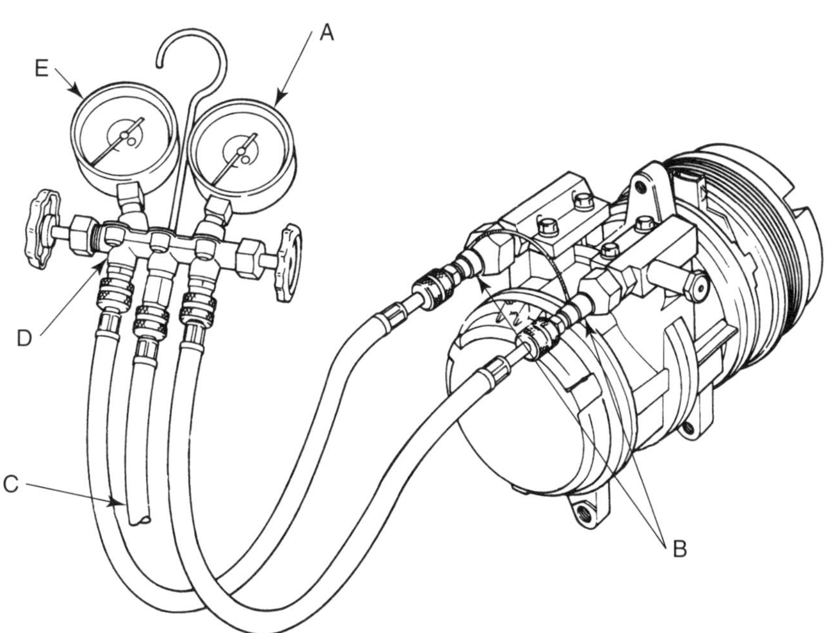

Completion

19. Air conditioning is the process performed by a closed refrigeration system that circulates _____ under pressure. 19. ______________

20. The refrigerant cycles from _____ to _____ to _____, absorbing heat from the warm air inside the passenger compartment and discharging it to the outside air. 20. ______________

21. The _____-_____ relationship works well with refrigerant in the system. The value of this relationship lies in the fact that pressure tests made on the "low side" will reveal the refrigerant temperature at this point in the system. 21. ______________

22. The _____ is the power unit of the air conditioning system. It pumps out refrigerant vapor under high pressure and high heat on the discharge side (high side of the system) and sucks in low-pressure vapor on the intake side (low side). 22. ______________

23. The _____ is the connecting link between the compressor pulley and compressor. 23. ______________

24. The _____ in the air conditioning system is a device used to change high-pressure refrigerated vapor to a liquid. 24. ______________

Name ______________________________

25. A _____ _____ provided for viewing the condition of the refrigerant charge is usually built into or adjacent to the top of the receiver-drier assembly. 25. ______________________

26. The _____ _____ _____ is a metering device that removes pressure from the liquid refrigerant so that it can expand and become refrigerant vapor in the evaporator. The metering action is performed by an orifice within the valve body. 26. ______________________

27. If an air conditioning system is contaminated by moisture, the best way to remove the moisture is by using a(n) _____ _____ to evacuate all traces of refrigerant, air, and moisture. 27. ______________________

28. The _____ _____ set is used to test pressure on the high and low sides of the compressor. 28. ______________________

29. Many automatic temperature control systems are controlled by a computer or _____. 29. ______________________

Short Answer

30. List the five major elements that do the job of circulating, condensing, and vaporizing the refrigerant.

31. Heat always flows (transfers) from hotter to colder objects by one or more of three methods. Name them.

32. Explain how heat is provided in an automobile's heating system.

33. Describe how the evaporator in the air conditioning system works.

Name ______________________________

34. Suppose you are a technician troubleshooting a heating system. List six possible causes of insufficient or no heat.

For questions 35–40, suppose you are a technician troubleshooting an air conditioning system.

35. List six possible causes of no refrigeration action.

36. List six possible causes of insufficient cool air.

37. List four possible causes of insufficient or no air discharge.

38. List two possible causes of the system running too cold.

39. List four possible causes of the system cooling intermittently.

Name ______________________________

40. List four possible causes of a noisy system.

____

____

____

____

Chapter 48

Safety Systems

Name ______________________________

Date ______________ Instructor ______________

Score________ Textbook pages 709–722

After studying the chapter in the text and completing this section of the workbook, you will be able to:

- ❑ List dozens of major advances in automotive safety.
- ❑ Describe current front seat lap/shoulder belt systems.
- ❑ Explain how automatic seat belt systems operate.
- ❑ Explain how air bags work.
- ❑ Compare the construction and function of the three major types of energy-absorbing bumper systems.
- ❑ Describe the operation of a modern anti-lock braking system.

Multiple Choice

1. Which of the following is one of the latest safety features being installed on vehicles?
   (A) High-mounted stop lamps.
   (B) Horns.
   (C) Emergency brakes.
   (D) Safety wheel rims.

   1. ______________________

2. Which of the following is not a typical air bag system component?
   (A) Impact sensor.
   (B) Coil assembly.
   (C) Control module.
   (D) Inertial retractor.

   2. ______________________

3. An air bag system deploys within _____ milliseconds of impact.
   (A) 10
   (B) 30
   (C) 50
   (D) 60

   3. ______________________

Name ____________________

4. By law, auto manufacturers are required to install bumper systems that will protect the vehicle safety systems in a barrier impact of _____ mile(s) per hour.
   (A) one
   (B) five
   (C) twenty
   (D) fifty-five

4. ____________________

5. Which of the following should be relieved of gas pressure before disposal?
   (A) Fluid/spring energy absorbing unit.
   (B) Fluid/gas energy absorbing unit.
   (C) Plastic pad/impact bar energy absorbing unit.
   (D) None of the above.

5. ____________________

Identification

Identify the components indicated on the typical air bag system shown below.

6. Coil assembly. 6. E
7. Driver's-side air bag module. 7. D
8. Control module. 8. C
9. Passenger-side air bag module. 9. B
10. Impact sensors. 10. A

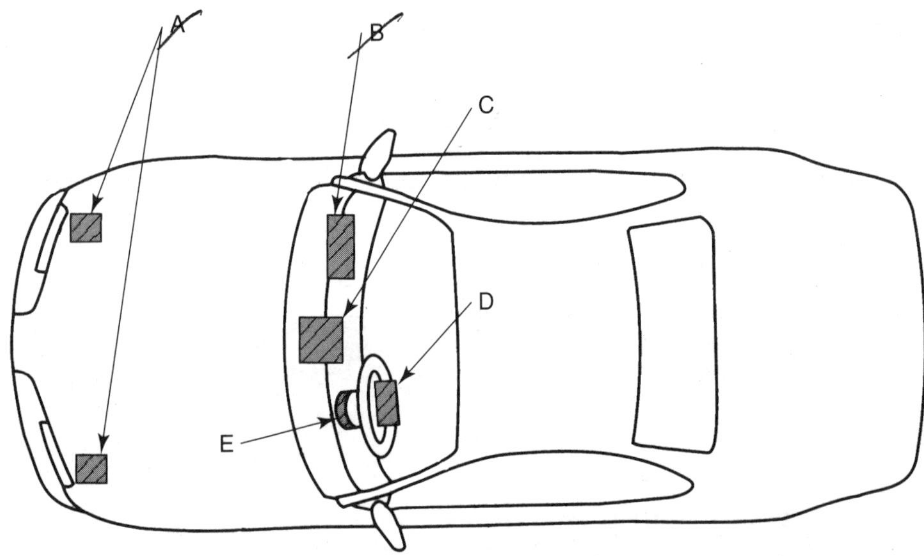

Identify the parts indicated on the passenger-side air bag module shown on the next page.

11. Ignitor. 11. D
12. Filter assembly. 12. G
13. Air bag. 13. A
14. Cover. 14. B
15. Gas generant. 15. F
16. Inflator body. 16. C
17. Ignitor housing. 17. E

Name ______________________

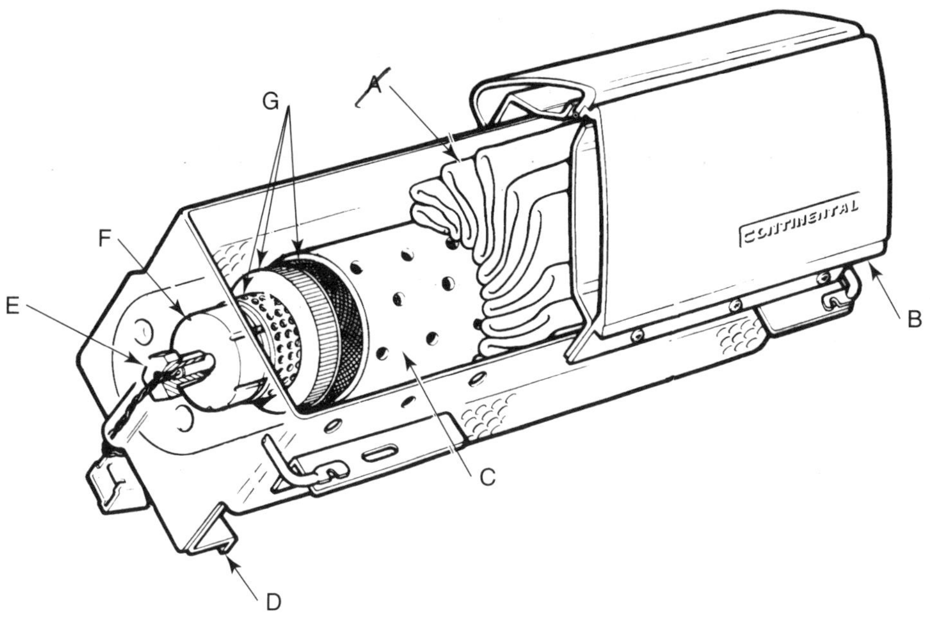

Completion

18. In most seat belt systems in U.S. cars, a mechanical inertial-locking _____ is used.

18. RETRACTOR

19. The _____ seat belt requires no buckling up or adjustments by the driver or front-seat passenger.

19. AUTOMATIC

20. Electronic _____ _____ systems basically are warnings to enhance those provided by instruments, lights, and buzzers.

20. VOICE ALERT

21. Speedometer cluster telltale _____ _____ on the instrument panel warn the driver of impending problems.

21. ______________________

Short Answer

22. List at least ten major advances in automotive safety.

Name ______________________________

23. List the three major types of energy absorbing bumper systems.

FLUID / GAS ENERGY ABSORBING UNIT

FLUID / SPRING ENERGY ABSORBING UNIT

PLASTIC PAD / IMPACT BAR ENERGY ABSORBING UNIT

Chapter 49
Lamps, Lighting Circuits, Wiring, Horns, Wipers, and Washers

Name ______________________________

Date ____________ Instructor ____________

Score_______ Textbook pages 723–744

After studying the chapter in the text and completing this section of the workbook, you will be able to:

- ❑ Explain how the complete automobile lighting circuit is divided into individual circuits and a common ground.
- ❑ State functions of electronic headlight dimming devices and headlight delay systems.
- ❑ Give service tips on headlamp and bulb replacement.
- ❑ Describe headlight aiming procedures.
- ❑ Explain wire gauge numbering system.
- ❑ Tell how the horn circuit operates and what tests and adjustments can be made.
- ❑ List the different types of wiper motor construction.
- ❑ Describe how the washer system works.

Multiple Choice

1. The lighting circuit includes _____.
   (A) the battery
   (B) the frame
   (C) all the lights and various switches that control their use
   (D) All of the above.

1. ______________________

2. Dim lights result from low voltage, which may be caused by _____.
   (A) loose or corroded terminals in the lamp circuit
   (B) a low charging rate
   (C) a defective battery
   (D) All of the above.

2. ______________________

3. When servicing composite headlamps for a halogen bulb burnout, handle the bulb by _____.
   (A) the glass portion
   (B) the metal parts
   (C) its plastic base only
   (D) None of the above.

3. ______________________

Name ______________________

4. The horn electrical circuit generally includes the _____. 4. ______________
   (A) battery, horn relay, and horn(s)
   (B) fuse or fusible link and steering column wiring harness
   (C) horn switch and body sheet metal
   (D) All of the above.

5. Failure of a windshield wiper to operate can be caused by a _____. 5. ______________
   (A) blown fuse or an open circuit
   (B) loose wiring harness connector or the wiper motor not being grounded
   (C) bad wiper switch or motor
   (D) All of the above.

Identification

Identify the parts indicated on the diagram below.

6. Headlamp bulb and retainer assembly. 6. ______________
7. Bulb. 7. ______________
8. Reflector and lens assembly. 8. ______________
9. Parking lamp assembly. 9. ______________
10. Wiring assembly. 10. ______________
11. Bulb assembly. 11. ______________
12. Wiring assembly. 12. ______________
13. Lamp assembly. 13. ______________

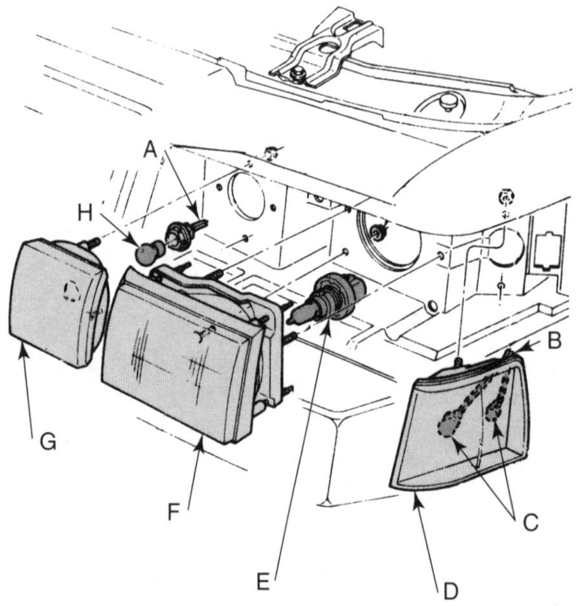

Name ______________________________

Identify the parts indicated on the diagram below.

14. Bulb socket. 14. ______________________
15. Reflector. 15. ______________________
16. Rear face of socket. 16. ______________________
17. Unlock. 17. ______________________
18. Flat side of plastic base. 18. ______________________
19. Bulb. 19. ______________________
20. Glass envelope. 20. ______________________
21. Bulb retaining ring. 21. ______________________
22. Mounting flange. 22. ______________________
23. Electrical connector. 23. ______________________
24. Lock. 24. ______________________

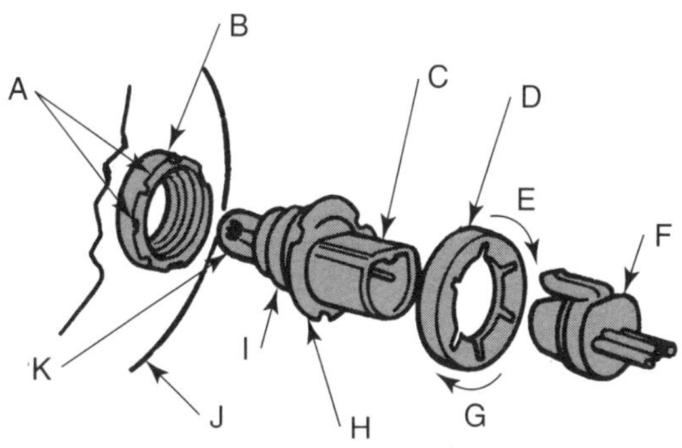

Identify the three different types of motors that can be used for windshield wipers as represented by the diagrams below.

25. Shunt wound motor that has field winding parallel with armature. 25. ______________________
26. Permanent magnet type motor. 26. ______________________
27. Compound motor that has field windings parallel to and in series with the armature. 27. ______________________

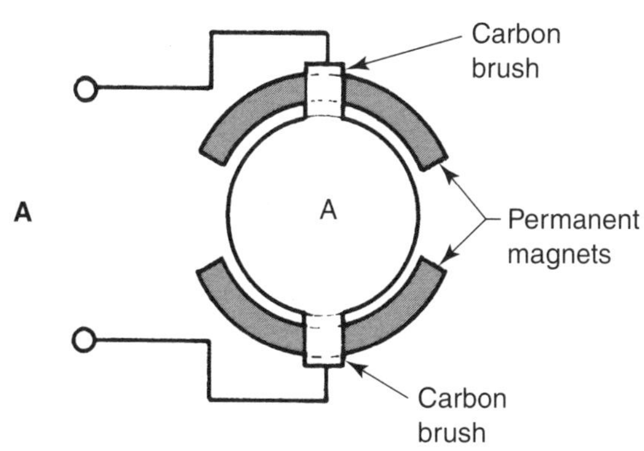

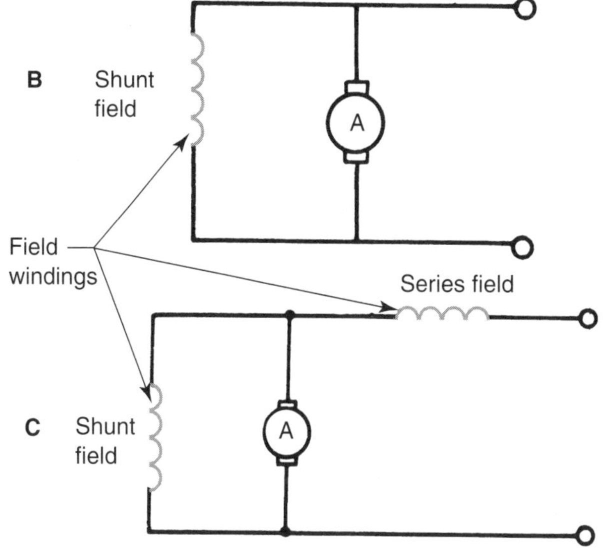

Name ______________________________

Identify the parts indicated on the wiper motor shown below.

28. Switch plate. 28. ______________________
29. Cam. 29. ______________________
30. Drive gear. 30. ______________________
31. Motor housing. 31. ______________________
32. Gear housing. 32. ______________________
33. Worm gear. 33. ______________________
34. Drive shaft. 34. ______________________
35. Drive link. 35. ______________________

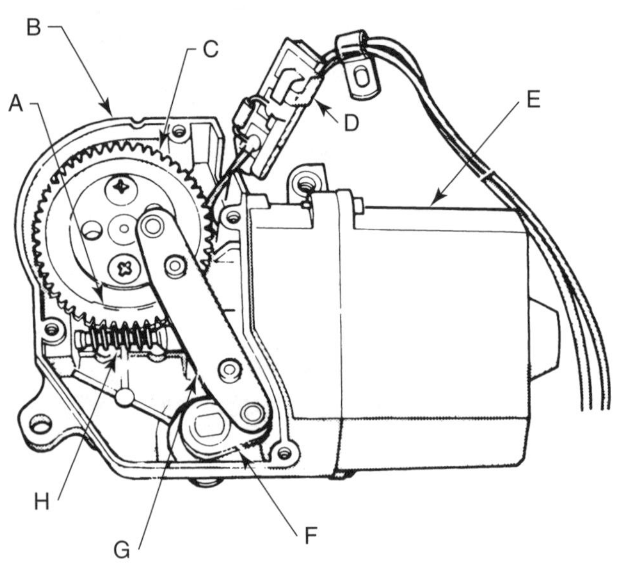

Completion

36. A _____ _____ is generally connected between the battery and the main lighting switch. It is often mounted on the driver's side of the firewall. 36. ______________________

37. The quest for reducing aerodynamic drag also resulted in the introduction of _____ headlamps. 37. ______________________

38. Headlamp _____ _____ automatically control headlamp on-off operation after the ignition switch and main lighting switch are turned off. 38. ______________________

39. Lighting outages in pairs (headlamps, parking lamps, and tail lamps) could be caused by a defective _____ lighting switch. 39. ______________________

40. Wires and cables are conductors of electricity. Usually, they are made of annealed _____. 40. ______________________

41. The _____ of a length of wire or cable decreases as its cross section increases. 41. ______________________

Chapter 50

Speedometers and Cruise Control Systems

Name ______________________________

Date ______________ Instructor ______________

Score_______ Textbook pages 745–756

After studying the chapter in the text and completing this section of the workbook, you will be able to:

- ❑ Explain how an analog speedometer operates.
- ❑ Describe how a digital speedometer operates.
- ❑ List the different types of digital display.
- ❑ Troubleshoot an analog speedometer/odometer, including the cable.
- ❑ Explain how the cruise control servo operates.
- ❑ List the components of a cruise control system.
- ❑ Describe the different cruise control systems.

Multiple Choice

1. In most cases, the speedometer is designed to convert _____ revolutions of the drive cable into one mile on the odometer.
   (A) 11
   (B) 101
   (C) 1001
   (D) 1111

   1. ______________________

2. The accuracy of a speedometer and odometer is affected by the _____.
   (A) size of the tires
   (B) rear axle ratio
   (C) gears used to drive the speedometer
   (D) All of the above.

   2. ______________________

3. Which of the following can cause incorrect speed indication?
   (A) Out of balance pointer.
   (B) Out of calibration.
   (C) Worn second or third gears.
   (D) Both A and B.

   3. ______________________

Name ______________________________

4. If the odometer readings are incorrect, wrong _____ might be the cause. 4. ______________________
   (A) tire size
   (B) stripped transmission drive gear
   (C) tire size or rear axle ratio
   (D) All of the above.

5. Which digital speedometer display is a semiconductor diode? 5. ______________________
   (A) Light emitting diode.
   (B) Liquid crystal display.
   (C) Vacuum fluorescent display.
   (D) Cathode ray tube.

Identification

Identify the parts indicated on the illustration below.

6. First gear. 6. ______________________
7. Total odometer. 7. ______________________
8. Third gear. 8. ______________________
9. Intermediate gear. 9. ______________________
10. Magnet shaft. 10. ______________________
11. Reset shaft. 11. ______________________
12. Second gear. 12. ______________________
13. Trip odometer. 13. ______________________

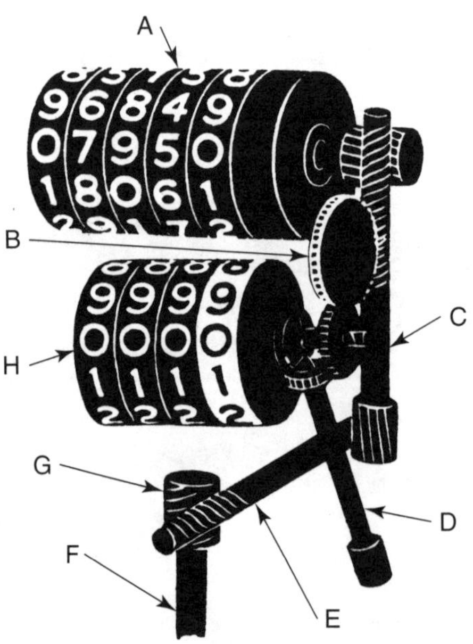

Name ______________________________

Identify the parts indicated on the illustration below.

14. Movable speed cup. 14. ______________________
15. Hairspring. 15. ______________________
16. Rotating magnet. 16. ______________________
17. Pointer. 17. ______________________
18. Stationary field plate. 18. ______________________
19. Spindle. 19. ______________________

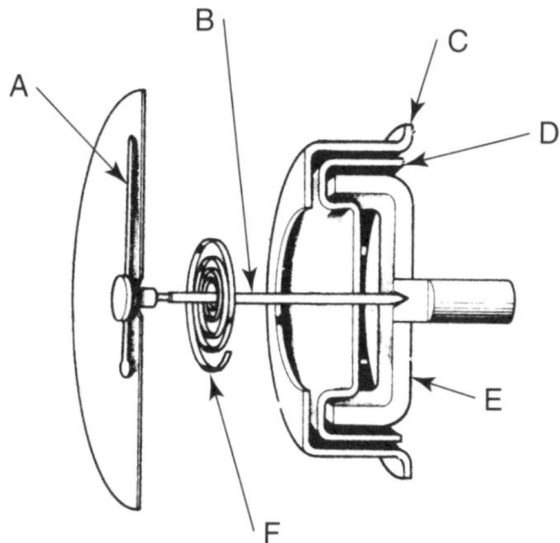

Identify the parts indicated on the illustration below.

20. Speed sensor. 20. ______________________
21. Speedometer cable. 21. ______________________
22. Transaxle. 22. ______________________

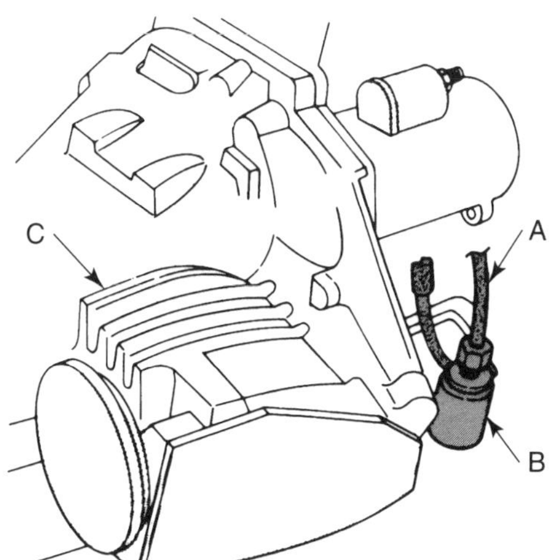

Name ______________________________

Identify the parts indicated on the vacuum servo shown below.

23. Diaphragm chamber. 23. ______________
24. Variable inductance position sensor. 24. ______________
25. Vacuum solenoid and valve. 25. ______________
26. Steel core. 26. ______________
27. Spring. 27. ______________
28. Coil. 28. ______________
29. Servo diaphragm. 29. ______________
30. Vent solenoid and valve. 30. ______________
31. Throttle attachment. 31. ______________

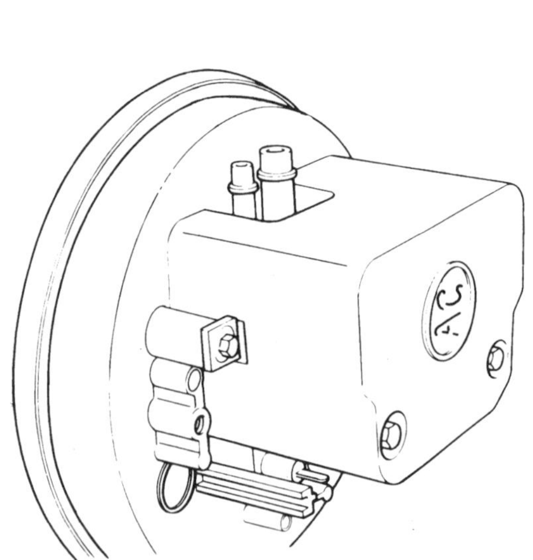

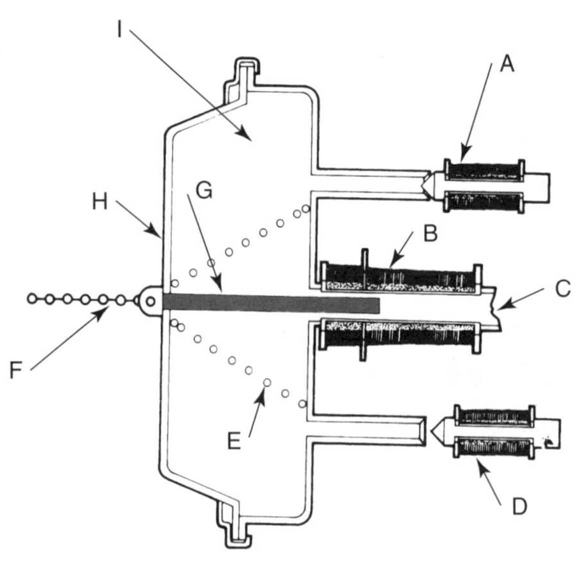

Internal view

Identify the parts indicated on the governor-type servo shown at the top of the next page.

32. Spring. 32. ______________
33. Atmospheric pressure. 33. ______________
34. Control valve. 34. ______________
35. To throttle linkage. 35. ______________
36. Vacuum port. 36. ______________
37. Speedo cable. 37. ______________
38. Servo housing. 38. ______________
39. Diaphragm. 39. ______________
40. Governor. 40. ______________

Name ______________________________

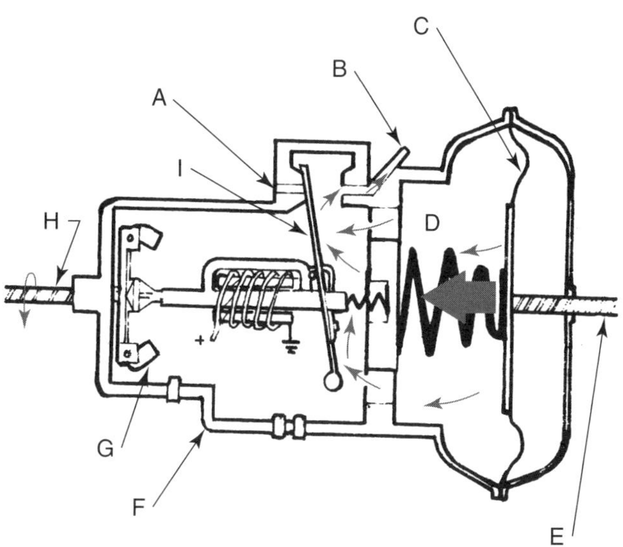

Completion

41. The speedometer adaptor must be positioned in relation to the number of _____ indicated on the drive pinion, or the indicated speed will be incorrect. 41. ______________________________

42. The digital odometer chip retains mileage in its _____. 42. ______________________________

Short Answer

43. What is being checked in the illustration below?

____

____

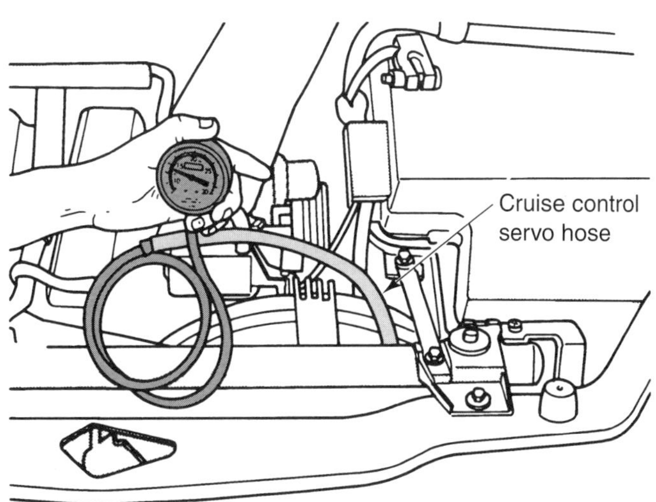

44. List three causes of an inoperative cruise control system.

____

____

____

Name ______________________________

45. A cruise control system will not disengage when the brakes are applied. List three possible causes.

____

____

____

Chapter 51

Body Repairing and Refinishing

Name ______________________________

Date ________________ Instructor ________________

Score________ Textbook pages 757–782

After studying the chapter in the text and completing this section of the workbook, you will be able to:

- ❑ Demonstrate the procedure for straightening a damaged panel.
- ❑ Explain how to replace a damaged panel.
- ❑ Describe the welding and cutting procedures used on late-model vehicles.
- ❑ Explain why it is important to properly prepare a surface before painting.
- ❑ Describe the most common spray gun types used for auto body work.
- ❑ Describe the various types of paints available for automotive refinishing.

Multiple Choice

1. When there is a major depression in a panel, followed by a buckled area and a series of ridges, apply pressure at the _____.
   (A) spot where the panel was struck first and where it is depressed most
   (B) ridge farthest from the point where the body was struck first
   (C) ridge closest to the point where the body was struck first
   (D) None of the above.

1. ______________________________

2. When using a hammer to straighten a damaged panel, the hammer blows should be at the rate of _____ per minute.
   (A) 10
   (B) 30
   (C) 60
   (D) 100

2. ______________________________

Name ______________________________

3. When mixing plastic body filler with hardener, a golf ball–size amount of filler needs about a _____ inch ribbon of hardener. 3. ______________________
   (A) 1/2
   (B) 1
   (C) 2
   (D) 3

4. For welding sheet metal, acetylene pressure should be _____. 4. ______________________
   (A) 5 psi and oxygen pressure should be 10 psi
   (B) 5 psi and oxygen pressure should be 5 psi
   (C) 10 psi and oxygen pressure should be 20 psi
   (D) None of the above.

5. Which of the following spray gun applies more paint to the surface than other guns and reduces over-spray by 75 to 80%? 5. ______________________
   (A) Pressure feed guns.
   (B) Siphon feed guns.
   (C) High-volume, low pressure (HVLP) guns.
   (D) Gravity feed guns.

Identification

Identify the dolly blocks shown below.

6. Utility. 6. ______________________

7. General purpose. 7. ______________________

8. Heel. 8. ______________________

9. Wedge. 9. ______________________

10. Mushroom. 10. ______________________

11. Toe. 11. ______________________

A B C

D E F

Identify the spray patterns shown at the top of the next page.

12. Air pressure too high. 12. ______________________

13. Not enough air pressure. 13. ______________________

14. Clogged wing port. 14. ______________________

15. Correct spray pattern. 15. ______________________

16. Fluid has dried around tip of nozzle. 16. ______________________

Name ____________________

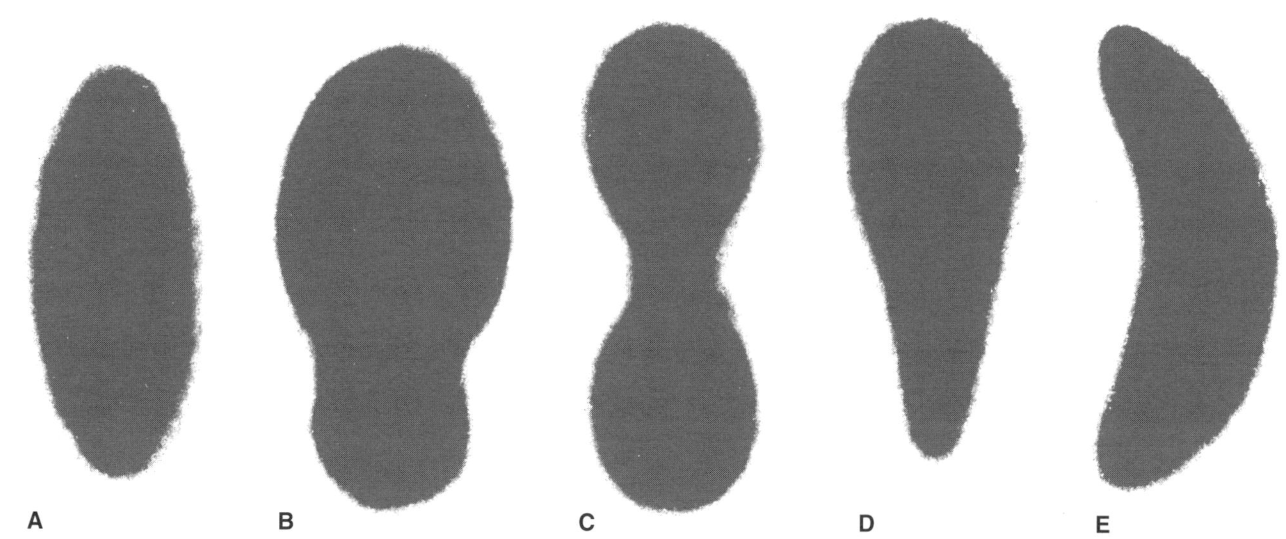

Identify the types of plastics illustrated below.

17. Vinyl group. 17. ____________________

18. Polypropylene. 18. ____________________

19. ABS group. 19. ____________________

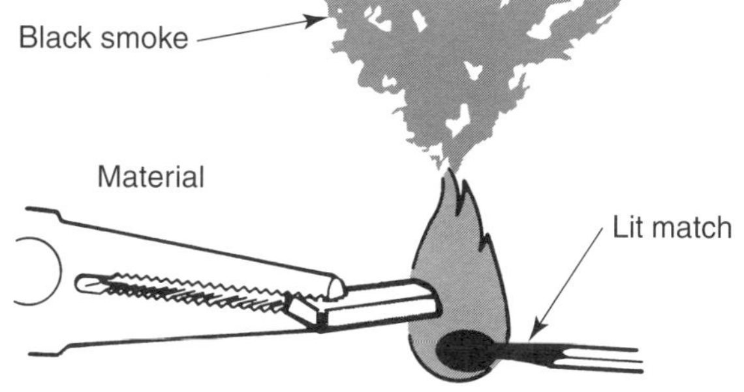

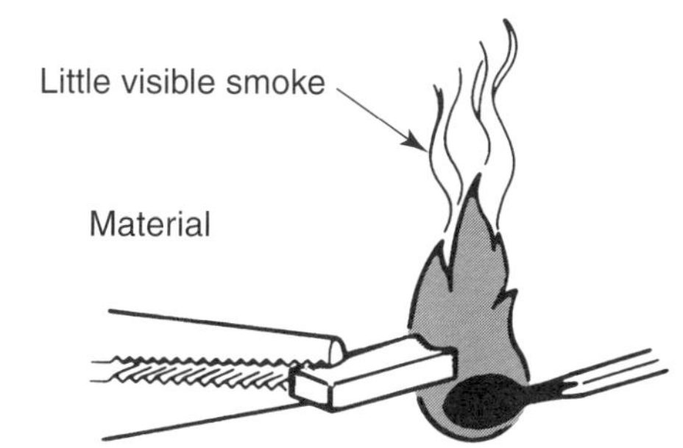

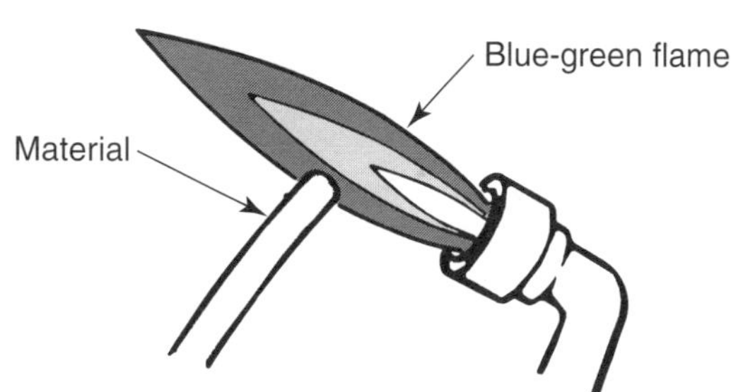

Name ______________________________

Completion

20. Body filler should not be thicker than _____″, or it will crack when dry. 20. ______________________

21. A disk sander should be held _____ degrees to the surface of the panel. 21. ______________________

Short Answer

22. Look at the illustration below. When straightening a wrinkled panel, pressure is first applied to what point?

____

____

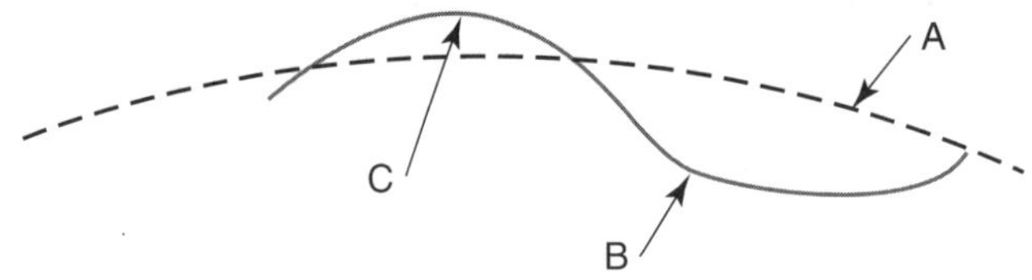

23. Name the type of tools shown below and describe their purpose.

____

____

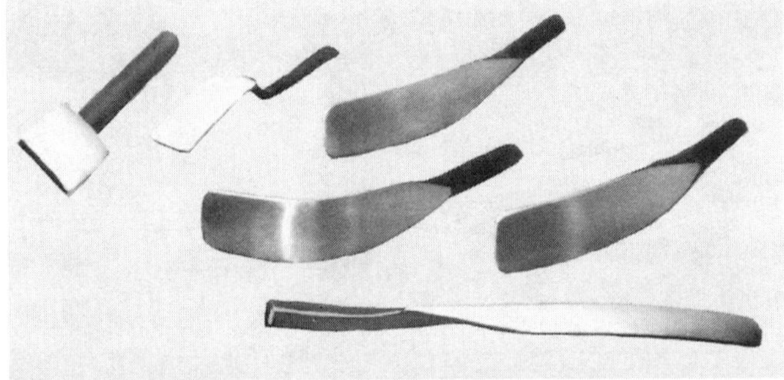

24. What is being done in the illustrations below?

(A)____

(B)____

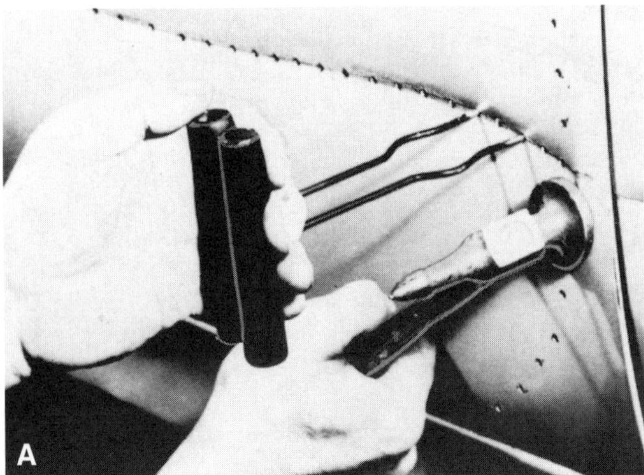

Name ______________________________

For questions 25–38, name the types of paint defects shown. Then list the cause and recommend a remedy.

25. ______________________________

____

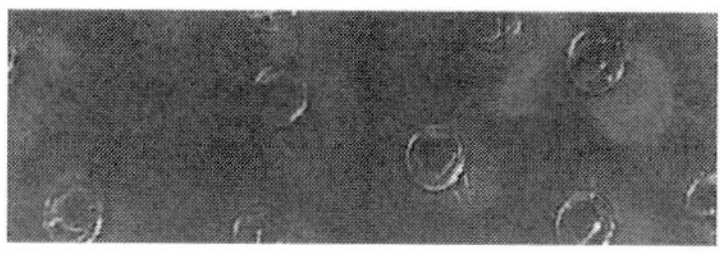

26. ______________________________

____

27. ______________________________

____

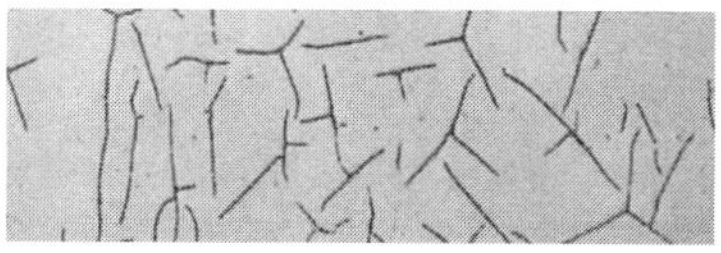

28. ______________________________

____

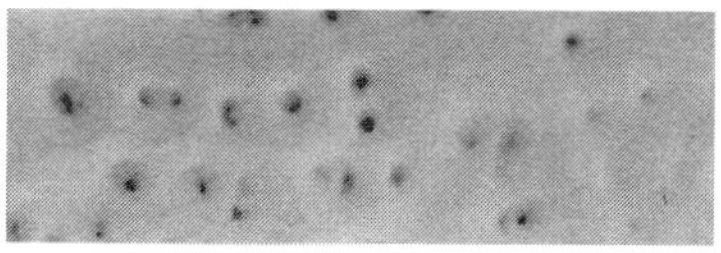

29. ______________________________

____

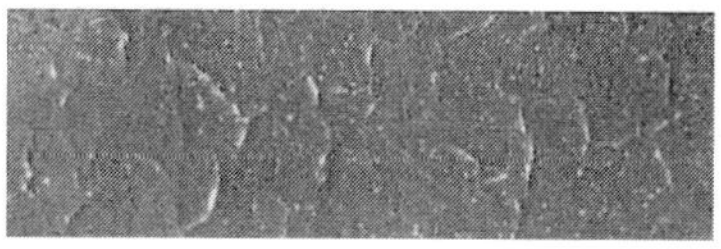

30. ______________________________

____

31. ______________________________

____

Name ______________________________

32. ______________________________

____

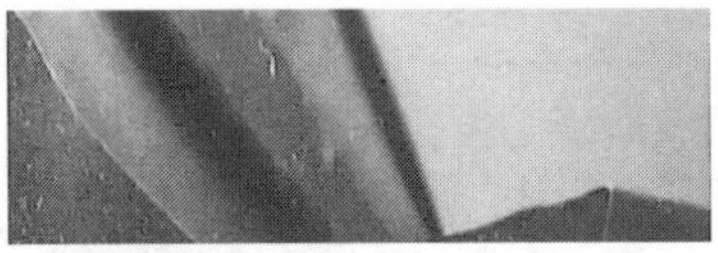

33. ______________________________

____

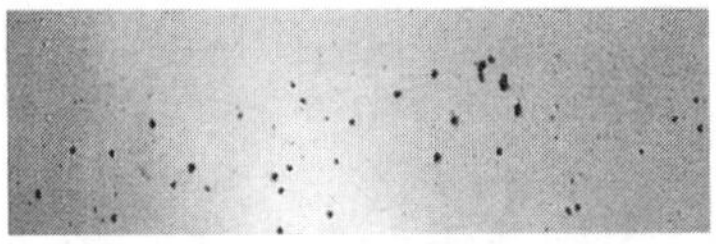

34. ______________________________

____

35. ______________________________

____

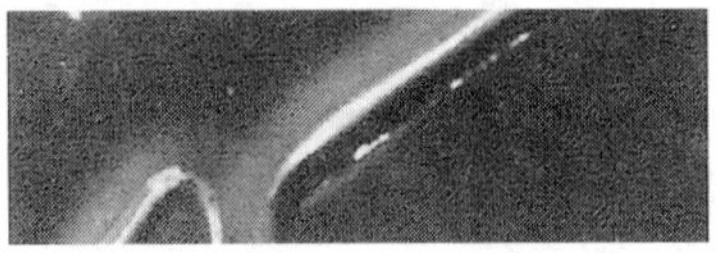

36. ______________________________

____

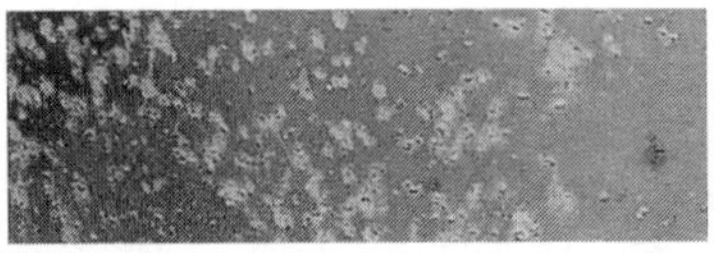

37. ______________________________

____

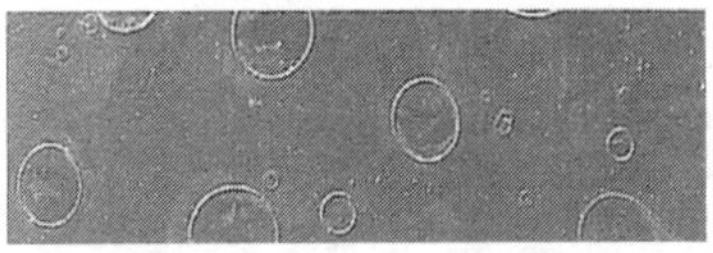

38. ______________________________

____

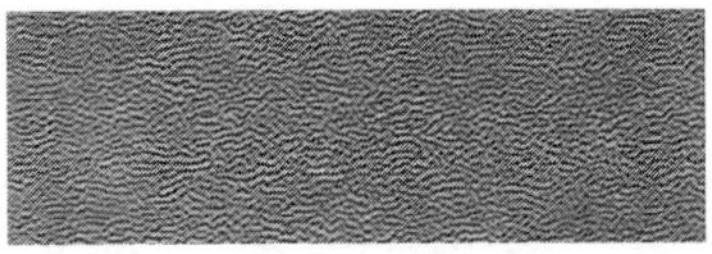

Chapter 52

Career Opportunities and Technician Certification

Name ______________________________

Date ____________ Instructor ____________

Score_______ Textbook pages 783–792

After studying the chapter in the text and completing this section of the workbook, you will be able to:

- ❑ Identify careers directly involved with automotive service.
- ❑ Describe duties of various levels of service technicians.
- ❑ Explain why specialty service technicians are necessary.
- ❑ Describe duties of supervisory and management level personnel in a car manufacturer's dealership.
- ❑ Name career opportunities in automotive service-related businesses.

Multiple Choice

1. The automotive field offers _____ career opportunities.
   (A) extremely limited
   (B) limited
   (C) almost unlimited
   (D) None of the above.

   1. C

2. Apprentice auto service technicians _____.
   (A) are involved in a three- or four-year training program
   (B) divide their work time between the classroom and the shop
   (C) often receive periodic raises in pay until they reach journeyman status
   (D) All of the above.

   2. D

3. Which of the following specialty service technicians analyzes problems with starting, charging, ignition, and lighting systems?
   (A) Auto electrical technicians.
   (B) Alignment technicians.
   (C) Auto radiator service technicians.
   (D) Automatic transmission service technicians.

   3. A

Name ____________________

4. An entrepreneur should have the ability to _____.
   (A) organize
   (B) manage
   (C) assume the risks of operating a business
   (D) All of the above.

4. D

5. A technician who passes one or more of the eight standard certification tests and has at least two years of work experience in the automotive field is _____.
   (A) not qualified for certification
   (B) certified as an ASE Automobile Technician
   (C) certified as a Master Automobile Technician
   (D) None of the above.

5. B

Matching

Match the following automotive careers to their descriptions. Place the corresponding letter in the blank.

K 6. Parts manager.
J 7. Motor vehicle salesperson.
C 8. Truck service technician.
O 9. Vocational teacher or auto technology instructor.
L 10. Jobber salesperson.
G 11. Shop supervisor.
I 12. Insurance adjuster or claim adjuster.
B 13. Specialty service technician.
R 14. Automotive dealer.
H 15. Service manager.
M 16. Car manufacturer's representative.
E 17. Master service technician.
Q 18. Owner of specialty repair shop.
P 19. Auto body and paint technician.
A 20. Sales manager.
N 21. Car factory/supplier employee.
D 22. General service technician.
F 23. Auto service advisor/writer.

(A) Must know how to diagnose trouble and maintain all systems of automobiles.
(B) Concentrates on a single phase of repair work.
(C) Uses service know-how plus special skills and strength to handle heavy parts and assemblies.
(D) Works on repeat comebacks, unusual symptoms, mysterious noises, etc.
(E) Performs auto body and chassis repair and realignment, along with carefully controlled refinishing procedures.
(F) Greets customers and writes repair orders based on symptoms described by the car owner.
(G) Is directly in charge of the service technicians: directing, routing, and scheduling service and repair work.
(H) Is the department head in charge of planning, supervising, and coordinating the activities of all shop employees.
(I) Explains the mechanical and electronic features of a car or truck to a potential customer and demonstrates it.
(J) Is in charge of the entire selling activity of a dealership.
(K) Orders, stocks, and sells replacement parts and accessories.
(L) Travels over a certain territory selling the products of several manufacturers to automotive repair and supply shops.
(M) Represents car manufacturers in various capacities, such as factory district manager, factory service instructor, etc.
(N) Works in factories in jobs such as subassembly, quality control, etc.
(O) Trains service personnel or students in trade schools, public schools, or vocational schools.
(P) Must have knowledge of auto body work, refinishing, and replacement parts pricing.
(Q) Operates franchises of specialty repair shops such as muffler shops, tire dealerships, fast oil change chains, etc.
(R) Owns a dealership that sells cars.

Name ______________________

Career Investigation

Instructions: Investigate a career of your choice in the automotive field. If possible, interview someone with that career. However, you may use library materials, information from your guidance counselor, etc. Find out the following information.

Career: MASTER TECHNICIAN

Education or training needed: 4 YEAR SCHOOL AN 4 YEARS TRAINING

Salary range: 50,000 YEAR

Description of duties: DIAGNOSIN UNUSUAL PROBLEM AND FIXING THEM

Hours: 7 HOURS A DAY

Working conditions: HARD AND STRESSFUL WORK

Advantages of this career: DIGINOS CAR EASY AND OTHER CAR COMP WILL WONT TO HIRE YOU

Disadvantages of this career: A LONG TIME TO LEARN THE TRADE

Other comments: ______________________

Name ______________________________

Filling out a Job Application

Instructions: Complete the following job application form.

EMPLOYMENT APPLICATION

NAME AND ADDRESS

First Name	Middle Name	Last Name	Social Security No.	Date of Application
KYLE	S	MACKIE		

PERMANENT MAILING ADDRESS				TELEPHONE NO.
Number and Street	City	State	Zip Code	(Area) Local Number
137 LOCUST St	BREA	CA	92821	714 366-8301

TEMPORARY MAILING ADDRESS (if different)				TELEPHONE NO.
Number and Street	City	State	Zip Code	(Area) Local Number

Are you over 18 years of age and less than 70? YES

JOB INTEREST

Type of work you are seeking (specify or check below)

Secretarial ☐ Clerical ☐ Supervisory ☐ Technical/Professional ☒

Production/Maintenance ☐ Other ☐

Full-Time ☐ Part-Time ☒ Permanent ☐ Temporary ☐ Summer ☐

Are you currently employed? Yes ☒ No ☐ Date available for work

Work location preferences or restrictions

Will you work overtime if asked? Yes ☒ No ☐ Will you work shifts? Yes ☒ No ☐

Approximate salary requested (per month)

EDUCATION AND TRAINING

Name and Address (City & State) of last Grade School Attended	Dates Attended	Major Studies	Did You Graduate? Yes ☒ No ☐
BREA AROVISTA			
Name and Address (City & State) of last High School Attended	**Dates Attended**	**Major Studies**	**Did You Graduate? Yes ☒ No ☐**
BREA OLIND HIGH			
Name of Business Career or Technical School (City & State) Attended	**Dates Attended**	**Major Studies**	**Did You Graduate? Yes ☐ No ☐**

STOP HERE IF YOU HAVE NOT ATTENDED COLLEGE (GO ON TO COMPLETE OTHER PAGES)

COLLEGE LEVEL AND ABOVE (Including Junior & Community Colleges)

SCHOOL NAME	SCHOOL LOCATION (City & State)	DATE GRADUATED (or Years Attended) Month/Year	TYPE OF DEGREE RECEIVED	MAJOR & MINOR FIELD OF STUDY

Your College Grade Point Average =

A = Lowest Passing =

List Below, Awards or Honors & Research:

Name ______________________

EMPLOYMENT RECORD

Please list last five employers (if you have had that many) starting with present or most recent employer.

Date	Name & Address—Employer	1 Position or Occupation 2 Department 3 Name of Supervisor	Describe Major Duties	Salary or Wages (Monthly)	Reason for Leaving
From 03 (Month) 06 (Year) To 00 (Month) 06 (Year)	TOYS R US	1 SALES 2 FLOOR 3 MIKE		Starting $ 6.75 Final $	STORE CLOSED
From Month Year To Month Year		1 2 3		Starting $ Final $	
From Month Year To Month Year		1 2 3		Starting $ Final $	
From Month Year To Month Year		1 2 3		Starting $ Final $	
From Month Year To Month Year		1 2 3		Starting $ Final $	

If you have served in the U.S. Armed Forces, indicate:

Branch ______ Special Training ______ Rank Attained ______ Years in Service ______ Honors or Awards ______

Date of Separation ______

REFERENCES (Do not list relatives)

Name	Address	Phone No.	Occupation	Years Known

ADDITIONAL DATA

Have you ever been convicted of a crime (other than traffic, game law or other minor violations)? Yes ☐ No ☐
If yes, give nature of offense and other circumstances regarding conviction

Are you a U. S. citizen? Yes ☒ No ☐
If "No," do you have an alien registration card or valid U. S. work permit? Yes ☒ No ☐

Non-English languages you read ______ speak ______ write ______

Other special skills, knowledges and abilities which support your qualifications for the position you are seeking ______

PHYSICAL STATUS

1. Are you presently or have you during the last six months been under a physician's care or in a hospital? Yes ☐ No ☒
2. Do you have any disabilities? Yes ☐ No ☒
3. Have you ever been compensated for, or do you currently have outstanding, a job-related injury or claim? Yes ☐ No ☒

If yes to any of the above, explain:

STATEMENT AND SIGNATURE

In completing, and submitting this application, I understand and agree: That any misstatement of material facts will be sufficient reason for immediate withdrawal of this application or, in the event of employment be deemed cause for dismissal. That my previous employers may be asked for information concerning my employment, character, ability, and experience. That no question on this application has been answered in such a manner as to disclose my race, color, religion, or national origin. That if employed, I may be required to furnish proof of age by birth or baptismal certificate.

Signature [signature]

Date of Application 9/26/06

Name ______________________

The Job Interview

Instructions: Questions that are often asked during a job interview are listed below. Pretend you are being interviewed. Answer these questions as you would during an interview.

Job for which you are applying:

Company:

1. Why do you want to work for this company?

   I THINK IT IS A GOOD COMPANY TO WORK FOR

2. Do you think you will like this kind of work? If so, why?

   I THINK I WOULD LIKE THIS KIND OF WORK BECUSE IT DO IT AT HOME AS WELL

3. How would you describe yourself?

   HARD WORKER, TRUSTY,

4. What are your best subjects in school?

   MATH & HISTORY

5. What are your worst subjects in school?

   ENG.

6. What other jobs have you had?

   TOY · R US, BORDERS

7. Have you ever been fired from a job? If so, why?

   NO

8. What is your best qualification for this job?

   I HAVE MANY SKILLS AND I LEARN FAST

9. What are your future plans?

   GO TO SCHOOL AND GET A GOOD JOB

10. Why should I hire you?

    I WORK HARD, ILL BE ON TIME, I CAN DO MANY THING FOR THE COMP.

Name ______________________

Entrepreneurship

Instructions: Complete the following activity about entrepreneurship.

1. In your own words, define entrepreneurship.
   A PERSONS ABILITY TO ORGANIZE, MANAGE
2. Does starting your own business appeal to you? Give two reasons for your answer.
   IT APPEAL TO ME, ONE I STARTED THE COMP, AND I LIKE THE FIELD IM IN
3. List at least three products or services you could sell.
   TYERS
   CAR PARTS
   BODY PARTS
4. Briefly describe the demand for your products or services. (Consider potential customers, competition, and your abilities.)
   THE DEMAND WILL BE HIGH
5. Based on your answer to Question 4, which product or service seems to offer you the best opportunity for success?
   ILL HAVE ONLY THE BEST PARTS
6. How much time would your business take to manage? 12 HR.
   Do you have enough time to manage? YES
7. How much money do you estimate it would cost to start and operate your business? (Consider equipment, supplies, advertising, etc.)
   100,000
8. Consider your answers to the above question. What are some advantages and disadvantages of becoming an entrepreneur?
   Advantages:
   DEMAND WILL BE HIGH AND SEALS GO UP MAKE MONEY
   Disadvantages:
   LOW DEMAND YOU LOSE THE MONEY TO START THE COMP.